# FEDERAL INCOME TAXATION OF CORPORATIONS AND STOCKHOLDERS

## IN A NUTSHELL

### FOURTH EDITION

By

## KAREN C. BURKE

Professor of Law
University of Minnesota Law School

## WEST GROUP

Bancroft-Whitney • Clark Boardman Callaghan
Lawyers Cooperative Publishing • WESTLAW® • West Publishing

*For Customer Assistance Call 1-800-328-4880*

COPYRIGHT © 1978, 1981, 1989 WEST PUBLISHING CO.
COPYRIGHT © 1996 By WEST PUBLISHING CO.
610 Opperman Drive
P.O. Box 64526
St. Paul, MN 55164–0526
1–800–328–9352

**Library of Congress Cataloging-in-Publication Data**

Burke, Karen C., 1951–
    Federal income taxation of corporations and stockholders in a
nutshell / by Karen C. Burke. — 4th ed.
        p.   cm. — (Nutshell series)
    Rev. ed. of: Federal income taxation of corporations and
stockholders in a nutshell / by Peter P. Weidenbruch, Jr. and Karen
C. Burke.   3rd ed. 1989.
    Includes index.
    ISBN 0–314–6641–1 (soft cover)
    1. Corporations—Taxation—Law and legislation—United States.
I. Weidenbruch, Peter P., 1929–    Federal income taxation of
corporations and stockholders in a nutshell.   II. Title.
III. Series.
KF6465.S58   1996
343.7305'267—dc20
[347.3035267]
                                                    95–43333
                                                         CIP

ISBN 0–314–06641–1

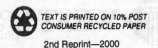

# PREFACE TO
# THE FOURTH EDITION

Since the third edition of this work appeared in 1989, federal income taxation of corporations and stockholders has undergone numerous changes. The fourth edition has been completely revised to reflect developments in the statute, regulations and case law through January 1996.

Despite significant changes in emphasis and direction, many of the basic principles of corporate taxation have proved remarkably durable. This edition retains the essential structure of its predecessors. Chapter 1 introduces several fundamental issues in the taxation of corporations and stockholders, and Chapter 2 focuses on the corporation as a taxable entity. Chapters 3 through 7 track the corporate life cycle from incorporation through complete liquidation, including nonliquidating distributions, redemptions and stock dividends. Chapters 8 through 11 address more advanced problems in corporate taxation, including taxable acquisitions, taxfree reorganizations and corporate divisions, and carryover of corporate tax attributes. Chapter 12 provides an overview of the taxation of S corporations. Finally, Chapter 13 discusses various reform proposals, with special attention to corporate-shareholder integration.

## *PREFACE TO THE FOURTH EDITION*

This work is intended to introduce students to the basic structure of corporate taxation. Students interested in pursuing specific topics in greater detail should consult the leading treatises on corporate taxation.

KAREN C. BURKE

Minneapolis, MN
January, 1996

# OUTLINE

## Chapter 4. Nonliquidating Distributions

## OUTLINE

## Chapter 5. Redemptions

## OUTLINE

X

## Chapter 6. Stock Dividends

## Chapter 7. Complete Liquidations; Collapsible Corporations

*OUTLINE*

## Chapter 9.  Reorganizations

## Chapter 11.  Carryover of Corporate Attributes

## Chapter 12.  Subchapter S

## Chapter 13. Integration

# TABLE OF CASES

## TABLE OF CASES

## TABLE OF CASES

# TABLE OF CASES

## TABLE OF CASES

## TABLE OF CASES

\*

# TABLE OF INTERNAL REVENUE CODE SECTIONS, REGULATIONS AND RULINGS

---

**UNITED STATES**

---

## UNITED STATES CODE ANNOTATED
### 26 U.S.C.A.—Internal Revenue Code

## TABLE OF INTERNAL REVENUE CODE SECTIONS

**UNITED STATES CODE ANNOTATED**
**26 U.S.C.A.—Internal Revenue Code**

## TABLE OF INTERNAL REVENUE CODE SECTIONS

### UNITED STATES CODE ANNOTATED
### 26 U.S.C.A.—Internal Revenue Code

**UNITED STATES CODE ANNOTATED**
**26 U.S.C.A.—Internal Revenue Code**

# TABLE OF INTERNAL REVENUE CODE SECTIONS

## UNITED STATES CODE ANNOTATED
### 26 U.S.C.A.—Internal Revenue Code

## TABLE OF INTERNAL REVENUE CODE SECTIONS

**UNITED STATES CODE ANNOTATED**
**26 U.S.C.A.—Internal Revenue Code**

## TABLE OF INTERNAL REVENUE CODE SECTIONS

### UNITED STATES CODE ANNOTATED
### 26 U.S.C.A.—Internal Revenue Code

# TABLE OF INTERNAL REVENUE CODE SECTIONS

## UNITED STATES CODE ANNOTATED
### 26 U.S.C.A.—Internal Revenue Code

**UNITED STATES CODE ANNOTATED**
**26 U.S.C.A.—Internal Revenue Code**

# TABLE OF INTERNAL REVENUE CODE SECTIONS

## UNITED STATES CODE ANNOTATED
### 26 U.S.C.A.—Internal Revenue Code

**UNITED STATES CODE ANNOTATED**
**26 U.S.C.A.—Internal Revenue Code**

## TABLE OF INTERNAL REVENUE CODE SECTIONS

**UNITED STATES CODE ANNOTATED**
**26 U.S.C.A.—Internal Revenue Code**

XLI

**UNITED STATES CODE ANNOTATED**
**26 U.S.C.A.—Internal Revenue Code**

**UNITED STATES CODE ANNOTATED**
**26 U.S.C.A.—Internal Revenue Code**

**UNITED STATES CODE ANNOTATED**
**26 U.S.C.A.—Internal Revenue Code**

**UNITED STATES CODE ANNOTATED**
**26 U.S.C.A.—Internal Revenue Code**

**UNITED STATES CODE ANNOTATED**
**26 U.S.C.A.—Internal Revenue Code**

**UNITED STATES CODE ANNOTATED**
**26 U.S.C.A.—Internal Revenue Code**

## TABLE OF INTERNAL REVENUE CODE SECTIONS

**UNITED STATES CODE ANNOTATED**
**26 U.S.C.A.—Internal Revenue Code**

## TABLE OF INTERNAL REVENUE CODE SECTIONS

**UNITED STATES CODE ANNOTATED**
**26 U.S.C.A.—Internal Revenue Code**

**UNITED STATES CODE ANNOTATED**
**26 U.S.C.A.—Internal Revenue Code**

**UNITED STATES CODE ANNOTATED**
**26 U.S.C.A.—Internal Revenue Code**

**UNITED STATES CODE ANNOTATED**
**26 U.S.C.A.—Internal Revenue Code**

# TABLE OF INTERNAL REVENUE CODE SECTIONS

**UNITED STATES CODE ANNOTATED**
**26 U.S.C.A.—Internal Revenue Code**

LV

**UNITED STATES CODE ANNOTATED**
**26 U.S.C.A.—Internal Revenue Code**

## TABLE OF INTERNAL REVENUE CODE SECTIONS

**UNITED STATES CODE ANNOTATED**
**26 U.S.C.A.—Internal Revenue Code**

## TABLE OF INTERNAL REVENUE CODE SECTIONS

**UNITED STATES CODE ANNOTATED**
**26 U.S.C.A.—Internal Revenue Code**

**UNITED STATES CODE ANNOTATED**
**26 U.S.C.A.—Internal Revenue Code**

# TABLE OF INTERNAL REVENUE CODE SECTIONS

## UNITED STATES CODE ANNOTATED
### 26 U.S.C.A.—Internal Revenue Code

# TABLE OF INTERNAL REVENUE CODE SECTIONS

## UNITED STATES CODE ANNOTATED
### 26 U.S.C.A.—Internal Revenue Code

**UNITED STATES CODE ANNOTATED**
**26 U.S.C.A.—Internal Revenue Code**

Burke Tax Corp 4th—3

## TABLE OF INTERNAL REVENUE CODE SECTIONS

### TREASURY REGULATIONS

**TREASURY REGULATIONS**

## *TABLE OF INTERNAL REVENUE CODE SECTIONS*

### TREASURY REGULATIONS

## TABLE OF INTERNAL REVENUE CODE SECTIONS

### TREASURY REGULATIONS

# TABLE OF INTERNAL REVENUE CODE SECTIONS

## TREASURY REGULATIONS

## REVENUE PROCEDURES

## TABLE OF INTERNAL REVENUE CODE SECTIONS

### REVENUE PROCEDURES

### REVENUE RULINGS

## TABLE OF INTERNAL REVENUE CODE SECTIONS

### REVENUE RULINGS

# TABLE OF INTERNAL REVENUE CODE SECTIONS

## REVENUE RULINGS

# FEDERAL INCOME TAXATION OF CORPORATIONS AND STOCKHOLDERS

## IN A NUTSHELL

### FOURTH EDITION

\*

# CHAPTER 1

# INTRODUCTION

## § 1. The Corporate Double Tax and the Tax Reform Act of 1986

(a) *Corporate Double Tax.* Subchapter C is premised on double taxation of distributed corporate earnings. A corporation is taxed as a separate entity on its taxable income, and shareholders are taxed on distributions of the corporation's after-tax earnings. Prior to the Tax Reform Act of 1986 (the "1986 Act"), corporate tax rates had historically been significantly lower than individual tax rates. From 1986 until 1993, the highest corporate rate exceeded the highest individual rate. The Revenue Reconciliation Act of 1993 (the "1993 Act") eliminated this "inversion" in the rate relationship by increasing the maximum individual rate (39.6%) above the maximum corporate rate (35%). Since 1986, the rate structures have substantially curtailed the benefit of sheltering income within the corporation and increased the burden of the double tax.

The combined corporate and individual tax burden on distributed corporate earnings may exceed 60%. For example, assume that a corporation earns income of $100 which is taxed at 35%. After payment of corporate tax of $35, the corporation has only $65 available for distribution. An individual shareholder in the highest tax bracket (39.6%) would pay a tax of $25.74 on the distribution. The maximum aggregate tax burden is thus more than $60 if the corporation's after-tax earnings are distributed as a dividend to individual shareholders. Traditionally, individual shareholders have sought to minimize the burden of the double tax through various strategies.

By contrast, dividend income distributed to a corporate shareholder is generally taxed at a lower rate than other corporate earnings. Intercorporate dividends qualify for a dividends-received deduction ranging from 20% to 100%. *See* § 243. *See also* Chapter 4. The dividends-received deduction mitigates the burden of multiple levels of corporate tax. It also creates an incentive for corporate shareholders to characterize income as a dividend.

(b) *Impact of the 1986 Act.* The 1986 Act created a "state of disequilibrium" by introducing several changes that generally strengthen the corporate double tax and lessen the attractiveness of the corporate business form. One important change was the repeal of the *General Utilities* doctrine that formerly permitted a corporation to distribute appreciated property to its shareholders without recognizing gain on the appreciation. *See* General Utilities & Operating Co. (1935). Congress believed that the *General Utilities* doctrine was subject to abuse and tended to undermine the corporate income tax.

Under Subchapter C, a corporation recognizes gain on both liquidating and nonliquidating distributions of property, as discussed in Chapters 4 and 7. Losses are recognized, however, only on liquidating distributions of property. The repeal of the *General Utilities* doctrine affects not only distributions of property, but also sales of assets prior to liquidation and stock purchases treated as asset purchases, as discussed in Chapter 8.

The 1986 Act briefly eliminated preferential capital gains rates for both individual and corporate taxpayers. The Revenue Reconciliation Act of 1990 restored a modest capital gains preference of 3 percentage points for individuals. The 1993 Act increased the differential between the maximum individual rate on ordinary income (39.6%) and the maximum individual rate on capital gains (28%) to 11.6%. Corporate capital gains and ordinary income are both subject to a maximum rate of 35%.

Prior to the 1986 Act, an issue of primary importance with respect to corporate distributions was whether the distribution would be taxed at the shareholder level as ordinary income (to the extent the distribution constituted a dividend) or as capital gain from a sale or exchange of stock. In the case of a redemption of stock treated as a sale or exchange, the shareholder is generally permitted to recover his basis in the redeemed stock tax free; only the excess is taxed as capital gain, as discussed in Chapter 5. Because capital gains are currently taxed at a lower rate than ordinary income, individual shareholders will prefer sale or exchange treatment. Even in the absence of a preferential capital gains rate, individual shareholders might still prefer capital gains in order to offset capital losses. Despite significantly reduced tax stakes, Subchapter C continues to contain several complex provisions designed to prevent shareholders from availing themselves of capital gains treatment in connection with a bailout of corporate earnings (including § 306, discussed in Chapter 6).

Since 1986, legislative activity in the Subchapter C area has been directed mainly toward preserving the integrity of the corporate tax base. In the area of corporate liquidations and divisions, for example, Congress has enacted measures to prevent taxpayers from circumventing the repeal of *General Utilities*. *See* Chapters 7 and 10. Although the double tax system is firmly entrenched in current law, several policy arguments against double taxation have recently gained ground.

## § 2.  Case Against Double Taxation

(a) *Incidence of the Corporate Tax*. The argument against double taxation often proceeds from considerations of vertical and horizontal equity. Since corporations have no independent taxpaying capacity apart from their shareholders, the burden ("incidence") of the corporate tax ultimately falls on individuals. Economists have long disagreed, however, about where the burden of the corporate tax ultimately comes to rest. In the short run, the corporate tax may be borne primarily by shareholders in the form of a lower return on corporate stock. In the long run, however, the burden of the corporate tax may be at least partially shifted to consumers, suppliers and labor. To the extent that the corporate tax is not fully shifted, it may be borne indirectly by owners of capital in corporate and noncorporate form through reduced returns on all investments.

Determining the incidence of the corporate tax is necessary to assess its overall distributional effect. If the corporate tax is shifted to labor or consumers, it has the effect of a wage or consumption tax, both of which are generally considered regressive. As a result, the corporate tax may frustrate efforts to develop an individual income tax that is progressive and vertically equitable. By reducing the attractiveness of investment in corporate form, the double tax may also induce investors to act in a manner that results in an overall welfare loss. Economists have argued that lifting the burden of the double tax would eliminate "deadweight loss," thereby yielding overall welfare gains.

(b) *Biases of the Double Tax System.* The Treasury has recognized the distorting impact of the double tax on several important financial decisions: (i) whether to conduct business in corporate or noncorporate form, (ii) whether to use debt or equity, (iii) whether to retain or distribute corporate earnings, and (iv) whether to make distributions in dividend or nondividend form. In turn, these distortions may lead to misallocation of resources and insufficient investment in the corporate sector.

The existing system is biased in favor of corporate financing through debt or retained earnings rather than issuance of new shares. To compensate for the burden of the double tax, new equity investment in corporate form requires a higher pre-tax return than a similar investment in noncorporate form. Although dividends on corporate stock are subject to tax at both the corporate and the shareholder level, interest payments on corporate debt are generally deductible at the corporate level. Thus, it will often be more advantageous for a corporation to borrow than to issue new shares. Corporations may also choose to finance new investments through retention of corporate earnings, thereby deferring the shareholder-level tax on distributions. Financing of corporate expansion through retained earnings was particularly advantageous when corporate rates were significantly lower than individual rates.

The bias in favor of debt may help to explain the increase in "leveraged buyouts" and "share repurchases" during the 1980's. *See* Chapter 13. Instead of undertaking comprehensive reform of the tax treatment of debt, Congress has generally responded to particular abuses by enacting narrowly-targeted provisions. Limitations on the corporate interest deduction in connection with taxable acquisitions and debt-equity conversions are discussed in Chapter 8.

(c) *Dividend Policy: Traditional and New Views*. Given the maximum aggregate tax burden of over 60% on dividend distributions, it is not surprising that shareholders prefer to extract corporate earnings in nondividend form whenever possible. Indeed, the bias against dividend distributions prompts the question of why corporations ever pay dividends. Economists have offered two differing views to explain corporate dividend policy: the "traditional view" and the "new view." Under the traditional view, corporations are assumed to pay dividends for nontax reasons—for example, to signal to the market that the corporation is financially sound. By contrast, the new view posits that corporations pay dividends not because of any nontax benefits but rather because they already have sufficient funds to finance corporate expansion and lack other profitable opportunities for investing surplus funds.

The new view of corporate dividend policy assumes that stock prices are already discounted by the market to reflect the burden of the corporate-level tax. Accordingly, if the burden of the corporate tax were lifted, stock prices would presumably increase and existing shareholders would receive a windfall. The amount of the potential windfall, however, is quite speculative. In any event, the windfall argument hardly justifies retaining the double tax, since any change in the existing tax structure will confer a benefit or impose a detriment on particular groups.

## § 3.  Corporate Tax and Deferral

(a) *Eliminating the Corporate Tax.* A separate corporate tax may be intended partly to address the problem of shareholder-level deferral. Merely eliminating the corporate-level tax would treat corporate investments more favorably than noncorporate investments. Corporations could invest at a pre-tax rate of return, while noncorporate businesses and sole proprietors would be able to invest only at an after-tax rate of return. Shareholders would not be subject to tax until distribution of income earned at the corporate level or disposition of their stock. Thus, shareholders would enjoy virtually unlimited deferral benefits, and might avoid tax altogether on appreciated stock by virtue of the § 1014 deathtime basis step-up.

*Example:* In Year 1, a sole shareholder (A) contributes $100 to X Corp., which earns a pre-tax return of 10% annually and reinvests all of its earnings. X pays no tax and A is taxed at a flat rate of 40%. At the end of Year 10, X makes a distribution of $259 to A, consisting of A's initial investment ($100) and accumulated earnings ($159). After paying tax of approximately $64 on the accumulated earnings ($159 × 40%), A is left with about $195 after tax. If A had instead invested the $100 outside the corporation and earned an after-tax return of 6%, she would have accumulated only approximately $179 at the end of Year 10. The difference of $16 ($195 less $179) represents the benefit of deferring the tax on the corporate earnings until ultimate distribution to A.

(b) *Corporate Tax as Surrogate.* Shareholder-level deferral could be eliminated by taxing shareholders on the annual changes in the value of their stock. Although such accrual taxation might be feasible for publicly traded or readily marketable stock, it would be administratively cumbersome and might raise liquidity concerns. It would also represent a significant departure from the traditional reluctance to tax unrealized income. An alternative approach would be to retain the corporate-level tax but to eliminate the shareholder-level tax on distributions. Since the former would function as a surrogate for the latter, no additional tax would be owed on distributed corporate income.

*Example:* The facts are the same as in the preceding example, except that X is taxed at a rate of 40% on its annual earnings. At the end of Year 10, X would have approximately $179 available for distribution to A who would treat the distribution as tax free. Thus, A ends up with the same after-tax amount ($179) at the end of Year 10 regardless of whether the investment is made in corporate or noncorporate form.

When corporate and individual income tax rates are identical, a corporate-level tax functions as a perfect substitute for a shareholder-level tax on reinvested earnings. A disparity between the corporate and individual income tax rates, however, will produce either a windfall or a detriment. In the above example, if A were in the 20% bracket, she would generally prefer to invest outside the corporation. If A invested $100 outside the corporation for 10 years at an 8% after-tax return, she would receive $216 after tax, leaving her better off by $37 ($216 less $179).

Eliminating the shareholder-level tax on distributions would not address the problem of undistributed corporate earnings. Potential double taxation would occur whenever gain on sale of corporate stock reflects unrealized appreciation in corporate assets. This problem could be eliminated by extending nonrecognition treatment to sales of corporate stock. Treating corporate stock differently from other appreciated assets seems unjustified, however, and would reintroduce unwarranted deferral opportunities. Alternatively, the corporation's basis in its assets could be adjusted to reflect shareholder-level gain or loss on a sale of corporate stock. By analogy, the partnership provisions provide an elective adjustment to the basis of partnership assets when a partner recognizes gain or loss from sale of his partnership interest. Basis adjustments would, however, prove administratively quite cumbersome when corporate stock is traded frequently.

*Example:* In Year 1, a sole shareholder (B) invests $100 in Y Corp., which uses the funds to purchase an asset that appreciates in value to $200 at the end of Year 10. If B sells her stock for $200, she will be taxed on a gain of $100. Since the basis of Y's asset remains unchanged, however, Y will also be taxed on the $100 of unrealized appreciation if it later sells the asset. Thus, the potential for double taxation remains unabated.

(c) *Distribution versus Retention.* A corporation's decision to retain its earnings or to distribute them as dividends has important tax consequences to shareholders. Annual distribution of corporate earnings ("full distribution") triggers an immediate shareholder-level tax, while retention of corporate earnings ("full retention") defers the shareholder-level tax. When the individual shareholder rate is significantly higher than the corporate rate, there is an incentive to retain earnings. The benefit of deferring the individual income tax may outweigh the burden of the corporate tax on future earnings. Conversely, when the individual shareholder rate is significantly lower than the corporate rate, full distribution will generally be preferable.

*Example:* At the beginning of Year 1, X Corp. has $100 available to invest or to distribute to A, X's sole shareholder. X and A are taxed at rates of 30% and 50%, respectively, and all investments earn a pre-tax return of 10%. If X invests the funds, X will have $7 after tax to distribute to A at the end of Year 1. After paying tax on the distribution, A will be left with $3.50. If X instead distributes the $100 immediately, A would have only $50 available to reinvest, which will yield only $2.50 after tax at the end of Year 1. Thus, A is $1 better off if the distribution is delayed.

In the above example, immediate distribution accelerates the individual tax, thereby reducing the funds otherwise available for investment. Any post-distribution earnings are taxed at the shareholder's higher individual rate. If A were instead taxed at a 20% rate, immediate distribution would leave her with $80 to reinvest, which would yield $6.40 after tax at the end of Year 1. Thus, low-bracket shareholders may benefit from elimination of the corporate-level tax, even though the distribution triggers an immediate shareholder-level tax. If the individual shareholder and corporate tax rates are equal, the tax results of full distribution and full retention are equivalent.

*Example:* In Year 1, X Corp. is capitalized with a $100 contribution from A, its sole shareholder; A and X are each taxed at a 30% rate and earn 7% after tax on all investments. For a 10–year period prior to liquidation, X will either (i) retain all earnings or (ii) distribute all earnings currently to A. At the end of Year 10, assuming that all earnings are retained, X will have available $197 to distribute to A. A will recover her initial investment ($100) tax free and the remaining distribution ($97) will trigger tax of $29 ($97 × 30%), leaving A with $168 after tax ($197 less $29). Alternatively, assuming that X distributes all earnings currently, A will receive 10 annual distributions of $7 each, or $4.90 after tax. At a 7% after-tax rate of return, the reinvested after-tax dividends will grow to $68 at the end of Year 10. Thus, A will receive $168 ($100 initial investment plus $68 after-tax savings) under either full retention or full distribution, provided that X and A are taxed at the same rate.

The above example is somewhat unrealistic because it ignores the possibility that nondividend distributions will be taxed at preferential rates. Thus, if A were taxed at a rate of only 20% on capital gains, full retention would be more advantageous than full distribution. At the lower rate, A would owe tax of $19 ($97 × 20%) on a liquidating distribution at the end of Year 10, assuming that all earnings are retained. Accordingly, A would receive $178 after tax ($197 less $19) instead of only $168 if liquidating distributions are treated more favorably than ordinary dividend distributions.

Such preferential treatment provides an incentive to distribute corporate earnings in nondividend form, thereby lowering the overall tax burden on corporate investments.

## § 4.  Integration

Several proposals have been advanced for "integrating" the treatment of corporations and shareholders in order to eliminate or reduce the burden of the double tax.  The goal of integration is to ensure that corporate income is taxed once and only once, regardless of whether such income is distributed or retained.  While other countries have successfully implemented corporate-shareholder integration, the United States has made relatively little progress in this direction.  Chapter 13 discusses various integration proposals and prospects for future corporate tax reform.

## § 5.  Choice of Business Entity

A form of full integration is already available in the case of so-called "S corporations," *i.e.*, certain corporations having relatively few shareholders and simple capital structures. *See* Chapter 12.  Subchapter S of the Code offers small business entities an alternative to the double tax system without sacrificing the non-tax advantages of doing business in corporate form.  In the case of electing corporations, both distributed and undistributed corporate earnings are generally taxed only at the shareholder level.  Thus, Subchapter S reflects the policy goal that federal income tax considerations should not unduly influence the choice of business form.

Choice-of-entity issues have become increasingly significant in light of the emergence of limited liability companies (LLCs), a hybrid form of business organization which combines both corporate and partnership characteristics. Partly in response to the growth of LLCs, the Treasury has announced that it is considering permitting an unincorporated business to elect to be treated for federal tax purposes either as a partnership or as a corporation. *See* Chapter 2. The criteria set forth in the existing classification rules for distinguishing double-tax from pass-through entities are widely viewed as unsatisfactory. It remains uncertain, however, whether an elective "check-the-box" approach will lead to substantial simplification. As long as the existing system remains unintegrated, the pressure for ad hoc integration is likely to continue.

## § 6. Fundamental Concepts

(a) *General.* Typically, Subchapter C prescribes mandatory statutory rules for taxation of business transactions. While mastery of the statutory rules is essential, it is also important to grasp the role of general tax principles and judicially-developed doctrines. The nonrecognition provisions of §§ 351 and 361, for example, are grounded in general concepts of realization and recognition. Even if the literal provisions of Subchapter C are satisfied, a transaction may still be challenged on nonstatutory grounds. Several judicial doctrines are available to recharacterize transactions that lack economic substance or fail to comport with statutory intent: the substance-over-form doctrine, the business purpose doctrine, and the step-transaction doctrine.

(b) *Nonrecognition.* The Code provides nonrecognition treatment for certain transactions which are viewed as mere changes in the form of an investment. Nonrecognition transactions include incorporation transfers (Chapter 3) and certain corporate rearrangements broadly described as reorganizations (Chapter 9). Typically, the nonrecognition provisions ensure that any realized gain or loss is temporarily deferred rather than permanently eliminated. Technically, deferral is accomplished by requiring that a taxpayer's basis in property received in a nonrecognition transaction be determined (in whole or in part) either by reference to the basis of other property formerly held by the same taxpayer ("exchanged basis") or by reference to the basis of the same property in the hands of a previous owner ("transferred basis"). For convenience, the general term "substituted basis" is used to refer to exchanged basis as well as transferred basis. *See* §§ 7701(a)(42)-(44). The strengthening of the double tax system has enhanced the importance of tax-free reorganizations as opposed to taxable acquisitions which trigger tax at both the corporate and shareholder levels.

(c) *Substance Over Form.* For tax purposes, the form in which the parties structure a corporate transaction is often controlling. Although the parties are free to choose the most advantageous form, they generally may not disavow their formal arrangement on the ground that it does not comport with economic substance. The government may invoke the substance-over-form doctrine, however, to challenge the form chosen by the parties. Given the pervasive nature of the substance-over-form doctrine, it is difficult to predict when courts will look behind the form of a transaction to determine its economic substance. If a transaction is motivated solely by a tax-avoidance purpose, it may be disregarded as a "sham."

(d) *Business Purpose*. The business purpose test is generally considered to stem from *Gregory v. Helvering* (S.Ct.1935), an early case involving a corporate spin-off. In *Gregory*, the Supreme Court determined that the absence of a business purpose removed the transaction from the intended scope of the reorganization provisions, since it was a mere device to avoid taxes. The business purpose test was subsequently incorporated in regulations governing tax-free divisions and reorganizations. *See* Chapters 9 and 10. The requirement of a business purpose is not confined to these specific areas, but crops up throughout Subchapter C. A transaction that lacks a legitimate business purpose is unlikely to withstand scrutiny.

(e) *Step Transaction*. Under the step-transaction doctrine, a series of formally separate steps may be collapsed and treated as if they constituted a single integrated transaction. In general, courts have applied three variants of the step-transaction doctrine: the "binding commitment" test, the "mutual interdependence" test, and the "end result" test. The first test looks to whether, at the time the initial transaction was entered into, there was a binding commitment to undertake the subsequent steps. *See* Intermountain Lumber Co. (Tax Ct.1976); Mc-

Donald's Restaurants of Illinois, Inc. (7th Cir.1982). Even in the absence of a binding commitment, the second test is relevant if the legal relations created by the initial transaction would have been meaningless without completion of the entire transaction. *See* American Bantam Car Co. (Tax Ct.1948). The third test focuses on whether the parties conceived of the various steps in the transaction as an integrated whole designed from the outset to reach a particular end result. Taken together, these three tests represent a continuum of the step-transaction doctrine from the relatively concrete "binding commitment" test to the amorphous "end result" test.

A recent case may indicate judicial reluctance to extend the scope of the step-transaction doctrine. *See* Esmark, Inc. (Tax Ct.1988). In *Esmark*, the court refused to apply the step-transaction doctrine even though the parties' arrangement was clearly intended to exploit a loophole under prior law. Rather than collapsing the existing steps, the government attempted to recast the transaction by creating a fictional step. The court found that the transaction did not involve any unnecessary steps and could not have been accomplished more directly by a different route. Since all of the steps had independent economic significance, the court respected the form of the transaction. It remains unclear whether the controversial decision in *Esmark* is confined to the particular facts involved or evinces broader judicial skepticism toward the step-transaction doctrine.

# CHAPTER 2

# CORPORATION AS TAXABLE ENTITY

## § 1. Definition and Classification

(a) *General.* Under § 7701(a)(3), the term "corporation" is defined to include associations. The § 7701 Regulations list six corporate characteristics to be taken into account in determining whether an unincorporated organization will be classified as an association for federal tax purposes: (i) associates, (ii) an objective to carry on business and divide the gains therefrom, (iii) continuity of life, (iv) centralized management, (v) limited liability, and (vi) free transferability of interests. The first two characteristics are essential: unless both are present, the organization cannot be classified as an association. In addition, to qualify as an association (as opposed to a partnership or trust, for example), the organization must have a majority of the four remaining corporate characteristics. Reg. § 301.7701–2(a)(3).

For example, a trust cannot be taxed as a corporation if it lacks either of the two essential corporate characteristics. *See* Morrissey (S.Ct.1935) (trust taxed as corporation); Bedell (Tax Ct.1986)(testamentary trust lacking "associates" could not be classified as an association). Similarly, a partnership is ordinarily not treated as an corporation for federal tax purposes unless, in addition to

18

the two essential corporate characteristics, it also has at least three of the remaining four corporate characteristics.

Under § 7704(a), certain publicly traded partnerships (PTPs) are treated as corporations for federal tax purposes. Congress was concerned that such investment vehicles offered an opportunity for active businesses previously conducted in corporate form to avoid the corporate-level tax. A PTP is defined as any partnership whose interests are (i) traded on an established securities market, or (ii) readily tradeable on a secondary market (or the substantial equivalent thereof). § 7704(b). Even if a partnership is a PTP, it will not be taxed as a corporation if at least 90% of its gross income for the taxable year is derived from interest, dividends and certain other forms of passive income. § 7704(c).

(b) *Hybrid Entities*. Recently, limited liability companies (LLCs) have emerged as a hybrid form of business organization that combines the corporate benefit of limited liability for its owners with pass-through tax treatment. After initial hostility, the Service ruled in 1988 that a Wyoming LLC would be classified as a partnership for federal tax purposes. *See* Rev. Rul. 88–76. The Service determined that the Wyoming LLC had, in addition to the two essential corporate characteristics, only two of the remaining corporate characteristics (*i.e.*, centralized management and limited liability); neither continuity of life nor free transferability was present. Typically, LLC statutes provide "default" rules that allow the parties to custom tailor their business arrangement through the LLC's operating agreement. Because of this flexibility, care must be exercised in organizing an LLC to ensure that it does not have a preponderance of corporate characteristics for federal tax purposes. Depending on the terms of its articles and operating agreement, an LLC may be classified for federal tax purposes as either a corporation or a partnership. *See* Rev. Rul. 93–38.

The Service has recently issued guidelines that provide a "safe harbor" for classification of LLCs. *See* Rev. Proc. 95–10. The classification standards vary depending upon whether the LLC is governed by all of its members or by so-called member managers, *i.e.*, persons designated or elected by the members to act on behalf of the LLC pursuant to the applicable state statute. Continuity of life is lacking if the LLC would technically dissolve upon the occurrence of certain specified dissolution events unless continued by the consent of the majority in interest of the remaining members. To lack continuity, each member manager or, in the absence of designated managers, each member must be subject to the specified dissolution events. Free transferability is lacking if members owning more than 20% of all interests in the LLC do not have an unrestricted right to transfer their interests. A valid transfer restriction may be conditioned on the consent of a majority of nontransferring member-managers or, in the absence of designated managers, a majority of nontransferring members.

The Service has abandoned its earlier position that an LLC automatically has centralized management if member managers are appointed. Under the guidelines, centralized management is lacking in a member-managed LLC if member managers in the aggregate own at least 20% of the interests in the LLC and certain other requirements are satisfied. Centralized management is always lacking if the LLC is managed by the members exclusively in their capacity as members. Although an LLC normally possesses limited liability, the Service will rule that this characteristic is lacking if at least one member validly assumes personal liability for all of the LLC's obligations.

In addition to LLCs, other hybrid entities such as "limited liability partnerships" (LLPs) have become increasingly popular. An LLP is essentially a general partnership in form, but its members typically are shielded from liability arising from acts of negligence or malfeasance by another member. In some states, an LLP can provide liability protection against contractual as well as tort claims. The rise of LLCs and LLPs has called into question the appropriateness of distinguishing double-tax from pass-through entities based on factors such as limited liability. The existing classification criteria, which depend largely on historical state-law differences between partnerships and corporations, are no longer adequate to deal with contemporary forms of business organization.

(c) *Simplification of Classification Rules*. The Treasury is considering simplified classification rules that would allow an unincorporated business to elect to be treated as either a corporation or a partnership for federal tax purposes. The Treasury's proposals recognize that as a practical matter classification as an association is largely elective under the existing rules. By choosing an appropriate organizational form and including appropriate terms in the governing instruments, most unincorporated businesses can obtain the desired tax classification. Thus, partnership classification is available for nonpublicly traded entities that are virtually indistinguishable from corporations. Allowing an express election would eliminate wasteful expenditure of resources in business planning and tax administration.

The Treasury's proposals would not affect the tax classification of existing entities. An entity organized as a corporation under state law would continue to be treated as a corporation for federal tax purposes. Absent an express election to the contrary, domestic unincorporated businesses would normally be classified as partnerships, and foreign business entities would be classified as associations, in accordance with the presumed preference of the owners. The Treasury's proposals leave numerous issues unaddressed, including possible restrictions on the ability of an existing business to change from one status to another. Although formal recognition of elective classification would permit greater flexibility within the existing income tax system, it is hardly an adequate substitute for a thoroughgoing reexamination of the existing classification rules, especially in light of integration proposals that would do away with the double tax on corporate earnings. *See* Chapter 13.

(d) *Corporate Alter Ego*. In some cases, taxpayers have argued that a corporation's income should be taxed directly to its shareholders, rather than to the corporation, on the theory that (i) the corporation's separate existence should be ignored or (ii) the corporation acts merely as the shareholders' agent. In *Moline Properties* (S.Ct.1943), the Supreme Court held that a corporation may be treated as a separate taxable entity even if it is wholly dominated by a single shareholder. The Court noted that the corporation was not merely the shareholder's alter ego, and its independent corporate existence was not fictitious. In *Bollinger* (S. Ct.1988), the Supreme Court addressed the argument that a corporation might act merely as the agent of its shareholders. The Court held that an agency relationship is sufficiently established if (i) the agency relationship is set forth in writing at the time the corporation acquires the relevant assets, (ii) the corporation functions as an agent with respect to those assets for all purposes, and (iii) the corporation's status as an agent is disclosed in all dealings with third parties relating to those assets. These cases indicate that agency status is essentially a factual matter to be determined by reference to criteria other than the control of the corporation inherent in the corporate-shareholder relationship.

## § 2.  Corporate Tax Rate Structure

(a) *General*. For taxable years beginning on or after January 1, 1993, a corporation's taxable income is taxed at the following graduated rates under § 11: 15% on the first $50,000, 25% on the next $25,000, 34% on the next $9,925,000, and 35% on taxable income in excess of $10,000,000.

The benefit of the 15% and 25% rates is phased out by a 5% surtax on taxable income between $100,000 and $335,000. The maximum surtax liability—5% of the amount of taxable income in the $235,000 phase-out range ($335,000 less $100,000), or $11,750—is exactly equal to the difference between a flat 34% tax on $75,000 ($25,500) and the tax imposed at the 15% and 25% rates ($13,750). Thus, a corporation with taxable income between $335,000 and $10,000,000 pays tax at an effective (as well as marginal) rate of 34%. The benefit of the 34% rate is phased out by a 3% surtax on taxable income between $15,000,000 and $18,333,-333, producing a maximum additional surtax of $100,000 (3% of $3,333,333). As a result, corporate taxable income over $18,333,333 is subject to an effective (as well as marginal) rate of 35%.

(b) *Capital Gains and Losses.* Before 1987, corporations were taxed on "net capital gain" at a rate equal to the lesser of the regular tax rates or a flat 28% rate. (Net capital gain is defined in § 1222(11) as the excess of net long-term capital gain over net short-term capital loss.) The 1986 Act eliminated this preferential treatment; for taxable years beginning on or after January 1, 1993, net capital gain is taxed at a flat 35% rate under § 1201(a). Although there is currently no difference between the maximum ordinary income rate and the net capital gain rate, an increase in ordinary income rates without a corresponding change under § 1201(a) would enhance the importance of capital gain treatment.

A corporation may deduct capital losses only to the extent of capital gains during the year. § 1211(a). Any excess capital losses may be carried back for 3 years and carried forward for 5 years. § 1212(a)(1).

## § 3.  Corporate Taxable Income

(a) *General.*  The gross income of a corporation is defined under § 61 in much the same manner as that of an individual, and corporate taxable income is determined under § 63(a) by subtracting allowable deductions from gross income.  Corporations may deduct their ordinary and necessary business expenses under § 162 and interest expense under § 163.  Corporations are also allowed deductions for security and debt losses under §§ 165 and 166. Corporate net operating losses are deductible subject to the 3–year carryback and 15–year carryforward provisions of § 172.  Section 291 imposes special limitations on the tax benefits available to a corporation from specified "preference items," such as the unrecaptured portion of accelerated depreciation deductions on certain real property under § 1250.  The passive loss limitations of § 469, enacted by the 1986 Act to curb tax shelters, do not apply to corporations (other than certain closely held corporations and personal service corporations). §§ 469(a)(2) and 469(j)(1)-(2).  In the case of an S corporation, the passive loss limitations are determined separately on the individual shareholders' tax returns.

Section 248 allows a corporation to elect to amortize certain organizational expenses over a 60–month period. § 248(a). Organizational expenses are defined as any expenditures which (i) are incident to creation of the corporation, (ii) are chargeable to capital account, and (iii) would otherwise be amortizable if the corporation had an ascertainable life. § 248(b). Organizational expenses include legal fees for drafting the corporate charter and by-laws, fees paid to the state for incorporation and necessary accounting fees. *See* Reg. § 1.248–1(b). However, expenses of issuing or selling stock and expenditures connected with transfer of assets to the corporation are specifically excluded. *See* Reg. § 1.248–1(b)(3).

(b) *Disallowed Deductions.* Section 162(m), added in 1993, disallows a deduction for compensation by publicly held corporations in excess of $1 million paid to a "covered employee," defined as an employee who (i) as of the close of the taxable year is the chief executive officer (CEO) of the corporation or (ii) is one of the four most highly compensated corporate officers (other than the CEO) for the taxable year. Section 162(m) does not apply to performance-based compensation if certain procedural requirements are satisfied and there is accountability to outside directors and shareholder approval. Thus, compensation in excess of $1 million may be deductible to the extent that it is keyed to an improvement in the corporation's overall performance or an increase in share prices.

Section 267(a)(1) disallows deductions for losses on sales or exchanges of property between certain related parties. Under § 267(b), an individual and a corporation are treated as related parties if the individual owns directly or indirectly more than 50% in value of the corporation's outstanding stock. For this purpose, stock ownership is determined under the constructive ownership rules of § 267(c).

The "matching" rules of § 267(a)(2) also defer the deduction for an item of expense or interest owed by an accrual-method taxpayer to a related party who uses the cash method, until the item is actually included in the payee's gross income (generally when paid). This provision is intended, for example, to prevent a corporation from deducting currently an amount for accrued but unpaid salary owed to a controlling shareholder-employee. The 1986 Act amended § 267(a)(2) to cover any shareholder-employee of a personal service corporation (as defined in § 441(i)(2)) as a related party, regardless of the amount of stock ownership.

(c) *Cancellation of Indebtedness.* Under § 108, a corporation may recognize cancellation of indebtedness income upon retirement of its debt for less than its adjusted issue price. If a corporation issues stock in exchange for its debt, it is generally treated as if it had satisfied the debt for an amount equal to the fair market value of the stock. § 108(e)(8). Under prior law, the so-called stock-for-debt exception permitted a bankrupt or insolvent corporation to avoid reducing its tax attributes under § 108 upon a cancellation of its indebtedness. In 1993, Congress repealed the stock-for-debt exception for transfers occurring after December 31, 1994.

## § 4.  Taxable Year and Method of Accounting

A corporation, like any other taxpayer, must choose a taxable year and method of accounting for tax purposes.  §§ 441 and 446.  Generally, corporations may adopt either a calendar or a fiscal year.  Under § 441(i), added by the 1986 Act, a personal service corporation (defined in § 269A as a corporation of which the principal activity is performance of personal services by its shareholders) may be required to use a calendar year unless it obtains the Service's approval to select a fiscal year.  Similarly, an S corporation is generally required to use a calendar year.  § 1378.  These rules are intended to eliminate the advantages of tax deferral arising from a difference between the taxable year of the corporation and that of its shareholders.

The Omnibus Budget Reform Act of 1987 (the "1987 Act") added three provisions that significantly modify these rules.  Section 444 allows S corporations and personal service corporations to elect to retain their previous fiscal years, or, if newly formed, to adopt fiscal years ending no earlier than September 30.  Section 7519 requires that S corporations that elect fiscal years must make certain payments on behalf of their owners to offset the advantage of tax deferral.  Finally, § 280H provides that personal service corporations which "disproportionately postpone" payments to employee-owners until after December 31 must postpone some or all of their deductions until the following fiscal year.  *See* Temp. Reg. § 1.280H–1T.

Section 448 requires most Subchapter C corporations to use the accrual method of accounting, except for certain farming corporations, "qualified personal service corporations" (as defined in § 448(d)(2)) and entities having average annual gross receipts of $5 million or less for the 3–year period preceding the taxable year. Qualified personal service corporations are defined as corporations substantially all of whose activities involve the performance of services in certain specified fields (including health, law and accounting), provided that substantially all of the stock in such corporations is owned by employees, retired employees or their estates. Temporary Regulations § 1.448–1T(e) provide guidance concerning when a corporation will be considered a qualified personal service corporation based on the type of services provided. Qualified personal service corporations are taxed at a flat rate of 35%, without the benefit of the graduated rates. § 11(b)(2).

## § 5. Allocation of Income and Deductions Among Related Taxpayers

Section 482 authorizes the Service to reallocate income, deductions and certain other items among two or more "organizations, trades, or businesses" under common control in order clearly to reflect the income of such organizations. The major purpose of § 482 is to prevent shifting or distortion of income or deductions reported by related parties. The term "organizations, trades or businesses" has been broadly construed to cover virtually any type of business structure having independent tax significance. *See* Keller (Tax Ct.1981). For example, § 482 clearly applies to transactions between a corporation and a sole proprietorship owned by a controlling shareholder. In *Foglesong* (7th Cir.1982), the Seventh Circuit considered whether § 482 applies to a taxpayer whose only trade or business is the performance of services for a controlled corporation. Because the taxpayer and the controlled corporation were engaged in the same business, the court held that the two-trades-or-businesses requirement of § 482 was not satisfied. *But see* Dolese (10th Cir.1987)(two separate trades or businesses found). The Service has announced that it will not follow the holding in *Foglesong* that § 482 does not apply to a shareholder-employee who works exclusively for a controlled corporation. Rev. Rul. 88–38. In the international context, the Service has invoked § 482 to reallocate income from a foreign subsidiary to a U.S. parent based on an arm's-length standard. *See* Bausch & Lomb, Inc. (2d Cir.1991).

Under § 269A, the Service may reallocate income or deductions between a personal service corporation and its employee-owners. Thus, § 269A sidesteps the issue of whether the rendering of services by an employee is a separate trade or business. This provision, however, applies only to a narrow category of personal service corporations performing services primarily for one other entity. In addition, the principal purpose for forming or using the corporation must be avoidance or evasion of federal income tax by reducing the income of, or securing tax benefits that would otherwise not be available to, an employee-owner.

Assignment-of-income principles may also be relevant in determining whether income should be taxed to a personal service corporation or its employee-owners. In *Sargent* (8th Cir.1991), the government sought unsuccessfully to tax income directly to professional hockey players who had formed personal service corporations that contracted with the hockey teams to provide their services. In refusing to apply assignment-of-income principles, the Eighth Circuit noted that the personal service corporations had the legal obligation to perform and legal control of the players. It rejected the Tax Court's "team control test" which looks to whether the team has the right to control the manner and means by which the taxpayer's personal services are performed. On similar facts, the Tax Court subsequently held in *Leavell* (Tax Ct.1995) that a professional basketball player was an employee of the basketball team and thus taxable on income paid to his personal service corporation.

## § 6.  Alternative Minimum Tax

(a) *Purpose of the AMT*. In addition to the regular corporate tax, a corporation may also be subject to the alternative minimum tax (AMT) imposed by § 55. The primary objective of Congress in enacting the AMT was to ensure that taxpayers with substantial economic income could not reduce their tax liability to nominal levels by using exclusions, deductions and credits allowable under the regular tax. Thus, the AMT tax base ("alternative minimum taxable income," or AMTI) is broader than regular taxable income and is intended to provide a better measure of the corporation's economic income.

(b) *Mechanics*. Section 55 imposes a tentative minimum tax of 20% on the corporation's AMTI, computed after allowance of a $40,000 exemption which is phased out between $150,000 and $310,000. *See* §§ 55(b) and 55(d). AMTI is defined in § 55(b)(2) as regular taxable income, adjusted as provided by §§ 56 and 58 and increased by the tax preference items listed in § 57. If the corporation's tentative minimum tax exceeds the regular tax for the taxable year, the excess amount is the AMT.

*Example:* X Corp. has a tentative minimum tax of $1.5 million and a regular tax of $1 million. X must pay total taxes (AMT and regular tax) of $1.5 million, comprising $1 million of regular tax and $.5 million of AMT. In this sense, the AMT is an "add-on" tax rather than an alternative tax. This distinction is important when the taxpayer computes its AMT credits under § 53 against the regular tax, discussed below. The § 53 credit is limited to the excess of the tentative minimum tax over the regular tax, or $.5 million in this example.

(c) *Adjustments Other Than ACE Adjustment*. Sections 56–58 specify the adjustments that must be made to taxable income in arriving at AMTI. For example, § 56(a)(1) generally requires use of a modified version of the alternative depreciation system under § 168(g) to determine depreciation deductions for AMT purposes. To the extent that the corporation's allowable depreciation deductions under the accelerated cost recovery system (ACRS) exceed the amount determined under § 56(a)(1), the excess is added back to the corporation's taxable income.  Under § 56(a)(1), real property is depreciated over a 40–year period using the straight-line method.  Tangible personal property (*e.g.*, machinery and equipment) is depreciated using the 150% declining balance method (rather than the 200% declining balance method under ACRS) over a longer useful life.  Other adjustments accelerate the timing of income from long-term contracts, disallow installment sale treatment of certain property, and require inclusion of interest on specified private activity bonds.  *See* §§ 56(a)(3), 56(a)(6) and 57(a)(5).  Section 56(d) also requires recomputation of net operating losses to reflect AMTI and limits the deductible portion to 90% of AMTI.

In addition, § 58 imposes special rules in computing AMTI for certain farming and passive activity losses, but these adjustments generally do not apply to corporations (except for personal service corporations).

(d) *Timing Differences*.  Many of the adjustments required in arriving at AMTI affect only the timing and not the amount of a corporation's deductions.  In effect, these adjustments represent a downpayment on the corporation's regular tax liability, since the AMT denies certain income tax deferrals and accelerated deductions that are allowable for regular tax purposes.  The corporation may receive no tax benefit from a corresponding reduction in AMTI in later years, however, if its regular tax reflects some items which generated AMT in earlier years.

In these situations, § 53 provides relief by allowing a credit against the corporation's regular tax for the AMT paid in earlier years.

*Example:* X Corp. owns depreciated residential real property which is used in its trade or business. For regular tax purposes, the depreciation will be taken ratably over 27.5 years under § 168. For AMT purposes, however, the recovery period for the property will be 40 years, resulting in smaller AMT deductions (and higher AMTI) in the early years. The basis of the property will be fully recovered for regular tax purposes at the end of 27.5 years, but the corporation will still be entitled to AMT depreciation deductions for another 12.5 years, resulting in lower AMTI. In this situation, § 53 would allow a credit against X's regular tax liability in later years for the AMT generated in the earlier years attributable to the timing differences in the depreciation deductions.

The amount of the § 53 credit is the corporation's alternative minimum tax liability for all prior years reduced by the § 53 credits allowable for prior years; the amount of the credit in any year may not reduce the regular tax below the AMT for the current year. Prior to 1989, no credit was allowed for AMT allocable to so-called exclusion preferences (*i.e.*, those items involving permanent exclusions rather than timing differences), since such items could never generate any regular tax liability. Under current law, however, a credit is allowed for the entire amount of the AMT, eliminating the distinction between timing and exclusion preferences. *See*

§ 53(d)(1)(B)(iv). For purposes of the § 53 credit, the taxpayer's AMT can be carried forward indefinitely (until applied against the regular tax), but may not be carried back. Since no credit carryback is permitted, § 53 does not provide relief if an item generates regular tax liability in an earlier year and also generates AMT liability in a later year.

(e) *Parallel Tax System.* In effect, the AMT is a separate tax system, and taxpayers must keep records of ongoing AMT adjustments even for years in which no AMT is payable. The AMT adjustments will affect the AMT basis of the corporation's property, which can have surprising results upon sale of the property in subsequent years.

*Example:* Assume that X Corp. in the above example has depreciated the basis of its real property to zero for regular tax purposes, but that the property still has a basis of $1,000 for AMT purposes. If the property is sold for $500, the corporation will have a $500 gain for regular tax purposes and a $500 loss for AMT purposes.

(f) *ACE Adjustment.* Despite the comprehensive AMT base, Congress was concerned that companies with substantial income for financial accounting purposes might still pay insufficient tax. To address these concerns, § 56(g) requires an upward adjustment to AMTI equal to 75% of the corporation's "adjusted current earnings" (ACE) over its AMTI (computed before the ACE adjustment and AMT net operating losses). In computing ACE, interim AMTI (determined before the ACE adjustment) is adjusted upward or downward to reflect more accurately the corporation's economic income.

§ 56(g)(4). Thus, an upward adjustment is required for certain items that are not included in interim AMTI but that increase a corporation's earnings and profits ("e & p"). For a discussion of e & p, *see* Chapter 4. Similarly, items that reduce taxable income but are nondeductible for purposes of computing e & p must generally be added back in determining ACE (other than the 80% and 100% dividends-received deduction under § 243). ACE adjustments may also reduce AMTI; if interim AMTI exceeds ACE, then AMTI is reduced by 75% of such excess. *See* § 56(g)(2).

## § 7. Capital Structure

(a) *Debt vs. Equity.* A corporation's capital structure often includes substantial amounts of debt in addition to the shareholders' equity. From the corporation's standpoint, interest payments on corporate debt give rise to a deduction while distributions with respect to stock do not. From the investor's standpoint, corporate debt is often preferable to stock because the repayment of principal at maturity or on redemption is generally tax free, while a redemption of stock may trigger recognition of ordinary income or capital gain to the shareholder. A corporate shareholder, however, may prefer to hold stock rather than debt, since a portion of the dividends received may be excludable under § 243.

In general, the parties are free to choose debt or equity financing or a combination of each. If the ratio of debt to equity in the corporation's capital structure is unreasonably high, however, the Service may treat purported debt instruments as stock for tax purposes, with the result that no deduction is allowed for payments reported as interest by the corporation. In 1969, Congress added § 385 to the Code which authorized the Treasury to issue regulations governing the classification of instruments as debt or stock for tax purposes. The Regulations issued under § 385 proved unworkable, however, and never became effective in final form. The debt-equity classification, therefore, depends on a judicially-developed facts-and-circumstances test. Under § 385(a), the Treasury has authority to issue regulations bifurcating a hybrid instrument into part debt and part stock. Section 385(c) provides generally that the issuer's initial characterization of an instrument is binding on all holders, although the Service may challenge such characterization. *See* Notice 94–47 (Service will closely scrutinize debt instruments that contain equity features, including unreasonably long maturity or repayment in the insurer's stock).

(b) *Gain or Loss on Investments.* Stock and debt instruments in the hands of a shareholder are generally capital assets, so that any gain or loss on disposition is capital gain or loss. Under § 1271, retirement of a debt instrument is treated as an exchange. Section 1276 may require a portion of the gain on so-called market discount bonds, however, to be reported as ordinary income rather than capital gain to the extent allocable to accrued market discount.

Worthless stock or debt is subject to the rules of § 165(g) or § 166. Generally, § 165(g) provides for capital loss treatment if a loss results from worth-lessness of stock or debt evidenced by a "security" which is a capital asset. If a loss is sustained on a debt not evidenced by a security, the bad debt deduction rules of § 166 are applicable. Business bad debts are treated as ordinary losses, while non-business bad debts are treated as short-term capital losses. §§ 166(a) and 166(d). If a shareholder-employee sustains a loss in his capacity as a credi-tor, nonbusiness bad debt treatment is virtually unavoidable. *See* Generes (S.Ct.1972)(shareholder-employee lacked "dominant" business motivation for loan to corporation). The nonbusiness bad debt rule of § 166(d) does not apply to corporations. Thus, a corporate creditor generally receives ordi-nary loss treatment under § 166(a), unless the debt is a "security" under § 165(g). A special rule, however, permits ordinary loss treatment for securi-ties in an "affiliated" corporation. § 165(g)(3).

If a corporation purchases stock in another corpo-ration, it may seek ordinary loss treatment on a sale of the stock on the ground that it purchased the stock predominantly for business rather than in-vestment purposes. In *Arkansas Best Corp.* (S.Ct. 1988), the Supreme Court denied ordinary loss treatment on a corporation's sale of stock in anoth-er corporation which it acquired and held for pur-poses of protecting its business reputation. The Court adopted a narrow reading of its earlier deci-sion in *Corn Products Refining Co.* (S.Ct.1955), which allowed an ordinary loss on certain futures contracts acquired as an integral part of the taxpay-

er's business. Since the stock held by the taxpayer
in *Arkansas Best* fell within the definition of a
capital asset in § 1221, the Court held that capital
loss treatment was appropriate regardless of the
taxpayer's motive in acquiring the stock.

(c) *Section 1244 Stock.* An individual investor in
a corporation which meets the requirements of
§ 1244 is entitled to treat up to $50,000 ($100,000
in the case of a joint return) of loss on "§ 1244
stock" as an ordinary (rather than a capital) loss for
the taxable year; losses in excess of the § 1244
ceiling amount are generally allowable as capital
losses. Section 1244 formerly applied only to common stock, but in 1984 this restriction was eliminated.

(d) *Qualified Small Business Stock.* Section
1202(a), added in 1993, permits a noncorporate
shareholder to exclude from gross income 50% of
eligible gain from sale or exchange of "qualified
small business stock," as defined in § 1202(c).
This provision is intended mainly to facilitate investment in small, active, operating businesses
whose gross assets do not exceed $50,000,000 imme-
diately after issuance of the qualifying stock.
§ 1202(d). The 50% exclusion is generally available
only if the shareholder acquired the qualifying stock
at its original issuance and has held such stock for
more than 5 years prior to disposition.
§§ 1202(b)(2) and 1202(c)(1)(B).

# § 8.  Special Corporate Taxes

In addition to the regular corporate tax and the
AMT, the Code also imposes special penalty taxes
(the accumulated earnings tax and the personal

holding company tax) on the undistributed income of certain corporations. The practical significance of these penalty taxes is greatly reduced as a result of the 1986 Act because corporations no longer offer significant income-sheltering opportunities. In view of the reduced importance of the penalty taxes, only their main outlines are summarized here.

(a) *Accumulated Earnings Tax.* The accumulated earnings tax imposed by § 531 is intended to penalize corporations with excessive accumulated earnings. When applicable, this penalty tax is imposed on "accumulated taxable income" at a flat 39.6% tax rate, corresponding to the maximum tax rate for individuals. Accumulated taxable income is defined in § 535 as taxable income, with specified adjustments, less a dividends-paid deduction and an accumulated earnings credit. Since the penalty tax is aimed only at undistributed corporate earnings, the dividends-paid deduction is allowed both for dividends actually paid and for so-called "consent dividends," that is, amounts treated as dividends with shareholder consent even though not actually distributed by the corporation. §§ 561–565. The accumulated earnings credit permits most corporations to accumulate at least $250,000 without incurring accumulated earnings tax liability. § 535(c). Prior to 1984, it was often assumed that the accumulated earnings tax did not apply to publicly held corporations, but the 1984 Act amended § 532(c) to make the tax applicable without regard to the number of shareholders.

The accumulated earnings tax is imposed only on a corporation "formed or availed of for the purpose of avoiding the income tax with respect to its shareholders...." § 532(a). The proscribed purpose is presumed in any case where earnings and profits are allowed to accumulate "beyond the reasonable needs of the business" (including "reasonably anticipated needs"), unless the corporation proves the contrary by a preponderance of the evidence. §§ 533(a) and 537(a)(1). This presumption may be determinative where tax avoidance is not the primary or dominant purpose for an accumulation, but only a contributing purpose. Donruss Co. (1969). The Regulations provide a nonexclusive list of factors for determining whether accumulations are reasonable. Reg. §§ 1.537–2(b) and 1.537–2(c). Although the reasonable needs of the business might ordinarily be financed with new equity capital or with borrowed funds, the courts tend to permit financing of operations and expansion entirely from retained earnings.

In a recent case, the Tax Court held that accumulations for the purpose of redeeming corporate stock were within the reasonable needs of the business but that accumulations beyond those needs were unreasonable. Technalysis Corp. (Tax Ct.1993). Nevertheless, the taxpayer successfully overcame the presumption that the unreasonable portion of the accumulations was for the proscribed purpose of avoiding shareholder income tax. The decision in *Technalysis* seems misguided for several reasons. First, the court arguably showed excessive deference to the director-shareholders' stated intent to accumulate only reasonable amounts as sufficient to overcome the statutory presumption of proscribed purpose. Second, accumulations for the purpose of future stock redemptions may well be outside the reasonable needs of the business. Accumulations to fund nondividend distributions tend to reduce shareholder income tax by allowing basis recovery and capital gain treatment.

(b) *Personal Holding Company Tax.* The personal holding company tax is imposed by § 541 on certain closely held corporations that might otherwise serve as vehicles to shelter passive income. Section 542 generally defines a personal holding company as a corporation of which more than half of the stock is owned (actually or constructively) by not more than 5 individuals, if at least 60% of the corporation's "adjusted ordinary gross income" (as defined in § 543(b)(2)) for the taxable year is "personal holding company income." *See* Rev. Rul. 89–20 (applying constructive ownership rules). Section 543 defines personal holding company income primarily as passive investment income (dividends, interest, rents, royalties and annuities). In addition, § 543(a)(7) includes certain personal service income in personal holding company income, in order to reach so-called "incorporated talents," *i.e.*, a corporation involved primarily in marketing the personal services of a professional athlete, actor, performer or other highly-compensated individual.

If the personal holding company provisions apply, § 541 imposes a tax of 39.6%, in addition to the regular corporate tax, on "undistributed personal holding company income," defined in § 545 as taxable income for the year with certain adjustments minus the dividends-paid deduction described in

§ 561. The adjustments to taxable income under § 545 include allowances for regular federal taxes and net capital gains (less taxes allocable thereto), as well as a disallowance of the § 243 dividends-received deduction. § 545(b). Thus, if a closely held corporation's sole annual income consists of $30,000 of fully deductible dividends, it will generally be a personal holding company subject to the § 541 tax unless it distributes all of its income to its shareholders each year.

The § 541 tax (but not interest or penalties) is subject to refund if the corporation follows the dividend-deficiency procedures contained in § 547. Thus, the effect of this tax is primarily to force distributions to shareholders rather than to raise revenue. To the extent that corporations no longer serve as effective tax shelters, the § 541 tax represents a trap for unwary corporations.

## § 9. Multiple Corporations and Consolidated Returns

The Code contains numerous provisions designed to prevent taxpayers from exploiting statutory allowances or graduated rates by conducting businesses through several corporations with similar ownership. *See, e.g.,* §§ 1551, 1561 and 1563. The narrowing of the corporate tax brackets under the 1986 Act has reduced the importance of some of these provisions.

A group of corporations related through one 80% "parent" corporation (an "affiliated group" under § 1504) may elect to file a consolidated return treating the group as a single unit for tax purposes. Thus, current losses of one corporation may, for example, be offset against current income of another corporation. The detailed rules for consolidated returns, contained in lengthy Regulations under § 1502, are beyond the scope of this work.

# CHAPTER 3

# INCORPORATIONS

## § 1. General

Section 351 reflects a longstanding policy that the incorporation of a business should generally be tax free both to the shareholders and to the corporation. This nonrecognition policy rests on the assumption that a contribution of property to a corporation represents a continuation in modified form, rather than a liquidation, of the shareholder's investment. At the shareholder level, § 351 provides that no gain or loss is recognized when "property is transferred to a corporation by one or more persons solely in exchange for stock in such corporation," if the transferor or transferors are in "control" of the corporation "immediately after the exchange." Section 357 generally preserves nonrecognition treatment at the shareholder level if the corporation assumes liabilities or takes property subject to liabilities in a § 351 transaction. Gain will be recognized at the shareholder level, however, under § 351(b), to the extent that the taxpayer receives "boot" as well as stock. At the corporate level, § 1032 provides that a corporation does not recognize gain or loss "on the receipt of money or other property in exchange for [its] stock (including treasury stock)." These nonrecognition provisions are accompanied by the basis provisions of §§ 358 and 362 which prescribe the basis of the stock (in the shareholder's hands) and the basis of the transferred assets (in the corporation's hands) generally by reference to the basis of the transferred assets in the shareholder's hands before the § 351 transfer, thus preserving any unrecognized gain or loss.

## § 2.  Requirements to Qualify for Tax–Free Exchange

Nonrecognition treatment is available under § 351 only if (i) one or more persons (the "transferors") transfer "property" to a corporation (the "transferee") in exchange for stock in the corporation and (ii) the transferors viewed as a group are in "control" of the corporation "immediately after" the transfer.

(a) *Property*.  Although the term "property" is not specifically defined, it is construed broadly to include cash, tangible property, accounts receivable, nonexclusive licenses and industrial know-how. The inclusion of cash does not specifically affect a person who transfers only cash, since he would recognize no gain or loss in any case.  The treatment of cash as property may be important to the other transferors, however, because it means that a person transferring cash will be counted in the group of property transferors for purposes of determining whether the control requirement is met.

The major exclusion from the definition of property is "services." § 351(d)(1).  The purpose of this exclusion is to ensure that a person who provides services will be taxed under § 61 or § 83 on the fair

market value of any stock (or other property) received from the corporation in exchange for the
services. This rule also prevents a person who
contributes only services from being counted in the
group of property transferors for purposes of the
control requirement. In some cases, it may be
possible to characterize a previously untaxed claim
for services as property, although the Service is
likely to challenge such a characterization. *See,
e.g.,* Stafford (11th Cir.1984)(real estate developer's
"letter of intent" treated as property under analogous provisions of § 721).

If the services were performed for a third party
and the service provider received stock from a corporation controlled by the third party, the stock
may be viewed as having been constructively issued
to the third party and then transferred to the
service provider (as compensation) in a taxable
transaction. If a transferor contributes a combination of property and services to a corporation in
exchange for stock as part of a mixed transaction,
the receipt of stock for property may qualify for
nonrecognition treatment if the other requirements
of § 351(a) are met. The receipt of stock attributable to services, however, will generally be treated
as a separate transaction outside the scope of § 351,
except for the limited purpose of determining
whether the control requirement (discussed below)
is met.

(b) *Stock.* Nonrecognition treatment is available
under § 351 only if the transferors receive stock of
the transferee corporation in the exchange. Under

prior law, § 351(a) applied to receipt of "stock or securities." Although the term "securities" was not defined, it was understood generally to include medium to long-term debt. *See, e.g.*, Bradshaw (Ct.Cl.1982)(notes maturing in 6.5 years or less not treated as securities). In 1989, Congress deleted the phrase "or securities" from § 351, so that receipt of a debt instrument will be taxable unless such debt is recharacterized as equity. Under the pre–1989 version of § 351, Congress was concerned that a taxpayer could avoid application of the installment sale rules by transferring appreciated property to a corporation in exchange for a combination of stock and securities. Receipt of securities, as opposed to stock, was considered inconsistent with the rationale for tax-free treatment under § 351(a).

Although § 351(a) provides for nonrecognition treatment if property is transferred "solely" in exchange for stock, this does not mean that the entire exchange will be taxable if the transferors receive cash or other property ("boot") in addition to stock. If some boot is received, § 351 nonrecognition treatment still applies to the receipt of stock, but the boot may trigger partial gain recognition under § 351(b). *See* § 3 below. Since § 351(a) by its terms no longer applies to receipt of securities, any debt instrument (whether short-term or long-term) will be treated as boot for purposes of § 351(b); the timing of the transferor's gain, however, will generally be determined under the installment sale rules of § 453. *See id.*

(c) *Control*. The transferor group must be in control of the corporation immediately after the transfer. For this purpose, "control" means direct ownership of stock possessing at least 80% of the total combined voting power of all classes of voting stock and at least 80% of the total number of shares of each class of nonvoting stock. § 368(c). *See* Rev. Rul. 59–259. The requisite percentage of stock must actually be owned by the transferors; the constructive ownership rules of § 318 do not apply to § 351.

There is no specific limit on the number of transferors or the timing of the transfers. For purposes of control, transfers need not be simultaneous, but may generally be aggregated as long as they are part of a prearranged plan and are carried out reasonably expeditiously. *See* Reg. § 1.351–1(a)(1). In a typical incorporation of a business in which the transferors receive 100% of the stock in exchange for property, the control test is easily satisfied. Moreover, § 351 also covers transfers to an existing corporation, if the transferors own the requisite amount of stock (including any stock previously owned and retained after the transfer) and the other requirements of § 351 are satisfied.

As noted above, if a transferor contributes a combination of property and services to a corporation in exchange for stock, the portion of the stock attributable to services is counted (along with the rest of the transferor's stock) in determining whether the control requirement is met. On the other hand, if the transferor contributes no property but only services, none of his stock is counted because the transaction falls entirely outside § 351.

*Example:* A transfers appreciated property worth $50,000, and B transfers appreciated property worth $15,000 and contributes services worth $35,-000, to X Corp. in exchange for all of the stock of X. A and B are each treated as transferors of property, and together they are in control of X. Neither A nor B will recognize any gain on the transferred property. B, however, will recognize $35,000 of ordinary income as compensation for her services. *See* Reg. § 1.351–1(a)(2), Example (3).

(d) *Nominal Transfers.* If a transferor contributes a nominal amount of property in exchange for stock, with the primary purpose of obtaining § 351(a) nonrecognition treatment for an exchange by another transferor, the Regulations provide that the nominal transferor will not be counted as part of the transferor group. Reg. § 1.351–1(a)(1). The transferred property will be considered to be of nominal value only if its fair market value is less than 10% of the fair market value of the stock already owned (or to be received in exchange for services) by the transferor. Rev. Proc. 77–37.

*Example:* X, a newly-formed corporation, issues 67% of its stock to A in exchange for appreciated property worth $67,000 and 33% of its stock to B in exchange for services worth $33,000. The transaction fails to qualify under § 351 since A, the only property transferor, lacks 80% control. As a result, A recognizes gain equal to the excess of the fair market value of the stock over A's basis in the transferred property; and B recognizes $33,000 of ordinary income. If B instead transferred $3,000 of cash in addition to $30,000 worth of services, the 10% safe-harbor rule would apply, and all of B's stock (including the 30% received for services) would count toward the control requirement. Because A and B together would receive 100% of the stock, A's transfer of appreciated property and B's transfer of cash would be tax free under § 351(a); B would still have $30,000 of ordinary income as compensation for services. If B transferred less than $3,000 cash, B's transfer would be considered nominal, and the entire transaction would fail to qualify under § 351(a).

A majority shareholder who makes a nominal transfer to enable a minority shareholder to qualify for § 351(a) treatment may have difficulty meeting the 10% safe-harbor test. *See, e.g.,* Estate of Kamborian (1972) (disregarding accommodation transfer because of lack of economic nexus).

*Example:* A owns 78% of the stock of X Corp., and B owns the remaining 22%; the total fair market value of the X stock is $100,000. If B wishes to make an additional tax-free transfer to X of property worth $22,000, under § 351(a) A must transfer an additional $7,800 in order to be included with B in the group of transferors.

(e) *Disposition of Stock.* Section 351(a) requires that the transferors be in control of the corporation immediately after the transfer. If some of the transferors promptly sell or dispose of their stock pursuant to a prearranged plan and fail to retain

sufficient stock to meet the 80% control requirement, the entire transaction may become ineligible
for nonrecognition treatment. In *American Bantam Car Co.* (Tax Ct.1948), the transferors contributed cash and other property to a new corporation
in exchange for 100% of its common stock; five
days later, the transferor-shareholders entered into
an agreement to transfer a portion of the common
stock to underwriters as compensation for their
services if the underwriters succeeded in selling the
corporation's preferred stock to the public. Upon
successful completion of the public offering approximately 15 months later, more than 20% of the
common stock was transferred to the underwriters.
The court held that the control requirement of
§ 351(a) was satisfied, despite the subsequent
transfer, because the § 351 exchange and the subsequent transfer to the underwriters were not "mutu-
ally interdependent" and therefore could not be
viewed as a single transaction.

For purposes of § 351, Proposed Regulations
treat a person who acquires stock from an underwriter pursuant to a "qualified underwriting transaction" as transferring cash directly to the corporation. Prop.Reg. § 1.351–1(a)(3). An offering is a
qualified underwriting transaction if the corporation issues stock for cash and the underwriter is an
agent of the corporation or the underwriter's stock
ownership is transitory. Thus, investors who acquire stock for cash in a qualified underwriting
transaction are treated as transferors for control
purposes, and the underwriter is disregarded. If a
third party purchases previously issued stock from a
member of the original control group, however,

control may be broken. *See, e.g.,* Intermountain Lumber Co. (Tax Ct.1976)(binding commitment by primary incorporator to sell 50% of the stock broke control).

(f) *Disproportionate Receipt of Stock.* When two or more transferors contribute property in exchange for stock, § 351 does not require as a condition for nonrecognition treatment that each transferor receive stock in proportion to the value of his respective property contribution. The Regulations, however, provide that the transaction may be recast "in accordance with its true nature." Reg. § 1.351–1(b)(1). Thus, the transaction may be treated as an initial proportionate issuance of stock, followed by a transfer between the shareholders in the nature of a gift or compensation.

*Example:* A and B transfer property of equal value to X, a newly-formed corporation, and in exchange A receives 60 shares of X stock and B receives 40 shares. The transaction may be treated as if A and B each initially received 50 shares of X stock and B then transferred 10 shares to A. If A and B are related family members, then B's transfer may be treated as a gift to A. Alternatively, if B is indebted to A for services, B's constructive transfer may be treated as compensation to A and relief of indebtedness to B. *See* Reg. § 1.351–1(b)(2), Example (1).

(g) *Investment Companies.* Section 351(e) denies § 351(a) nonrecognition treatment for transfers to an "investment company." This provision is aimed at so-called "swap funds" in which unrelated investors seek to achieve a tax-free diversification of their investment by transferring appreciated, readily marketable stock in exchange for stock of a newly-formed corporation. The Regulations provide that § 351(e) applies if (i) the transfer results, directly or indirectly, in diversification of the transferors' interests and (ii) the transferee is a regulated investment company, a real estate investment trust, or a corporation more than 80% of whose assets (other than cash and nonconvertible debt) consists of readily marketable stock, securities or similar assets held for investment. Reg. § 1.351–1(c)(1). If two or more persons transfer identical assets to a newly-formed corporation, the transfer will generally not be treated as resulting in diversification, unless it is part of a plan to achieve diversification without recognition of gain. Reg. § 1.351–1(c)(5); Rev. Rul. 88–32. If § 351(e) applies, losses as well as gains will be recognized. *See* Rev. Rul. 87–9.

## § 3. Boot

(a) *General.* Section 351(b) applies when a transferor receives cash or other property ("boot") in addition to stock qualifying for § 351(a) nonrecognition treatment. Under § 351(b), the transferor recognizes gain to the extent of cash and the fair market value of any other boot received. Any gain recognized with respect to receipt of debt instruments, however, may generally be deferred under the installment sale rules. Both the shareholder's basis in the stock received and the corporation's basis in the transferred property is increased to reflect any gain recognized by the transferor under § 351(b). *See* §§ 5 and 6 below. The transferor recognizes no loss in a § 351 transaction regardless of whether any boot is received. § 351(b)(2). Any unrecognized loss is preserved in the shareholder's adjusted basis in the stock received and in the corporation's basis in the transferred property. *See* §§ 5 and 6 below.

*Example:* In a § 351 transaction, A transfers land with an adjusted basis of $10,000 and a fair market value of $50,000 to a corporation in exchange for consideration consisting of $20,000 stock, $10,000 securities, $5,000 cash and $15,000 of other property. A's realized gain is $40,000 ($50,000 aggregate fair market value of consideration received less $10,000 basis in the transferred property), but A recognizes only $30,000 gain (fair market value of boot, consisting of $10,000 securities, $5,000 cash and $15,000 of other property). Deferral may be available under the installment sale rules, however, for the $10,000 of gain attributable to the securities. If A's basis in the transferred property were $40,000 instead of $10,000, the entire $10,000 of gain would be recognized since it does not exceed the amount of boot received. If A's basis in the transferred property were instead $60,-000, A would realize a loss of $10,000, but none of the loss would be recognized.

(b) *Character of Gain.* The character of any recognized gain is determined by reference to the nature of the transferred assets. Recognized gain is treated as ordinary income to the extent that it represents depreciation recapture under § 1245 or § 1250. In addition, § 1239 may require ordinary income treatment if the transferor owns, actually or constructively, more than 50% of the corporation's

stock and the property is depreciable in the corporation's hands.

(c) *Allocation*. If a transferor transfers several
different assets and receives some boot (in addition
to stock), it is necessary to allocate the consideration received separately to each asset for purposes
of determining the amount and character of gain
recognized. *See* Rev. Rul. 68–55, amplified by Rev.
Rul. 85–164. Any loss realized on an asset is not
recognized and cannot be offset against gain realized on any other asset.

*Example:* A transfers two assets in exchange for
$50,000 stock and $50,000 of cash in a § 351 transaction. Each of the assets has a basis of $20,000,
but Asset # 1 has a fair market value of $10,000
and Asset # 2 has a fair market value of $90,000.
The stock and cash must be allocated between the
two assets in proportion to their respective fair
market values. Accordingly, A is treated as receiv-
ing $\frac{1}{10}$ of the stock and cash for Asset # 1 and $\frac{9}{10}$ for
Asset # 2. Thus, A receives $5,000 of cash and
$5,000 stock for Asset # 1, and $45,000 of cash and
$45,000 stock for Asset # 2. A's realized loss of
$10,000 on Asset # 1 ($20,000 adjusted basis less
$10,000 consideration received) is not recognized.
A's realized gain of $70,000 on Asset # 2 is recog-
nized only to the extent of the boot received ($45,-
000). An alternative approach might be to allocate
the boot to the appreciated property (Asset # 2) to
the extent of the gain realized on that asset. Under
this approach, A would recognize $50,000 gain on
Asset # 2.

(d) *Installment Treatment.* If a transferor receives a combination of stock and debt in a § 351 transaction, the debt constitutes boot. Assuming that the debt qualifies for § 453 installment sale treatment, the shareholder may be able to defer recognition of gain. § 453(f)(6). *See* Prop. Reg. § 1.453–1(f)(3)(ii). The installment sale gain will normally be taxed only when the transferor receives payments on the debt rather than upon receipt of the debt. Under § 453(i), the shareholder must report gain immediately, however, to the extent of any depreciation recapture. Any deferred gain may be treated as ordinary or capital gain as payments are received, depending on the nature of the assets transferred. If the transferor reports gain under § 453, the transferee corporation's basis in the transferred property is not stepped up until the transferor recognizes gain. Prop. Reg. § 1.453–1(f)(3)(ii). If the transferee corporation disposes of the transferred property before making the subsequent installment payments, the benefit of the basis adjustment is not lost; instead, as payments are made, the transferee corporation is allowed a deductible loss equal to the amount of the basis step-up that it would have obtained had it still owned the transferred property. Prop. Reg. § 1.453–1(f)(3)(iii), Example (1).

## § 4. Relief of Liabilities

(a) *General.* If a corporation assumes a liability or acquires property subject to a liability in a § 351 transfer, the transferor must include the liabilities relieved in the amount realized. § 1001. Section 357(a), however, provides that the assumption of liabilities or acquisition of property subject to liabil-

ities is not treated as the receipt of boot, and does
not disqualify the transaction from nonrecognition
treatment under § 351. The principal effect of
§ 357(a) is to prevent the transferor from recognizing gain immediately on relief of liabilities. Instead, recognition of gain attributable to relief of
liabilities is deferred under § 358, which requires a
downward adjustment in the shareholder's basis in
the stock or securities received to reflect the relief
of liabilities. *See* § 5 below.

*Example:* A transfers property with a basis of
$50,000 and a fair market value of $100,000, subject
to a liability of $20,000, to X Corp. in exchange for
stock worth $80,000 (the net value of the trans-
ferred property). A will realize gain of $50,000
(total consideration of $100,000, consisting of $80,-
000 of stock and $20,000 of liabilities relieved, less
$50,000 adjusted basis). A will recognize no gain,
however, since § 357(a) does not treat the relief of
liabilities as boot. A's basis in the stock received
will be $30,000 under § 358 ($50,000 adjusted basis
of the transferred property, less $20,000 of liabili-
ties relieved).

(b) *Tax-Avoidance Transactions.* An important
exception to the general rule of § 357(a) is provided
in § 357(b) for certain tax-avoidance transactions.
Section 357(b) treats as taxable boot the entire
amount of liabilities assumed (or taken subject to)
by the corporation, if the transferor's principal purpose was tax avoidance or was not a bona fide
business purpose. Section 357(b) is intended to
prevent the transferor from bailing cash out of a
corporation by borrowing against the property im-

mediately before the transfer with the intention of keeping the borrowed funds and arranging for the corporation to pay the liability. Section 357(b) might apply, for example, if a taxpayer borrowed against business assets shortly before a § 351 transfer and used the borrowed proceeds to purchase a personal residence. If the borrowing is incurred in the course of the taxpayer's business or is used to acquire or improve the contributed property, however, § 357(b) should not apply because the borrowed funds are not retained by the transferor for a prohibited purpose. If § 357(b) applies, then all of the liabilities (not merely the liabilities with respect to which a prohibited purpose exists) are treated as cash boot. Reg. § 1.357–1(c).

*Example:* The facts are the same as in the previous example, except that A incurs the $20,000 of liabilities shortly before the § 351 transfer to purchase an automobile for personal use. Under § 357(b), the $20,000 relief of liabilities will be treated as cash boot. Accordingly, A's realized gain of $50,000 will be recognized to the extent of the $20,000 boot.

(c) *Liabilities in Excess of Basis.* Section 357(c)(1) provides another important exception to the general rule of § 357(a). Under § 357(c)(1), any liabilities relieved (or taken subject to) in excess of the transferor's basis are treated as gain from the sale or exchange of the transferred property. This provision is necessary to prevent the transferor's substituted basis in stock or securities from being reduced below zero under § 358. Section 357(c)(1) applies even if the transferor remains personally liable (usually as a guarantor) on a liability assumed by the corporation. *See* Smith (Tax Ct.1985); Owen (9th Cir.1989). If a transferor contributes his own note to the corporation, the issue arises whether the transferor can claim an increased basis to offset excess liabilities assumed. Generally, the courts and the Service have denied a basis increase on the ground that the transferor has a zero basis in his own note. *See* Alderman; Rev. Rul. 68–629.

In *Lessinger* (2d Cir.1989), the taxpayer transferred the assets of a sole proprietorship with a negative net worth to a newly-formed corporation; the corporation showed an open account from the transferor equal to the excess of the sole proprietorship's liabilities over the basis of its assets. The open account was subsequently formalized as a promissory note from the transferor. The Second Circuit agreed, in *Lessinger*, that the transferor had no basis in his own note, but then held that the transferor's basis for purposes of § 357(c) must be determined by reference to the transferee corporation's basis in the note, *i.e.*, a basis equal to the face value of the note. Accordingly, it held that the transferor recognized no gain from assumption of liabilities in excess of basis.

As a matter of statutory interpretation, *Lessinger* is clearly wrong in determining the transferor's basis under § 357(c) by reference to the transferee's basis. Since the transferee corporation takes a basis under § 362(a) equal to the transferor's basis in the transferred assets (increased by any gain recognized), the court's reasoning is circular. A literal application of *Lessinger* would leave the transferor with a negative basis under § 358 in the stock received, since no gain is recognized under § 357(c). As a practical matter, the result in *Lessinger* has superficial appeal because a transferor can generally avoid gain under § 357(c) by contributing additional cash (borrowed, if necessary, from a third party) in the § 351 exchange.

Section 357(c)(1) applies to each transferor separately, not to the transferors as a group. Each transferor may aggregate the basis of all assets transferred by him, however, for purposes of § 357(c)(1). Reg. § 1.357–2(a). The amount and character of any recognized gain must be allocated among the assets in proportion to their respective fair market values if more than one asset is transferred. Reg. § 1.357–2(b). To the extent that *Lessinger* applies, a transferor may avoid § 357(c) gain relatively easily avoid by contributing his own note in an amount equal to the excess liabilities. Alternatively, gain attributable to excess liabilities may normally be avoided by transferring additional cash or other property.

*Example:* A transfers two assets to a corporation in a § 351 transaction in exchange for stock worth $30,000. Asset # 1 has a basis of $15,000 and a fair market value of $30,000, and is subject to a liability of $20,000; Asset # 2 has a basis of $15,000 and a fair market value of $50,000, and is subject to a liability of $30,000. Under § 357(c)(1), A will recognize $20,000 of gain ($50,000 total liabilities relieved, less $30,000 total basis). If Asset # 1 is a capital asset and Asset # 2 is an ordinary income asset in A's hands, $7,500 of the gain will be capital gain allocable to Asset # 1 ($20,000 × $30,000/$80,000) and the remaining $12,500 will be ordinary income allocable to Asset # 2 ($20,000 × $50,000/$80,000). A could avoid recognizing any gain by transferring an additional $20,000 of cash (or unencumbered property with a basis of $20,000) to the corporation.

If the purpose for assumption of the liability is tax avoidance or is not a bona fide business purpose, however, § 357(b) applies instead of § 357(c)(1), and the entire liability (not merely the excess over total adjusted basis) is treated as taxable boot. *See* § 357(c)(2)(A).

*Example:* In the previous example, if A had a tax-avoidance purpose with respect to the transfer of Asset # 1 (subject to the $20,000 liability), then the entire $50,000 of liabilities relieved would be recognized as cash boot under § 357(b), rather than the $20,000 of excess liabilities over basis that would have been recognized if § 357(c)(1) applied. *See* Reg. § 1.357–1(c). The result would be the same if A contributed additional cash.

(d) *Certain Liabilities Excluded.* Section 357(c)(3) contains an exception to the rule of § 357(c)(1) for liabilities that would have given rise to a deduction if paid directly by the transferor. If § 357(c)(3) applies, the liability is not taken into account as an excess liability under § 357(c)(1). Section 357(c)(3) was intended to remedy the problem arising when a cash-method taxpayer transfers zero-basis receivables and accounts payable in a § 351 exchange. If the accounts payable were taken into account as liabilities under § 357(c)(1), the transferor would recognize gain equal to their full amount because he would have no basis in the receivables to offset the accounts payable. The transferor would have done better if he had received additional cash from the corporation and used it to pay the accounts payable directly; although the additional cash would have been taxable as boot, the transferor would at least receive an offsetting deduction on paying the accounts payable. In order to mitigate the disparity in tax treatment, § 357(c)(3) avoids taxing the gain from relief of excess deductible liabilities. Courts had reached a similar result even prior to enactment of § 357(c)(3). *See, e.g.,* Bongiovanni (2d Cir.1972); Focht (Tax Ct.1977). The special rule of § 357(c)(3) does not apply, however, to any liability which gave rise to or increased the transferor's basis in any property when incurred. § 357(c)(3)(B).

Although § 357(c)(3) literally applies only to "deductible" liabilities, the Service has permitted similar treatment for liabilities that would give rise to a capital expenditure. Rev. Rul. 95–74. In determining the amount of liabilities assumed for purposes of § 357(c)(1), the Service disregarded contingent environmental liabilities that had not yet given rise to a deduction or an increase in the transferor's basis in any property. *Id.* The principles underlying § 357(c)(3) justify excluding such liabilities in order to avoid "overstatement" of the transferor's liabilities and recognition of gain when the transferor has not received a corresponding tax benefit or deduction.

If only receivables and no offsetting accounts payable are transferred, the Service might assert that the transferor (rather than the corporation) should be taxed when the receivables are collected, under assignment-of-income principles. In the absence of a tax-avoidance purpose, however, the Service has ruled that it will not apply assignment-of-income principles to a cash-basis taxpayer's transfer of receivables in a § 351 transaction. Rev. Rul. 80–198. Thus, the corporation will be taxed on collection of the receivables, not the transferor. The corporation is also entitled to a deduction when it pays the accounts payable even though the transferor has already in effect received a deduction under § 357(c)(3). *Id.* *See* Rev.Rul. 95–74 (assumed environmental liabilities give rise to deductible or capital expenditure). Now that the maximum corporate rate is again lower than the maximum individual rate, a taxpayer may wish to retain the accounts payable to ensure that the deduction will be at the shareholder's marginal rate. By analogy to Rev. Rul. 80–198, however, the Service might seek to reallocate the accounts receivable to the transferor if the transfer is not for a bona fide business purpose.

## § 5. Transferor's Basis and Holding Period

(a) *General.* As a corollary to § 351(a) nonrecognition treatment, § 358(a)(1) provides that the transferor's basis in the stock (the "nonrecognition property") is determined by reference to his basis in the transferred property. The transferor's substituted basis in the stock is calculated as (i) the adjusted basis of the property transferred, (ii) decreased by the amount of cash and the fair market value of any other boot received, and (iii) increased by the amount of any gain recognized by the transferor on the exchange. The transferor's basis in different classes of stock is allocated in proportion to fair market value. Reg. § 1.358–2(b)(2). The transferor takes a basis in boot received (other than securities reported under the installment method) equal to its fair market value under § 358(a)(2); cash boot is in effect assigned a basis equal to its face amount.

*Example:* A transfers property with an adjusted basis of $20,000 and a fair market value of $100,000 in exchange for $75,000 worth of common stock and $25,000 worth of preferred stock. The common and preferred stock together will have an aggregate basis equal to A's basis in the transferred property ($20,000), allocated among the different classes of stock in proportion to their relative fair market values. Since the common stock accounts for 75% of the value of the consideration received, it receives a basis of $15,000 (75% of $20,000). The remaining basis of $5,000 (25% of $20,000) is allocated to the preferred stock.

(b) *Receipt of Boot.* If the transferor receives boot in addition to nonrecognition property, the basis computation under § 358(a)(1) will often leave the transferor with an aggregate basis in the nonrecognition property equal to his original basis in the transferred property. This is because the downward adjustment to basis for boot received is frequently offset by the upward adjustment for gain recognized. It is nevertheless important to calculate each separate step of the computation, since the recognized gain may be less than the fair market value of the boot received.

*Example (1):* A transfers property with an adjusted basis of $10,000 and a fair market value of $50,000 for total consideration of $50,000, consisting of stock ($30,000), cash ($5,000) and property ($15,000) other than securities. A realizes $40,000 gain, but recognizes only $20,000 of the gain (the fair market value of the boot). A's basis in the stock will be $10,000, calculated as: (i) the adjusted basis of the transferred property ($10,000), (ii) decreased by the cash and other boot received ($20,-000), and (iii) increased by the gain recognized ($20,000). Under § 358(a)(2), A's basis in the boot will be $20,000 ($5,000 cash and $15,000 fair market value of the other property).

*Example (2):* The facts are the same as in Example (1), except that A has a basis of $35,000 in the transferred property. A will realize, and hence recognize, only $15,000 of gain, even though she receives $20,000 of boot. A's basis in the stock will be $30,000, calculated as: (i) the adjusted basis of the transferred property ($35,000), (ii) decreased by the cash and other boot received ($20,000), and (iii) increased by the gain recognized ($15,000). A will still take a basis of $20,000 in the boot ($5,000 cash and $15,000 fair market value of the other property).

*Example (3):* The facts are the same as in Example (1), except that A has a basis of $55,000 in the transferred property. A will realize, but not recognize, a loss of $5,000. A's basis in the stock will be $35,000, calculated as: (i) the adjusted basis of the transferred property ($55,000), (ii) decreased by the cash and other boot received ($20,000), and (iii) increased by the gain recognized ($0).

If a transferor receives a combination of stock and debt in a § 351 transaction, the debt may qualify for installment reporting. *See* § 453(f). Solely for purposes of determining the transferor's basis in the stock under § 358, the deferred gain on the installment obligation is treated as if recognized immediately. *See* Prop. Reg. § 1.453–1(f)(3)(ii). The transferor's basis in the transferred property is allocated first to any stock received up to the fair market value of the stock; to the extent that the basis of the transferred property exceeds the fair market value of the stock received, the excess basis is allocated to the installment obligation. The basis, if any, allocated to the installment obligation reduces the amount of gain reportable upon payment of the installment obligation. *See* Prop. Reg. § 1.453–1(f)(3)(iii), Examples.

*Example (1):* In a § 351 transaction, A transfers property with an adjusted basis of $30,000 and a fair market value of $100,000 in exchange for $40,-000 worth of stock and a $60,000 note. A realizes

$70,000 gain, but recognizes only $60,000 of the gain (the fair market value of the note). Although the note constitutes boot under § 351(b), A's recognized gain is deferred under the installment sale rules. A's basis in the stock is $30,000, calculated as: (i) the adjusted basis of the transferred property ($30,000), (ii) decreased by the fair market value of the boot received ($60,000), and (iii) increased by the recognized but deferred gain ($60,000). A will recognize $60,000 of gain when the note is paid; A's remaining realized gain of $10,000 is preserved in the basis of her stock.

*Example (2):* The facts are the same as in Example (1), except that A receives $20,000 worth of stock and an $80,000 note. Since A's basis in the transferred property ($30,000) exceeds the fair market value of the stock ($20,000), the "excess basis" of $10,000 is allocated to the installment obligation. A's realized gain of $70,000 will be recognized when the installment obligation is paid ($80,000 note less $10,000 basis). A's $20,000 basis in the stock is calculated as: (i) the adjusted basis of the transferred property ($30,000), (ii) decreased by the fair market value of the boot received ($80,000), and (iii) increased by the recognized but deferred gain ($70,000). If A later sells the stock for its fair market value of $20,000, she will recognize no gain since her entire realized gain is preserved in the note.

(c) *Effect of Liabilities.* Solely for purposes of determining the transferor's basis, liabilities relieved (other than liabilities subject to § 357(c)(3))

are treated as money received by the transferor.
§ 358(d). This means that the transferor's basis is
adjusted downward for liabilities relieved, even if
such liabilities do not give rise to recognition of gain
under § 357(a). To the extent that the transferor
recognizes gain under § 357(b) or § 357(c), however, the upward adjustment in the transferor's basis
for the recognized gain will cancel the downward
adjustment for liabilities relieved.

*Example:* A transfers property with an adjusted
basis of $40 and a fair market value of $55, subject
to a liability of $30, in exchange for all of the stock
of X Corp., which has a fair market value of $25.
Assuming that no gain is recognized on relief of
liabilities, A's basis in the stock is $10, calculated
as: (i) the adjusted basis of the property transferred
($40), (ii) decreased by liabilities relieved ($30), and
(iii) increased by the gain recognized ($0). A's
built-in gain of $15 in the transferred property (fair
market value of $55 less adjusted basis of $40) is
preserved in A's basis in the stock (the difference
between the fair market value of $25 and the sub-
stituted basis of $10). If § 357(b) applied to the
transaction, the $30 relief of liabilities would be
treated as cash received and A's recognized gain
would be $15 (amount of realized gain); A's basis in
the nonrecognition property would be $25, calculat-
ed as: (i) the adjusted basis of the transferred
property ($40), (ii) decreased by deemed boot re-
ceived ($30 of liabilities relieved), and (iii) increased
by gain recognized ($15).

In the case of liabilities subject to § 357(c)(3), § 358(d)(2) provides that such liabilities are not treated as cash received for purposes of determining the transferor's basis. Thus, no gain results from relief of such liabilities, and the transferor's basis is not adjusted downward.

*Example:* A, a cash-basis taxpayer, transfers receivables, with a basis of zero and a fair market value of $50, and accounts payable of $30 to X Corp. in exchange for all of its stock, which has a fair market value of $20. Under § 357(c), A recognizes no gain on the transfer even though the $30 of accounts payable transferred to X exceeds A's zero basis in the receivables. A's basis in the stock received is zero, the same as her basis in the transferred receivables.

(d) *Holding Period.* The transferor's holding period for stock received in a § 351 transaction is determined by reference to his holding period for the transferred assets (a "tacked" holding period), provided that the transferred assets are capital gain property or § 1231 assets. § 1223(1). If a taxpayer transfers both capital gain and non-capital gain property, he might seek to assign a tacked holding period to some of the shares received in the exchange and a holding period commencing on the date of exchange to other shares received. The Service, however, has ruled that each share must be allocated a split holding period in proportion to the fair market value of the transferred assets. Rev. Rul. 85–164, amplifying Rev. Rul. 68–55. The character of the transferred assets (*i.e.,* ordinary or capital) does not determine the character of the stock received, which will generally be a capital asset (long-term or short-term) in the recipient's hands.

*Example:* A transfers a long-term capital asset (with an adjusted basis of $40 and a fair market value of $60) and inventory (with an adjusted basis of $20 and a fair market value of $40) to X Corp. in a § 351 transaction, and receives in exchange X stock with a fair market value of $100. Three months later, A sells the X stock for $120. Since the inventory is not a capital asset or a § 1231 asset, the holding period of the stock received in exchange for the inventory is not tacked. Each share of A's stock will be considered to have a split holding period based on the respective fair market values of the transferred assets. Thus, $^{60}/_{100}$ of A's stock will be treated as received in exchange for the long-term capital asset and $^{40}/_{100}$ for inventory. Of the total amount realized on the sale ($120), A will be treated as receiving 60% ($72) for a long-term capital asset (with a substituted basis of $40), and 40% ($48) for a short-term capital asset (with a substituted basis of $20). Accordingly, A will recognize a long-term capital gain of $32 ($72 less $40 basis) and a short-term capital gain of $28 ($48 less $20 basis) on the sale.

## § 6. The Transferee Corporation

(a) *Nonrecognition Treatment.* Section 1032 provides that a corporation recognizes no gain or loss on receipt of money or other property for its stock (including treasury stock). Although § 1032 refers only to receipt of "money or other property," the

Regulations extend § 1032 nonrecognition treatment to an exchange of stock for services. Reg. § 1.1032–1(a). Thus, a corporation recognizes no gain when it uses its stock to pay for services; the payment (to the extent of the fair market value of the stock) may be deducted as an ordinary and necessary business expense under § 162 or treated as a capital expenditure under § 263, depending on the nature of the services. *See* Rev. Rul. 62–217, modified by Rev. Rul. 74–503.

Section 351(f) treats a transfer by the transferee corporation (referred to as the "controlled corporation") to its shareholders in a § 351 exchange (other than an exchange pursuant to a plan of reorganization) as if it were a nonliquidating distribution governed by § 311. *See* Chapter 4. Because § 311 permits nonrecognition treatment of a distribution of a corporation's own stock or obligations, § 351(f) will not trigger gain to the controlled corporation if a shareholder receives only stock or the corporation's own obligation in the exchange, preserving the result under § 1032. If the shareholder receives boot (other than the corporation's own obligation), however, the controlled corporation will recognize gain (but not loss) under the recognition rules of § 311(b) for distributions of appreciated property. The exchanging shareholder may also recognize gain on receipt of the boot property (including the corporation's own obligation) under the general provision of § 351(b).

(b) *Transferee Corporation's Basis.* Under § 362(a)(1), the corporation takes a substituted basis in the assets received in a § 351 transaction, determined as (i) the transferor's basis in the transferred property, (ii) increased by any gain recognized to the transferor. This computation parallels the basis computation for stock received by the shareholder under § 358(a)(1); liabilities relieved or boot paid, however, have no effect on the corporation's basis except indirectly to the extent that the shareholder is required to recognize gain. Under §§ 358 and 362, the transferor's basis is essentially preserved both in the property transferred to the corporation and in the stock received by the shareholder; as a result, the same gain or loss may be recognized once when the corporation sells the property and again when the shareholder sells the stock.

*Example:* A transfers property with a basis of $40 and a fair market value of $30 in exchange for $30 of stock in a transaction qualifying under § 351(a). Under § 362(a), the corporation's basis in the transferred property is $40, the same as the basis of the transferred property in the shareholder's hands. Under § 358(a), the shareholder's basis in the stock received is also $40, the same as the basis of the transferred property. If the corporation then sells the transferred property for $30, its fair market value, the corporation will recognize a loss of $10. Similarly, the shareholder will also recognize a loss of $10 if she sells her stock for its fair market value of $30.

(c) *Allocation of Transferee Corporation's Basis*. If the transferor recognizes no gain on the § 351 exchange, the corporation's basis in each asset received is the same as the transferor's basis in the particular asset. When the transferor recognizes gain, however, there is no indication in the Code or the Regulations of how any increase in basis is allocated among the transferred assets in the hands of the corporation. One possible method of allocation would be simply to increase the basis of each asset by the amount of the transferor's gain recognized on the particular asset, by analogy to the asset-by-asset allocation of boot under Rev. Rul. 68–55. For example, if the transferor were taxed on $100 of boot allocated 60% to one transferred asset and 40% to another based on the respective fair market values of the transferred assets, it seems reasonable to increase the basis of the first asset by $60 and that of the second asset by $40.

(d) *Holding Period.* The corporation may tack the transferor's holding period in each transferred asset for purposes of determining the corporation's holding period for the asset. § 1223(2). Tacking occurs regardless of the character of the asset in the transferor's hands.

## § 7. Avoiding § 351

(a) *General.* Although § 351 is nominally a mandatory provision, its effects can often be avoided by appropriate planning. For example, a taxpayer may wish to avoid § 351 by structuring a transaction as a sale of property rather than a tax-free contribution, in order to allow the transferor to recognize a loss. Alternatively, the taxpayer may desire to recognize gain on appreciated property, thereby stepping up the basis of the property in the corporation's hands. The relatively modest capital gains preference (11.6% spread between capital gains and ordinary income) is unlikely to cause many transactions to be structured as sales. *But see* Bradshaw (Ct.Cl.1982)(sale of undeveloped real estate to corporation when capital gains preference was substantial; less ordinary income realized on subsequent sale of developed parcels). A sale may also be attractive if the transferor has offsetting capital losses against which to use the capital gain.

To the extent that a transferor receives debt in a § 351 exchange, gain will be recognized because debt (whether short-term or long-term) is considered boot for purposes of § 351(b). Under prior law, a taxpayer who desired sale treatment had to be careful to ensure that debt was not treated as a non-boot security. Although under current law receipt of any bona fide debt instrument will trigger gain recognition, the step-up in the corporation's basis in the transferred property will be deferred if the shareholder reports the gain under the installment method. If the transferee corporation is thinly capitalized, a purported installment note may be recharacterized as equity. *See, e.g.*, Burr Oaks (7th Cir.1966)(treating the transaction as a contribution to capital in exchange for preferred stock).

(b) *Limitations on Sale Treatment*. Several Code provisions also limit the benefits of sale treatment. Section 1239 treats any gain from sale of property between related parties (*e.g.*, a corporation and a more-than-50% shareholder) as ordinary income if the property is depreciable in the hands of the related transferee. § 1239(a). Moreover, § 453(g) generally requires that gain be recognized immediately in the case of an installment sale of depreciable property between related parties; the purchaser's basis in the acquired property is not stepped up until the gain becomes includible in the seller's income. *See also* § 453(i)(requiring recognition of any recapture income under § 1245 or § 1250). In addition, § 453(e) treats a subsequent sale of property received in an installment sale from a related party as a "second disposition" which triggers the installment gain to the transferor. Finally, § 267 prevents recognition of loss on a sale between a corporation and a more-than-50% shareholder.

## § 8. Contributions to Capital

(a) *General.* Section 118(a) excludes capital contributions from the gross income of a corporation. Thus, if a corporation obtains additional capital through voluntary pro-rata contributions from shareholders, the contributions do not constitute gross income, even though the outstanding shares of the corporation are not increased. Reg. § 1.118–1. In the case of pro-rata contributions, § 118(a) serves a purpose analogous to the nonrecognition provision of § 1032 when a corporation issues its stock for property. Section 118 also applies to contributions to capital by non-shareholders, such as property contributed by a governmental unit or civic group in order to induce a corporation to locate in a particular area. Reg. § 1.118–1. The exclusion from gross income does not apply, however, to payments for goods or services by customers or potential customers. *See id.;* § 118(b).

Under § 362(a), the corporation's basis for contributed capital is generally the same as the transferor's basis in the contributed property. Section 362(c), however, provides a special rule for contributions to capital by non-shareholders: § 362(c)(1) gives the corporation a zero basis in property (other than cash) contributed by non-shareholders; in the case of a cash contribution, § 362(c)(2) requires that the basis of property acquired within the 12–month period following the contribution be reduced by the amount of the cash contribution. If the amount of cash or property received from non-shareholders is treated as a payment for goods or services, § 362(c) does not apply and no basis adjustment is required.

A shareholder who contributes capital receives an increased basis in his stock. *See* Reg. § 1.118–1. If the shareholder contributes property rather than cash, the basis of the shareholder's stock is increased by the basis of the contributed property. *See* Fink (S.Ct.1987)(non-pro-rata surrender of stock treated as a capital contribution).

(b) *Overlap With § 351.* If a sole shareholder contributes property to a wholly-owned corporation, § 351 applies rather than § 118 even though no new shares are issued. *See* Lessinger (2d Cir.1989). In *Lessinger*, the court indicated that receipt of new stock in this situation would have been a meaningless gesture. Since § 351 applies, § 358 determines the shareholder's basis with respect to the stock constructively received. Section 351 treatment is also significant because, if the contributed property is subject to debt, §§ 357(b) and 357(c) may apply.

## § 9. Midstream Income Problems

The assignment-of-income doctrine and the tax-benefit rule may apply if assets of an existing busi-

ness are incorporated. The Service has indicated
that the assignment-of-income doctrine generally
does not apply to a transfer of receivables, unless a
tax-avoidance purpose is present. *See* § 4 above.
The tax-benefit rule requires a taxpayer to include
in income the tax benefit received from an earlier
deduction if a subsequent event is "inconsistent"
with the earlier deduction. *See* Hillsboro Nat.
Bank (S.Ct.1983); *see also* Rojas (Tax Ct.1988). In
the § 351 context, the Service has used this doctrine to require that transferors include in income a
bad debt reserve associated with transferred receivables. The Supreme Court, however, has held that
if the receivables were transferred for consideration
equal to their book value net of the reserve, there is
no "recovery" and hence no includible income. *See*
Nash (S.Ct.1970). By implication, *Nash* seems to
require income inclusion to the extent that the
transferor receives stock and other consideration
worth more than the net book value of the receivables.

## § 10.  Section 351 and Acquisitive Transac-
tions

Section 351 may overlap with the provisions governing corporate reorganizations. *See* Chapter 9.
For example, assume that A owns 20% of corporation X, and the remaining stock of X is owned by
other shareholders. Y, a publicly owned corporation, wishes to acquire X. Together, A and Y form
a new corporation Z in a § 351 exchange, with A
contributing her X stock and Y contributing cash

equal to 80% of the value of X.  Z transfers the cash to a newly-formed subsidiary which is then merged into X, with X's remaining shareholders (other than A) receiving cash for their X stock.  Although the transaction does not qualify as a reorganization because more than 50% of the X shareholders receive cash for their stock, the Service has ruled in a similar situation that A's initial contribution of the X stock to Z nevertheless qualifies as a valid § 351 transaction.  *See* Rev. Rul. 84–71.

# CHAPTER 4

# NONLIQUIDATING DISTRIBUTIONS

## § 1. General

Section 301 of the Code prescribes the treatment of nonliquidating distributions of cash or other property to shareholders. Under § 301(c)(1), a § 301 distribution is included in the shareholder's gross income to the extent that it constitutes a "dividend," as defined in § 316. Section 316, in turn, defines a dividend for income tax purposes generally as a distribution out of current or accumulated earnings and profits ("e & p") of the distributing corporation. To the extent that a § 301 distribution exceeds e & p, it is treated under § 301(c)(2) as a tax-free return of the shareholder's capital and any amount in excess of basis is treated under § 301(c)(3) as gain from a sale or exchange. The character of the gain will be capital if the stock is a capital asset in the shareholder's hands. The tax definition of a "dividend" thus bears no fixed relation to a "dividend" in the corporate law context, though the two terms often overlap.

Nondividend treatment offers the advantage of tax-free recovery of the shareholder's basis. Moreover, the restoration of preferential treatment for capital gains has enhanced the tax stakes in this area. A corporate shareholder may, however, prefer dividend treatment because of the dividends-received deduction of § 243. *See* § 7.

It should be noted that § 301 applies only to payments to a shareholder in his capacity as such; payments to a shareholder in any other capacity (*e.g.*, as an officer, employee or bondholder) are not treated as § 301 distributions unless such payments are excessive and are held to be disguised dividends. Reg. § 1.301–1(c). It is important to understand treatment of nonliquidating distributions before approaching the topics of redemptions, stock dividends and reorganizations discussed in later chapters.

## § 2.  Dividends

Under the two-part definition of § 316, a distribution is a dividend if it is out of either (i) earnings and profits of the current taxable year, computed at the end of the year without reduction for distributions during the year ("current e & p") or (ii) earnings and profits accumulated after February 28, 1913 and before the current taxable year ("accumulated e & p"). A distribution is treated as coming first from current e & p. Thus, if current e & p are sufficient to cover all distributions during the taxable year, such distributions are dividends and it is unnecessary to consider accumulated e & p. If the aggregate distributions during the taxable year exceed current e & p, a pro-rata portion of each distribution is treated as coming from current e & p. If one class of stock has priority over other classes of stock in receiving distributions, *e.g.,* preferred stock, current e & p is allocated first to distributions on such stock. *See* Rev. Rul. 69–440.

*Example:* M Corp. has current e & p of $3,000 and no accumulated e & p. The common shareholders receive a distribution of $1,000 on January 1 and $1,000 on April 15; the preferred shareholders receive a distribution of $2,500 on December 31. The $2,500 distribution to the preferred stockholders will be treated as a dividend, and will leave only $500 of current e & p to be allocated to the distributions to the common stockholders. One-quarter of each of the distributions on common stock ($500/$2,000) will be treated as a dividend; and the remainder of these distributions ($1,500) will be treated as tax-free return of capital or taxable gain under § 301(c)(2) and (3).

Accumulated e & p is relevant only if current e & p are insufficient to cover distributions during the year. Distributions in excess of current e & p are dividends to the extent of accumulated e & p; the balance is treated as return of capital to the extent of the shareholder's basis in his stock, and any excess is treated as taxable gain. Accumulated e & p is allocated among distributions in chronological order. Reg. § 1.316–2(b). If a corporation has a deficit in accumulated e & p, it does not reduce current e & p; thus, distributions are still treated as dividends to the extent of current e & p.

*Example:* X Corp. has current e & p of $20,000 and accumulated e & p of $55,000. During the taxable year, X makes quarterly cash distributions of $25,000 each to its shareholders. One-fifth ($20,000/$100,000) of each distribution ($5,000) is treated as a dividend out of current e & p. The remainder of each of the first two distributions ($20,000 each) and $15,000 of the third distribution are treated as a dividend out of accumulated e & p. As a result, $5,000 of the third distribution and $20,-000 of the fourth distribution are treated as tax-free basis recovery or taxable gain. *See* Reg. § 1.316–2(c).

If a corporation has accumulated e & p and a deficit in current e & p, the deficit in current e & p reduces the amount of the accumulated e & p. The Regulations imply that the full amount of the deficit in current e & p may be taken into account if it is traceable to a period ending on or before the date of a particular distribution. Reg. § 1.316–2(b). The Service, however, appears to take the position that any deficit in current e & p must be prorated over the entire year, even if traceable to a specific period. Rev. Rul. 74–164.

*Example:* X Corp. has accumulated e & p of $50,000 at the beginning of the current year, and distributes $25,000 to its shareholders on July 1 of the current year. If X has a loss of $70,000 during the first half of the year but ends up with current e & p of $5,000 at the end of the year, the entire $25,000 distribution is a dividend ($5,000 from current e & p and $20,000 from accumulated e & p). If X instead ends up with a deficit of $10,000 in current e & p for the year (with $70,000 of losses in the first half of the year), the entire $25,000 is still a dividend, assuming that the $10,000 loss is prorated over the entire year under Rev. Rul. 74–164; as of the July 1 distribution, accumulated e & p would be reduced by $5,000 (one-half of the $10,000 loss), leaving $45,000 of accumulated e & p to cover the distribution. Under the tracing approach of the Regulations, however, the $70,000 loss allocable to the first half of the year would more than offset the $50,000 of accumulated e & p as of the July 1 distribution; thus, the entire $25,000 distribution would be treated as tax-free basis recovery to the extent of basis and then as taxable gain.

## § 3.  Nondividend Distributions

To the extent that a distribution is not covered by either current e & p or accumulated e & p, it is treated as a nondividend distribution under § 301(c)(2) and (3). Any such distribution in excess of the shareholder's basis in his stock triggers taxable gain; loss is recognized only if the stock becomes worthless or is redeemed or otherwise disposed of without full basis recovery. If a shareholder receives nondividend distributions with respect to several blocks of shares which were acquired at different times with different bases, the distribution apparently must be allocated ratably among all the shares. Thus, a shareholder may recognize gain on certain shares before recovering all of his basis in other shares; he is not permitted to defer gain until the aggregate basis of all of his shares has been recovered. *See* Johnson (4th Cir.1971).

*Example:* X Corp. has accumulated e & p of $100,000 and no earnings or losses for the current year. X distributes $300,000 cash pro rata to its shareholders. A, an individual, has two equal blocks of shares with adjusted bases of $8,000 and $22,000, respectively, and receives a $30,000 distribution. A must report $10,000 as a dividend, representing the ratio of the total distribution ($100,000/$300,000) covered by accumulated e & p. Of the remaining $20,000, A allocates $10,000 to each block of shares. With respect to the low-basis shares, A recovers her full basis ($8,000) tax free and recognizes $2,000 of gain. With respect to the high-basis shares, A reduces her basis by $10,000 and is left with an adjusted basis of $12,000.

## § 4. Earnings and Profits

Although § 312 provides for certain adjustments to e & p, the Code does not specifically define "earnings and profits." The starting point for determining e & p is taxable income. Generally, four types of adjustments are necessary to derive e & p from taxable income:

(a) *Items Excluded From Taxable Income But Included in E & P.* Some items excluded from taxable income must be included in e & p because they increase the dividend-paying capacity of the corporation without impairing its original capital. For example, Regulations § 1.312–6(b) provide that certain tax-exempt income (*e.g.*, municipal bond interest and life insurance proceeds exempt under §§ 103 and 101(a), respectively) is included in e & p. Section 312(f)(1) provides that realized gains and losses are not included in e & p until recognized in computing taxable income. Thus, e & p is not increased by the gain on nonrecognition transactions (*e.g.*, § 1031 like-kind exchanges) until such gain is recognized.

(b) *Items That Reduce Taxable Income But Do Not Reduce E & P.* Certain "artificial" deductions allowed in computing taxable income are added back in computing e & p, since they do not represent actual expenses and therefore do not impair dividend-paying capacity. For example, the full amount of dividends received is included in e & p, despite the § 243 dividends-received deduction.

(c) *Timing Differences.* Although the corporation's method of accounting normally determines when items are included in e & p, certain timing adjustments are necessary to ensure that e & p more accurately reflect economic gain or loss. For example, § 312(k) generally disallows accelerated depreciation in computing e & p and extends the recovery period applicable for this purpose. Similarly, § 312(n)(5) requires that income from installment sales must be computed for purposes of determining e & p as if the corporation did not use the installment method, *i.e.*, such income must be included currently in e & p without regard to any deferral under § 453. Section 301(e) makes the § 312(k) and (n) adjustments generally inapplicable to certain distributions to 20%-or-more corporate shareholders, if the distributee would otherwise be entitled to a dividends-received deduction under § 243. The significance of ignoring these timing adjustments is to reduce the distributing corporation's e & p solely for the purpose of determining the amount of any dividend to a corporate distributee.

(d) *Items That Reduce E & P But Do Not Reduce Taxable Income.* Some items not allowed as deductions in computing taxable income are allowed in computing e & p, since they clearly reduce the corporation's dividend-paying capacity. Thus, items disallowed by § 162(c), (f) and (g)(certain illegal payments, fines and penalties), § 265 (expenses allocable to tax-exempt income), § 1211(a)(excess capital losses over capital gains) and § 162(a)(1)(unreasonable compensation), as well as federal taxes and prior years' dividend distributions, are subtracted in determining e & p.

It should be noted that, for purposes of determining the amount of a dividend under § 316(a)(2), current distributions do not reduce current e & p (for the year in which the distribution occurs); and that under § 312(a) distributions reduce e & p only "to the extent thereof," *i.e.,* distributions cannot create a deficit in current or accumulated e & p. Thus, if a corporation has no current e & p or accumulated e & p, operating losses may further reduce e & p, but distributions to shareholders have no effect on e & p. Current income that increases e & p above zero represents a potential source of dividends.

*Example:* X Corp. suffers a loss of $300,000 in its first year of operations. In Year 2, X has earnings of $100,000 and distributes $50,000 to its shareholders. The $50,000 distribution is treated as a dividend because it is covered by current e & p. At the beginning of Year 3, X's accumulated e & p deficit is $250,000 ($300,000 deficit from Year 1 reduced by the $50,000 of undistributed earnings from Year 2). In Year 3, X has no current e & p and again distributes $50,000 to its shareholders. No portion of the distribution is treated as a dividend because X has neither current e & p nor accumulated e & p; the distribution has no effect on X's accumulated e & p deficit of $250,000 carried over to the beginning of Year 4. In Year 4, X has $300,000 of current e & p and makes no distributions. X's accumulated deficit of $250,000 is eliminated by the $300,000 of current e & p, leaving X with accumulated e & p of $50,000 at the beginning of Year 5. In Year 5, X has no current e & p and distributes $50,000 to its shareholders. The entire distribution is a dividend from accumulated e & p, leaving X with no accumulated e & p at the beginning of Year 6.

## § 5.  Distributions in Kind

(a) *Treatment of the Distributing Corporation.* Section 311(a) provides generally that a corporation does not recognize gain or loss on a distribution of property with respect to its stock. This nonrecognition rule is often called the *General Utilities* doctrine, an allusion to a case in which the government argued unsuccessfully that a distribution of appreciated property resulted in taxable gain to the distributing corporation. General Utilities & Operating Co. (S.Ct.1935). In deciding *General Utilities*, however, the Supreme Court did not consider it necessary to address this issue. Even before 1986, the exceptions to nonrecognition had virtually swallowed up the "general rule" of § 311(a). The 1986 Act repealed the *General Utilities* rule with respect to distributions of appreciated property, so that in effect § 311(a) now operates only to deny recognition of loss on nonliquidating distributions.

Section 311(b), relating to distributions of appreciated property, provides that the distributing corporation recognizes gain on a distribution of appreciated property (other than the distributing corporation's own obligation) as if such property were sold to the distributee at its fair market value. It should be noted that the distributing corporation recognizes gain even if the appreciation is attributable to pre-incorporation increases in value. In addition, if property is distributed subject to a liability or the shareholder assumes the liability, then the fair market value of the distributed property is deemed to be not less than the amount of such liability. § 311(b)(2) (borrowing from § 336(b) the rules for distributions of property subject to liabilities in excess of fair market value).

It should be noted that § 311(b) applies only to distributions covered by §§ 301–304 (*e.g.*, dividends, redemptions and partial liquidations); it does not apply to distributions governed by other Code provisions (*e.g.*, tax-free reorganizations and spin-offs). Moreover, distributions in complete liquidations are governed by a special set of rules, discussed in Chapter 7.

*Example:* X Corp. distributes property with a basis of $100 and a fair market value of $150, subject to a liability of $200. Under § 311(b)(2), the fair market value of the distributed property is deemed to be $200 (the amount of the liabilities) and X recognizes gain of $100. This rule applies equally to recourse and nonrecourse liabilities, with the result that the corporation must recognize gain whether the shareholder assumes the liability or merely takes property subject to the liability.

On an issue of first impression, the Tax Court held that the fair market value of distributed property for purposes of § 311 is "determined as if it had been sold in its entirety." Pope & Talbot, Inc. (Tax Ct.1995)(transfer of corporate assets to a newly-formed limited partnership followed by a distribution of partnership units). Thus, fair market value is determined by reference to "the entire property interest ... being taken out of corporate solution" rather than the "fractional interests received by the shareholders." Where the shareholders receive undivided fractional interests in property, the aggregate value of their interests may be less than the value of the property in the corporation's hands. In such cases, the Tax Court's approach suggests that the value of the distributed property for purposes of § 311 exceeds the value of the property received by shareholders for purposes of §§ 301 and 302.

The character of the corporation's gain is presumably determined as if the distribution were an actual sale. In the case of property (other than inventory-type property) used in the corporation's trade or business, the gain will generally be capital gain. §§ 1221 and 1231. Where property is distributed to a more-than-50% shareholder, however, § 1239(a) treats the gain recognized by the distributing corporation as ordinary income if the property is depreciable in the hands of the distributee.

Section 311(b)(3) authorizes the Treasury to issue Regulations to address potential abuses in connection with nonliquidating distributions of an interest in a partnership to which the corporation has previously contributed built-in loss property. The Regulations may provide that the amount of gain recognized by the distributing corporation under § 311(b) is determined by disregarding any loss attributable to property contributed to the partnership for the principal purpose of recognizing such loss on the distribution.

Even before the 1986 Act, a corporation might have been required to recognize gain on a nonliquidating distribution under assignment-of-income principles or the tax-benefit doctrine. *See, e.g.,* First State Bank of Stratford (5th Cir.1948)(corporation taxed on collectibles distributed to shareholders). Under present law, § 311(b) generally reaches the same result by expressly treating a nonliquidating distribution of appreciated property as a deemed sale at fair market value. Thus, the government is less likely to invoke assignment-of-income principles or the tax-benefit doctrine. *See* Chapter 7.

Since a distribution is treated as a recognition event, a corporation may prefer to sell appreciated property to its shareholder for the shareholder's own note. If the transaction qualifies for installment sale treatment under § 453, the corporation may be able to defer gain, and the shareholder will avoid dividend treatment. *But see* § 453(g) (installment sale of depreciable property between related persons). If the shareholder later defaults on the note, the shareholder will have cancellation-of-indebtedness income, but the corporation may be entitled to a bad debt deduction under § 166. As a result, the shareholder will be left in much the same position as if he had received a dividend, but the corporation may be better off.

In the case of loss property, it is almost always more advantageous for the corporation to sell, rather than distribute, property in order to recognize the loss. If the property is sold to a shareholder who (directly or by attribution under § 267(c)), owns more than 50% of the corporation's stock, however, § 267(a)(1) disallows a deduction to the corporation for its loss. Nevertheless, any loss disallowed by § 267(a)(1) to a seller on an actual sale of property to a related purchaser is preserved and may be used by the purchaser to offset gain on a later sale of the property. § 267(d).

*Example:* X Corp. distributes property with a basis of $500 and a fair market value of $200, to A, a more-than-50% shareholder. Under § 311(a), X's loss of $300 is disallowed, and A takes a basis in the property equal to $200, its fair market value. If the property appreciates and A subsequently sells it for $700, A will recognize a gain of $500 ($700 minus $200). By contrast, if the original transaction had been an actual sale rather than a distribution, the $300 loss on the initial sale would still be disallowed to X but would reduce A's gain on the subsequent sale from $500 to $200 under § 267(d).

Thus, even where a corporation is unable to recognize a loss on a sale because of § 267(a)(1), the relief available to the purchaser under § 267(d) generally makes a sale more attractive than a nonliquidating distribution of the loss property under § 311(a). This is because § 311(a) flatly disallows a deduction for the loss, without providing for deemed sale treatment; the shareholder-distributee's basis in the distributed property is limited to its fair market value, with no potential relief on a subsequent sale.

Under prior law, the government sometimes argued that a transaction structured as a distribution to a shareholder followed by the shareholder's sale of the distributed property should be recast as a sale of the property by the corporation followed by a distribution of the sale proceeds to the shareholder. *See* Court Holding Co. (S.Ct.1945). Because the distribution itself is now taxable to the corporation, it is no longer necessary to impute a shareholder-level sale to the corporation. In the case of loss property, however, the government may seek to recharacterize purported corporate-level sales to third parties as distributions followed by shareholder-level sales, permanently disallowing loss recognition.

(b) *Effect of Property Distributions on E & P.* A distribution of property in kind generally reduces the distributing corporation's e & p by the adjusted basis of the distributed property in the corporation's hands, but not below zero. In the case of a distribution of appreciated property, § 312(b) reaches the same end result by requiring that the corporation's e & p be first increased by the appreciation (excess of fair market value over basis) and then decreased (but not below zero) by the fair market value of the distributed property. The purpose of the special rule of § 312(b) is to ensure that the appreciation generates positive current e & p for purposes of determining dividend treatment. *See* § 316(a)(distributions out of current e & p, determined without reduction for distributions during the taxable year, treated as dividends). Any corporate tax liability attributable to the distribution will also reduce e & p.

*Example:* X Corp. distributes to A, an individual shareholder, property with a basis of $1,000 and a fair market value of $200. X has current e & p from other transactions of $100 and no accumulated e & p. The distribution reduces X's current e & p to zero, but A is treated as receiving a dividend of $100 (determined prior to the reduction for the current year's distributions). The remaining $100 of the distribution is treated as basis recovery or taxable gain under § 301(c)(2) and (3). Assume instead that the basis of the property is $200 and its fair market value is $1,000; ignoring the effect of corporate income taxes, X's current e & p will be increased to $900 ($100 plus $800 of appreciation) and then reduced to zero. A, however, will be treated as receiving a dividend of $900 under §§ 312(b) and 316(a)(2). The remaining $100 of the distribution is treated as basis recovery or taxable gain under § 301(c)(2) and (3).

If a corporation recognizes gain on a distribution of appreciated property, the timing of the reduction in e & p for the corporate income taxes is unclear. In the case of an accrual-basis corporation, the tax liability attributable to the distribution is fixed at year-end and presumably reduces current e & p for the year of the distribution. In the case of a cash-basis corporation, however, the tax liability apparently does not reduce e & p until the following year, when the taxes are actually paid. *See* Reg. § 1.312–6(a)(e & p generally determined under taxpayer's tax accounting method). This timing mismatch may be advantageous for a corporate shareholder, to the extent that the portion of the distribution eligible for the dividends-received deduction of § 243 in the year of distribution is overstated.

If a shareholder assumes a corporate liability in connection with a distribution (or takes distributed property subject to a liability), § 312(c) requires "proper" adjustments to e & p. The decrease in e & p attributable to the distribution is reduced by the amount of such liabilities. Reg. § 1.312–3.

*Example*: X Corp. distributes property with a basis of $400 and a fair market value of $1,000,

subject to a liability of $800. X has accumulated e
& p of $1,800 and no current e & p. Ignoring the
effect of corporate income taxes, X's e & p will be
increased by $600 and then reduced by $200 ($1,000
fair market value less $800 liability), leaving X with
e & p of $2,200. If the basis of the property were
instead $1,200, X's e & p would be reduced by $400
($1,200 basis less $800 liability), leaving X with e &
p of $1,400.

In determining the adjustments to e & p, the
treatment of liabilities in excess of the fair market
value of the distributed property is not entirely
clear. Although § 311(b)(2) is not expressly applicable, one approach would be to treat the fair
market value of the distributed property as not less
than the amount of such liabilities. Thus, e & p
would be increased by the amount of gain recognized; ignoring the effect of corporate income taxes,
e & p would not be further adjusted because the net
distribution is zero (the deemed fair market value
less the amount of liabilities).

*Example*: X Corp. distributes property with a
basis of zero and a fair market value of $700,
subject to a nonrecourse liability of $1,000. X has
no current or accumulated e & p at the time of the
distribution. Applying § 311(b)(2), X's e & p is
increased to $1,000 ($1,000 deemed fair market
value less zero basis); ignoring the effect of corporate income taxes, X's e & p is not further adjusted
($1,000 deemed fair market value less $1,000 liability).

(c) *Treatment of Shareholders.* If property is distributed to a shareholder (including a corporate shareholder), § 301(b)(1) provides that the amount of the distribution is the fair market value of the property. Section 301(b)(2) requires that the amount of the distribution be reduced (but not below zero) by any liabilities assumed by the shareholder in connection with the distribution (or subject to which the property is distributed). Under § 301(d), the basis of the distributed property in the hands of a shareholder (including a corporate shareholder) is equal to its fair market value.

*Example:* X Corp. distributes property with a fair market value of $4,000, subject to a liability of $3,000, to a shareholder. The amount of the distribution will be $1,000 under § 301(b)(2)(the fair market value of the property reduced by the liability), but the shareholder's basis in the property will be its fair market value of $4,000 under § 301(d). Accordingly, X's basis in the property is relevant only for purposes of determining X's gain (if any) on the distribution and the corresponding e & p adjustment under § 312(b).

Suppose instead that the liability in the above example is $6,000 and X's basis in the property is $1,000. Assuming that the property is still worth only $4,000, X recognizes gain of $5,000, since the fair market value is treated as not less than the amount of the liability. §§ 311(b)(2) and 336(b). The distribution to the shareholder, however, would be zero under § 301(b)(2), since the liability exceeds the fair market value of the property. It is not entirely clear whether the shareholder's basis under

these circumstances is fair market value ($4,000) or
the amount of the liability ($6,000). If the share-
holder assumes personal liability for the debt, then
presumably the basis should be $6,000, despite the
statutory fair-market-value limitation. If the liability is nonrecourse, however, the shareholder's basis
may be limited to fair market value. *See* Estate of
Franklin (9th Cir.1976); Pleasant Summit (3rd Cir.
1988).

## § 6. Distribution of Corporation's Own Obli- gations

Some special considerations apply if a corporation
makes a § 301 distribution of its bond or note to a
stockholder. Obligations of the distributing corporation are not excluded from the broad definition of
"property" in § 317(a), and are therefore treated as
property. *See* § 312(a)(2). Accordingly, both the
amount of the distribution and the basis of the
distributed obligation in the hands of the shareholder are equal to the fair market value of the obligation. §§ 301(b)(1) and 301(d). The distribution
of the corporation's obligation, however, does not
trigger gain at the corporate level under § 311(b).
Finally, § 312(a)(2) requires that the distributing
corporation's e & p be reduced by the principal
amount (or the issue price, in the case of an obligation having original issue discount) of the obligation. Section § 312(b) does not apply to a distribution of a corporation's own obligation; thus, such
a distribution will not increase the corporation's e
& p.

*Example:* X Corp., which has $10,000 of e & p, issues to its shareholders a note with a principal amount of $10,000. The note matures in 3 years and bears no interest. The note has a fair market value of $7,500, assuming an applicable discount rate of approximately 10%. X will not recognize any gain on distribution of the note under § 311(b). The shareholders are treated as receiving a distribution of $7,500 (the fair market value of the note), which is also their basis in the note. The issue price of the note, also $7,500, reduces X's e & p under § 312(a)(2). Since X has sufficient e & p to cover the amount of the distribution, the entire $7,500 is a dividend to X's shareholders.

## § 7. Intercorporate Dividends

(a) *Section 243.* Dividends received by a corporate shareholder normally qualify for the dividends-received deduction under § 243. Section 243 is intended to mitigate the effect of multiple levels of taxation on intercorporate dividends. Generally, the § 243 deduction ranges from 70% to 100% of dividends received, depending on the percentage of the distributing corporation's stock owned by the distributee corporation. §§ 243(a) and 243(c). If the distributee corporation owns at least 20% of the distributing corporation's stock, either an 80% or 100% dividends-received deduction is allowed. The 100% deduction generally applies only if both corporations are members of the same affiliated group within the meaning of § 1504(a). These basic rules are illustrated as follows:

| Percentage Ownership of Distributing Corporation | § 243 Dividends– Received Deduction |
|---|---|
| Less than 20% | 70% |
| At least 20% but less than 80% | 80 |
| At least 80% and same affiliated group | 100 |

Under § 243, the effective maximum tax rate on dividends eligible for the 80% deduction is only 7%; that is, a 35% tax is imposed on 20% of the dividends received.

(b) *Sales of Stock Ex-Dividend.* Section 246(c) denies any dividends-received deduction unless the corporation has held the stock on which the dividend is paid for more than 45 days (90 days in the case of certain preferred stock). This provision is intended to prevent a corporation from buying stock just before a dividend becomes payable (at a price reflecting the full value of the dividend) and then immediately selling the stock after payment of the dividend in order to claim a deductible loss in addition to the dividends-received deduction.

(c) *Basis Reduction for Extraordinary Dividends.* Section 1059 requires a corporate shareholder to reduce its basis to the extent of the deductible portion of any "extraordinary dividend." Generally, an extraordinary dividend is defined by § 1059(c) as a dividend equalling or exceeding 10% (5% for preferred stock) of the shareholder's adjusted basis in the underlying stock. In applying the percentage threshold, the taxpayer may elect to use the fair market value of the stock (rather than its adjusted basis) if such value can be determined satisfactorily. § 1059(c)(4). The basis of the stock

cannot be reduced below zero by the § 1059 basis
adjustment. If this special limitation applies,
§ 1059(a)(2) treats the remainder as gain at the
time of sale. A basis reduction is generally not
required, however, if the underlying stock has been
held for more than 2 years before the dividend
announcement date or if certain other conditions
are met. The 2–year safe harbor does not apply to
any amount treated as a dividend which is part of a
partial liquidation or non-pro-rata distribution. *See*
§ 1059(e)(1); *see also* § 1059(f)(dividends on so-
called self-liquidating preferred stock).

*Example:* P Corp. purchases T Corp.'s preferred
stock for $100 and T immediately distributes to P a
$10 dividend. If P is entitled to an 80% dividends-
received deduction under § 243, the deductible portion of the dividend is $8. Under § 1059, P would
be required to reduce its basis in the T stock to $92.
Assuming that P immediately thereafter sells the T
stock for $90 (the value of the T stock after the
dividend has been paid), P would be entitled to a
loss of $2 on its investment, which equals the $2
portion of the earlier distribution taxed to P. This
result is economically correct because the transaction produces a "wash" for P, *i.e.,* P has just
recovered its initial $100 investment through the
$10 distribution and $90 sales proceeds. If P were
not required to reduce its basis for the untaxed
portion of the dividend, P would have an additional
artificial loss of $8 on the sale (the difference be-
tween the cost basis of $100 and the reduced basis
of $92).

(d) *Debt-Financed Portfolio Stock Dividends*. Section 246A, enacted in 1984, is aimed at "tax arbitrage" arising when a corporation borrows funds to acquire stock and claims deductions both for interest paid on the debt under § 163 and for dividends received on the stock under § 243. In this situation, the § 243 deduction is reduced by a percentage equal to the portion of the stock which is debt financed. For example, if 60% of the stock basis is debt financed, only 40% of the § 243 deduction is allowed. The reduction, however, cannot exceed the amount of deductible interest on the debt financing attributable to the stock. Section 246A applies only if the indebtedness is "directly attributable" to the investment in the stock, *i.e.*, where the indebtedness is clearly incurred for the purpose of acquiring or carrying the stock. *See* § 246A(d)(3); Rev. Rul. 88–66. A recipient corporation is not subject to the § 246A reduction if it owns at least 50% of the stock of the distributing corporation (or owns at least 20% of the stock and 5 or fewer corporations own at least 50% of the stock).

## § 8.  Disguised Dividends

Shareholders generally prefer to draw economic benefits out of a corporation in ways that are tax free to themselves or deductible to the corporation (or both, if possible). The problem of disguised dividends is particularly likely to arise in closely held corporations from transactions such as the following: loans made by a corporation to its shareholders under circumstances indicating there is no intention of repayment; bargain sales of property by a corporation to its shareholders; excess compensation paid by a corporation to its shareholders for goods or services provided by the shareholders in their capacity as employees, lessors or contractors; and free use by shareholders, for personal rather than business purposes, of corporate property (*e.g.*, automobiles, yachts and airplanes).

In the case of below-market demand loans, § 7872(a) recharacterizes the "foregone" interest (determined on an annual basis) as a constructive distribution from the corporation (lender) to the shareholder (borrower) and a constructive interest payment in the same amount from the shareholder back to the corporation. As a result, the shareholder is treated as having ordinary income to the extent of the constructive dividend (possibly offset by a matching interest deduction) and the corporation is treated as having interest income (with no offsetting deduction because the constructive dividend is nondeductible). Any loan that is not transferable and is conditioned on performance of substantial services by an individual is generally treated as a demand loan. § 7872(f)(5). If the loan is not a demand loan, the difference between the amount loaned and the present value of all required payments under the terms of the loan is treated as a constructive distribution to the shareholder at the time the loan is made. *See* § 7872(b).

Although payments are most likely to be recharacterized as disguised dividends if made to shareholders on a pro-rata basis, even a non-pro-rata payment may be so treated if made to a shareholder who obtains an economic benefit that is not available to other shareholders, regardless of whether the corporation intended to distribute a dividend. *See* Honigman (6th Cir.1972). Occasionally, a constructive dividend to a controlling shareholder may be found if the corporation makes a payment to a third party under circumstances indicating that the corporation is acting merely to serve the controlling shareholder's personal wishes. *See* Rev. Rul. 79–9 (charitable contribution by closely held corporation taxable as a distribution if shareholders or their families receive economic benefits from the contribution). A shareholder's withdrawals from his wholly-owned professional corporation were held to be disguised dividends rather than loans based on a finding that there was no intention of repayment. Jaques (6th Cir.1991).

If a shareholder diverts corporate funds to himself, the issue arises whether the diverted funds are taxable under § 61 or as constructive dividends under § 301. In *Truesdell* (Tax Ct.1987), the court treated the diverted funds as constructive dividends taxable only to the extent of the corporation's e & p. The court distinguished cases holding that unlawful diversions from third parties constitute taxable income, regardless of e & p. *See, e.g.,* Miller (9th Cir.1976).

In the case of S corporations, the government may seek to recharacterize purported dividends as salary. *See* Rev. Rul. 74–44. As discussed in Chapter 12, S shareholders are generally permitted to receive distributions tax free until their stock basis is fully recovered. By arranging compensation for services in the form of dividends rather than salaries, S shareholders may attempt to avoid social security taxes, unemployment taxes and withholding taxes. In the absence of reasonable compensation for services, courts have recharacterized such purported dividends as wages for employment tax purposes. *See, e.g.*, Spicer Accounting, Inc. (9th Cir.1990).

# CHAPTER 5
# REDEMPTIONS

## § 1. General

A "redemption" occurs when a corporation acquires its stock from a shareholder in exchange for money or other property (other than stock of the corporation). § 317(b). Section 302(a) provides that a redemption will be treated as an exchange of stock for property if the requirements of § 302(b) are satisfied; § 302(d) provides that any other redemption will be treated as a nonliquidating distribution under § 301. Even without preferential treatment for capital gains, exchange treatment under § 302(a) would be attractive. The redeeming shareholder may recover his basis immediately and offset capital gain on the redemption against any capital losses that the shareholder may have from other transactions. Corporate taxpayers, however, generally prefer § 301 distribution treatment rather than exchange treatment, since the amount of the distribution may be wholly or partially excluded under the dividends-received deduction of § 243.

This Chapter first considers the § 302(b) requirements for redemptions treated as exchanges, including partial liquidations and constructive ownership rules, and then describes the related provisions of

§ 303 (redemptions to pay death taxes) and § 304 (redemptions through related corporations). Redemptions in connection with sale of a corporate business are considered separately. Finally, certain ancillary problems (computation of the shareholder's gain or loss, basis, and corporate-level tax consequences) are discussed.

## § 2.  Substantially Disproportionate Redemptions:  § 302(b)(2)

Section 302(b) contains four alternative tests for determining whether a redemption will be treated as an exchange. Of the four statutory tests, the first three (§ 302(b)(1)–(3)) focus on the effect of a redemption at the shareholder level, while the fourth (§ 302(b)(4)) focuses on the effect at the corporate level. Section 302(b)(1) allows exchange treatment whenever the redemption is "not essentially equivalent to a dividend." This ill-defined test can be better understood after considering the mechanical "safe harbor" rules of § 302(b)(2)(substantially disproportionate redemptions) and § 302(b)(3)(redemptions in complete termination of a shareholder's interest).

Section 302(b)(2) permits exchange treatment if the distribution is "substantially disproportionate with respect to the shareholder," *i.e.*, if the shareholder's interest in the corporation is substantially reduced by the redemption. In order to meet this test, the shareholder, immediately after the redemption, must: (i) own less than 50% of the voting power of the corporation; (ii) own less than 80% of his percentage ownership of voting stock immediately before the redemption; and (iii) own less than 80% of his percentage ownership of common stock immediately before the redemption. If the corporation has only voting common stock outstanding, both 80% tests will be satisfied if either one is met. If the corporation has more than one class of common stock outstanding (*i.e.*, both voting and nonvoting common stock), the 80% test described in clause (iii) above is applied in the aggregate, rather than on a class-by-class basis. Rev. Rul. 87–88.

*Example:* X Corp. has outstanding 10 shares of voting common and 30 shares of nonvoting common stock. A, an individual, owns 6 shares (60%) of the voting common and all 30 shares of the nonvoting common. Thus, A owns a total of 36 of the 40 shares of the common stock, or 90%. Each share of voting and nonvoting common stock is equal in value. If X redeems 3 of A's voting shares and 27 of A's 30 nonvoting shares, the redemption will satisfy the "substantially disproportionate" requirements of § 302(b)(2). After the redemption, A will own 3 of the 7 outstanding shares of voting common stock (42.9%) and 6 of the 10 outstanding shares of common stock in the aggregate (60%). A will own 71.5% (42.9%/60%) of her former percentage ownership of the voting common stock, and 66.7% (60%/90%) of her former percentage ownership of the common stock in the aggregate. Thus, both 80% tests of § 302(b)(2) are satisfied. In addition, A will also own less than 50% of the voting power of X (42.9%) after the redemption.

A redemption of nonvoting preferred stock from a shareholder who owns only nonvoting preferred stock will not satisfy the § 302(b)(2) test, since there is no reduction in the shareholder's voting power. If the corporation redeems sufficient voting stock from a shareholder to meet the § 302(b)(2) test independently, however, a redemption of the same shareholder's nonvoting preferred stock in the same transaction will also qualify for exchange treatment. Reg. § 1.302–3(a). In other words, the nonvoting preferred stock can be "piggybacked" onto an otherwise qualifying redemption of voting stock meeting the requirements of § 302(b)(2). A redemption of voting preferred stock from a shareholder who owns no common stock can also qualify under § 302(b)(2). *See* Rev. Rul. 81–41 (common-stock test applies only if shareholder owns common stock).

For purposes of § 302(b)(2), the shareholder whose stock is redeemed is treated as owning stock actually or constructively owned by him under the attribution rules of § 318. § 302(c). The reduction in the shareholder's percentage stock ownership is affected both by changes in the number of shares owned by the shareholder and by changes in the total number of outstanding shares, which may in turn reflect simultaneous redemptions from other shareholders.

*Example:* A and B, unrelated individuals, each own 60 of the 120 outstanding shares of voting common stock of X Corp., which has no other stock outstanding. Before the redemption, A owns 50%

($^{60}/_{120}$) of the voting common stock. If X redeems 20 of A's shares, A will own 40% ($^{40}/_{100}$) of the voting common stock, or exactly 80% (40%/50%) of her percentage of stock ownership before the redemption. Although the redemption will meet the less-than-50% test, it will not meet the less-than-80% tests, and thus will not satisfy the "substantially disproportionate" requirements of § 302(b)(2). If 21 of A's shares were redeemed instead, A's percentage ownership after the redemption would be slightly less than 80% of her percentage of stock ownership prior to the redemption; the redemption would thus qualify under § 302(b)(2) because A would meet the less-than-50% test and both less-than-80% tests. If X simultaneously redeemed 5 of B's shares, however, the redemption would not be substantially disproportionate with respect to either shareholder under § 302(b)(2).

A redemption will not be treated as substantially disproportionate under § 302(b)(2) if it forms part of a series of redemptions pursuant to a plan with a result that is not substantially disproportionate (in the aggregate). § 302(b)(2)(D). For example, the Service has held that § 302(b)(2) does not apply to a redemption of stock from a majority shareholder where a second redemption from another shareholder was designed to restore the majority shareholder's control. Rev. Rul. 85–14. Similarly, even if a redemption of stock from one shareholder is substantially disproportionate, when viewed by itself, it will presumably not qualify under § 302(b)(2) if other shareholders have agreed to sell sufficient shares to the first shareholder to render the redemption (viewed together with the sales as a single transaction) not substantially disproportionate.

## § 3. Termination of Shareholder's Interest: § 302(b)(3)

Section 302(b)(3) provides for exchange treatment for a "complete redemption of all of the stock of the corporation owned by the shareholder." The chief importance of the complete termination rule of § 302(b)(3) is the waiver of the § 318 family attribution rules. A complete termination may also be helpful if § 302(b)(2) is unavailable, *e.g.*, if the shareholder owns only nonvoting preferred stock.

Without the exception to the family attribution rules under § 302(c)(2), it would often be extremely difficult to obtain exchange treatment for a redemption of stock in a closely held family corporation. For example, assume that a parent and a child each own 50% of the stock of a family corporation, and that the corporation redeems all of the parent's stock. Under the family attribution rules, discussed below, the parent would be treated as owning 100% of the stock both before and after the redemption. In order to facilitate exchange treatment in such situations, § 302(c)(2)(A) provides that the family attribution rules do not apply to a shareholder whose stock is completely redeemed if each of the following requirements is met: (i) immediately after the redemption, the shareholder has no interest in the corporation (including an interest as an officer, director or employee) other than as a creditor; (ii) the shareholder does not acquire such a prohibited interest (other than stock acquired by bequest or inheritance) within 10 years from the date of the redemption; and (iii) the shareholder files an agreement to notify the Service of any prohibited interest acquired within the 10–year period. If the shareholder acquires a prohibited interest within the 10–year period, the waiver is retroactively invalidated and the statute of limitations is automatically tolled.

It should be noted that the waiver only applies to complete terminations under § 302(b)(3), and that constructive ownership rules other than the family attribution rules of § 318(a)(1) cannot be waived. If the corporation distributes its own note to a shareholder in redemption of all of the shareholder's stock, it may be unclear whether the note represents a true debt obligation or a disguised equity interest. *See* Reg. §§ 1.302–4(d) and 1.302–4(e). The Service will generally not rule on the tax consequences of a redemption if the payment period on a corporation's obligation extends beyond 15 years. Rev. Proc. 95–3. The obligation must bear a market rate of interest and should not be subordinated to other corporate debts.

In *Lynch* (Tax Ct.1984), the Tax Court held that an interest as an independent contractor was not a prohibited interest, at least where the actual services performed were infrequent. It focused on whether the retained interest gave the shareholder a financial stake in, or continuing control of, the corporation. The Ninth Circuit, however, reversed the Tax Court's decision, reasoning that Congress intended to establish a "bright-line" test in this area. Lynch (9th Cir.1986). The Service takes the position that actual performance of services, whether or not compensated, constitutes a prohibited interest; but an interest as an officer or director is not a prohibited interest if the former shareholder actually performs no duties and receives no compensation. *See* Lewis (Tax Ct.1966). The Service has also ruled that a § 302(c)(2) waiver is valid if the shareholder retains an interest as a lessor, provided that rental payments are not dependent on earnings and are determined at arm's length. Rev. Rul. 77–467. *See also* Rev. Proc. 95–3.

The waiver of family attribution rules is subject to a 10–year look-back period. § 302(c)(2)(B). The family attribution rules may not be waived if (i) any of the redeemed stock was acquired within 10 years of the redemption from a related person (within the meaning of § 318(a)), or (ii) any related person owning stock at the time of the redemption acquired such stock from the terminated shareholder within 10 years of the distribution, unless such stock is also redeemed. This limitation on waiver of the family attribution rules does not apply, however, if such acquisition of stock by or from the terminated shareholder did not have tax avoidance as one of its principal purposes. § 302(c)(2)(B)(last sentence).

For example, if a parent gives part of his stock to a child for the purpose of shifting control of the corporation to the child, and the corporation then redeems the rest of the parent's stock, tax avoidance is not a principal purpose of the transaction and the child's stock ownership is not attributed to the parent for purposes of § 302(b)(3). *See* Lynch (9th Cir.1986). The Service has also held that a tax-avoidance purpose is not present if the transfer to a related party "was not in contemplation of redemption of the balance of the transferor's stock nor of the stock transferred to the transferee." Rev. Rul. 85–19. In Revenue Ruling 85–19, a father reacquired stock that he had previously transferred to his son and the son's remaining stock was redeemed; since the net effect was merely to restore the original pattern of stock ownership, the son's waiver of the family attribution rules was valid.

In the case of a § 302(b)(3) redemption of stock owned by an entity (*i.e.,* a corporation, partnership, estate or trust), the entity can waive the family attribution rules if the additional requirements of § 302(c)(2)(C) are met. Under § 302(c)(2)(C), each person whose stock ownership would otherwise be attributed to the entity (under § 318(a)(3)) as well as the entity itself must meet the requirements of § 302(c)(2)(A) (no interest other than as a creditor; no acquisition of a prohibited interest for 10 years; agreement to notify the Service of any prohibited interest) and must agree to be jointly and severally liable for any deficiency resulting from acquisition of a prohibited interest. A waiver by an entity serves to break the chain of attribution from a related family member to an entity's beneficial owner (and hence to the entity itself).

*Example:* The stock of X Corp. is owned 50% by
P and 50% by T, a trust having C (P's child) as its
sole beneficiary. If X redeems all of T's stock, the
redemption will not qualify as a complete termination of T's interest. The stock owned by P is
attributed to C under § 318(a)(1), and is in turn
reattributed to T under § 318(a)(3)(B). *See*
§ 318(a)(5)(A). If T waives the family attribution
link (from P to C), however, the redemption of T's
stock will qualify for exchange treatment because T
will no longer be treated as owning P's shares.

## § 4.  Redemptions Not Essentially Equivalent to a Dividend: § 302(b)(1)

A redemption that fails to meet the mechanical
"safe harbor" tests of § 302(b)(2) or (3) may nevertheless qualify for exchange treatment if it is "not
essentially equivalent to a dividend." Although
this test is too amorphous to be used as a planning
device, its contours were clarified to some extent by
the Supreme Court in the *Davis* case (S.Ct.1970).
In *Davis,* a corporation redeemed preferred stock
held by the taxpayer at a time when the taxpayer
and his family owned all of the stock of the corporation. The corporation had originally issued the
preferred stock to the taxpayer in exchange for a
$25,000 capital contribution, which was necessary
to increase the corporation's working capital in
order to secure a loan from a third party to the
corporation. It was understood at the time of the
$25,000 capital contribution that the preferred
stock would be redeemed upon repayment of the

loan. The Supreme Court held that the redemption
did not qualify for exchange treatment under
§ 302(b)(1). It held specifically that (i) the taxpayer was considered to own 100% of the corporation's
stock both before and after the redemption for
purposes of § 302(b)(1), by virtue of the family
attribution rules; (ii) the redemption of a sole
shareholder's stock is always essentially equivalent
to a dividend; (iii) the corporation's business purpose is irrelevant; and (iv) exchange treatment is
available only if the redemption results in a "meaningful reduction of the shareholder's proportionate
interest in the corporation."

The "meaningful reduction" standard may be
helpful in qualifying a redemption of nonvoting
preferred stock from a shareholder owning only
nonvoting preferred stock. Reg. § 1.302–2(a)(third
sentence). *See also* Rev. Rul. 77–426 (redemption
of even a small amount of nonvoting preferred stock
qualifies, if shareholder does not own stock of any
other class actually or constructively). If a shareholder owns stock of another class as well as nonvoting preferred stock, a redemption of the nonvoting preferred may not qualify if the shareholder's
voting power is not reduced. *See* Rev. Rul. 85–106
(redemption of ⅖ of a trust's nonvoting preferred
stock was essentially equivalent to a dividend where
the trust owned constructively 18% of the voting
common stock both before and after the redemption). In Revenue Ruling 85–106, the Service found
dividend equivalency even though the redemption
concededly resulted in a reduction in the sharehold-

er's economic interest. This view seems inconsistent with the Second Circuit's approach in *Himmel* (2d Cir.1964), where the court emphasized that stock ownership involves three important rights: (i) the right to exercise control through voting rights, (ii) the right to participate in current earnings and accumulated surplus, and (iii) the right to share a distribution of assets on liquidation. Revenue Ruling 85–106 states that the Service will not follow *Himmel* to the extent inconsistent with *Davis*.

If the shareholder's voting power is reduced as a result of the redemption, the crucial question is whether the reduction is meaningful. This essentially factual determination is of limited use in planning. The Service has held, however, that a meaningful reduction occurs if a shareholder goes from a position of majority control (57%) to a deadlock position (50%). Rev. Rul. 75–502. *See also* Rev. Rul. 76–364 (reduction from 27% to 22.27% meaningful where shareholder lost the ability to control the corporation in concert with only one other shareholder). A reduction in the shareholder's interest from 90% to 60% was not considered meaningful, however, where no corporate action requiring a vote of more than 60% was anticipated. Rev. Rul. 78–401. Finally, a redemption from a minority shareholder whose stock interest is minimal and who exercises no control over the corporation may be meaningful even though it results in a minimal reduction. *See, e.g.*, Rev. Rul. 76–385 (reduction of shareholder's interest from .0001118% to .0001081%). If no reduction in the minority shareholder's interest occurs, however, the distribution will be treated as essentially equivalent to a dividend. *See, e.g.,* Rev. Rul. 81–289 (minority shareholder's interest was .2% before and after the redemption).

It is not clear whether family discord should be taken into account in applying the family attribution rules under § 302(b)(1). *Compare* Metzger Trust (5th Cir.1982)(discord not taken into account) *with* Haft Trust (1st Cir.1975)(discord "might negate the presumption" of family attribution). The Tax Court has taken the position that family discord may be relevant in testing dividend equivalency after application of the family attribution rules. Cerone (Tax Ct.1986). Under the Tax Court's view, the attribution rules should be applied to determine whether any reduction in the taxpayer's percentage interest has occurred; evidence of family discord may be relevant in determining whether any such percentage reduction is meaningful. In *Patterson Trust* (6th Cir.1984), the Sixth Circuit also found that a percentage reduction from 97% to 93% was meaningful in view of family hostility.

## § 5. Attribution of Stock Ownership: § 318

(a) *General.* For purposes of determining stock ownership under § 302(b)(1)–(3), the attribution rules of § 318 are generally applicable. These rules, which fall into four categories, treat an individual as constructively owning stock that is actually owned by related parties.

(b) *Family Attribution: § 318(a)(1)*.  An individual is generally treated as constructively owning the stock actually owned by his spouse, children, grandchildren or parents.  There is no attribution, however, between siblings or from a grandparent to a grandchild.

(c) *Entity-to-Beneficiary Attribution: § 318(a)(2)*.  Stock owned by a partnership or estate is treated as constructively owned proportionately by the partners or beneficiaries, and stock owned by a trust is attributed to the beneficiaries in proportion to their actuarial interests (in the case of a grantor trust, the grantor is treated as the sole beneficiary).  Stock actually owned by a corporation is treated as constructively owned by any shareholder owning 50% or more in value of the corporation's stock, in proportion to such shareholder's percentage stock ownership.  There is no attribution from the corporation to a shareholder owning less than 50% of the corporation's stock.

*Example:*  A, an individual, actually owns 50 of the 100 shares of the outstanding stock of X Corp., and the other 50 shares are owned by M Corp.  The stock of M is owned 60% by A and 40% by B, an unrelated party.  If X redeems 30 of A's 50 shares of X stock, A's actual percentage ownership is reduced from $^{50}/_{100}$ to $^{20}/_{70}$.  The redemption fails to qualify under § 302(b)(2), however, because A is treated as constructively owning 60% of M's 50 shares of X stock (30 shares) both before and after the redemption.  Accordingly, A's percentage ownership (both actual and constructive) of X stock falls from $^{80}/_{100}$ (80%) to $^{50}/_{70}$ (71.4%).

(d) *Beneficiary-to-Entity Attribution:* § *318(a)(3).* A partnership or estate is treated as constructively owning stock actually owned by its partners or beneficiaries. Stock owned by a trust beneficiary is attributed to the trust, unless the beneficiary's interest is a "remote contingent interest." § 318(a)(3)(B)(i). Stock owned by a 50%-or-more shareholder of a corporation is attributed to the corporation. When beneficiary-to-entity attribution applies, all stock owned by a beneficiary is treated as constructively owned by the entity; this differs from the attribution of only a proportionate part of an entity's stock to its beneficiaries under the entity-to-beneficiary rules.

*Example:* The facts are the same as in the example above, except that A does not sell any of her stock and X redeems 30 of its shares from M. Before the redemption, M is treated as owning 100% of X's stock (50 shares directly and 50 shares constructively from A, a 60% shareholder of M). After the redemption, M continues to own 100% of X's stock (20 shares directly and 50 shares constructively from A). Accordingly, the redemption will be treated as a § 301 distribution rather than an exchange; M will be entitled to a dividends-received deduction under § 243 if X has sufficient e & p.

(e) *Option Attribution:* § *318(a)(4).* A person holding an option to acquire stock is treated as owning the underlying stock. This rule may have the effect of decreasing the percentage of stock owned by all shareholders other than the owner of the option, if it increases the total number of shares considered outstanding. Thus, the option rule may actually facilitate exchange treatment for a shareholder whose percentage reduction would not be meaningful in the absence of the option rule. *See, e.g.,* Patterson Trust (6th Cir.1984)(applying the option rule in the context of a § 302(b)(1) redemption). Section 318(a)(4) applies even if the option is exercisable only after a lapse of time. *See* Rev. Rul. 89–64 (option to repurchase redeemed stock prevented redemption from qualifying under § 302(b)(2)).

(f) *Reattribution of Stock: § 318(a)(5).* The "operating rules" of § 318(a)(5) generally provide for "chain" attribution running from the actual owner to an ultimate constructive owner by way of one or more intermediate constructive owners. In order to prevent an unduly tenuous chain of constructive ownership, the operating rules contain two important limitations. The first limitation prevents "double family attribution" by providing that stock attributed once from one individual family member to another family member (under the family attribution rules) cannot be reattributed to a third family member under the family attribution rules. § 318(a)(5)(B). The second limitation prevents "sidewise attribution" by providing that stock attributed once from a beneficiary to an entity (under the beneficiary-to-entity attribution rules) cannot be reattributed from the entity to another beneficiary under the entity-to-beneficiary rules. § 318(a)(5)(C). In addition, option attribution takes precedence over family attribution if both rules apply. § 318(a)(5)(D).

*Example:* P, an individual, owns 30 of the 100 shares of stock of X Corp. D (P's daughter) and S

(P's son) each own directly 30 shares of X stock; the remaining 10 shares are owned by T, a trust in which D and S each have a one-half beneficial interest. Under § 318, P will be treated as owning 100 shares of X stock: 30 directly, 30 by attribution from D, 30 by attribution from S and 10 by chain attribution from T (5 by way of D and 5 by way of S). T will also be treated as owning 100 shares: 10 directly, 30 by attribution from D, 30 by attribution from S, and 30 by chain attribution from P (by way of D or S; P's stock is counted only once). D and S, however, are each treated as owning only 65 shares: 30 directly, 30 by attribution from P and 5 by attribution from T. Neither child will be treated as owning any part of the 30 shares owned directly by the other child, since § 318(a)(5)(B) prevents double family attribution by way of P and 318(a)(5)(C) prevents sidewise attribution by way of T.

## § 6.  Partial Liquidations:  § 302(b)(4)

(a) *General.*  Section 302(b)(4) permits exchange treatment for redemptions of stock held by noncorporate shareholders if the redemption is in "partial liquidation" of the corporation. Partial liquidations are defined in § 302(e). Under § 302(e)(1), a distribution may be treated as in partial liquidation if the distribution "is not essentially equivalent to a dividend." Unlike the identical phrase in § 302(b)(1), which refers to the effect of a redemption at the shareholder level, § 302(e)(1) focuses on the effect at the corporate level. The definition of a partial liquidation embodies the concept of a "corporate contraction," *i.e.*, a reduction in the size of the business. *See, e.g.,* Imler (Tax Ct.1948)(distribution of fire insurance proceeds).

(b) *Termination-of-Business Safe Harbor.* The "safe-harbor" provisions of § 302(e)(2) mitigate the vagueness of the "corporate contraction" requirement by providing mechanical rules for distributions attributable to termination of an active business. To qualify under § 302(e)(2), the distribution must be attributable to the corporation's ceasing to conduct a 5–year–old active business, and immediately after the distribution the distributing corporation must be engaged in a separate 5–year–old active business. §§ 302(e)(2) and 302(e)(3). The 5–year requirement is designed to prevent temporary investment of accumulated earnings in a business in anticipation of a bailout disguised as a corporate contraction. The additional requirement of an active business forestalls a bailout of passive investments. The requirement of two 5–year–old active businesses (one terminated and one continuing) raises problems similar to those encountered under § 355 in the context of business separations. *See* Chapter 10. *See also* Rev. Rul. 88–19. It is unclear whether the separate business test under § 302(e) is as liberal as the similar requirement for corporate separations under the most recent version of the § 355 regulations.

To qualify under § 302(e)(2), the distribution must consist of the assets of the terminated business or proceeds from the sale of such assets. If a subsidiary's business is discontinued, the subsidiary may distribute its assets (or sale proceeds) to its parent in complete liquidation; the parent's distribution of the subsidiary's assets (or sale proceeds)

to its shareholders will qualify as a partial liquidation of the parent. *See* Rev. Rul. 75–223, clarified by Rev. Rul. 77–376. *But see* Rev. Rul. 79–184
(parent's distribution of subsidiary stock, or proceeds from sale of such stock, does not qualify).

(c) *Other Requirements.* A distribution will qualify as a partial liquidation only if it is "pursuant to
a plan and occurs within the taxable year in which
the plan is adopted or within the succeeding taxable
year." § 302(e)(1)(B). Although pro-rata distributions would preclude exchange treatment under
§ 302(b)(1)–(3), § 302(e)(4) specifically permits exchange treatment for a partial liquidation meeting
the safe-harbor test of § 302(e), without regard to
whether the distribution is pro rata. Moreover, a
constructive redemption is deemed to occur where
there is a genuine corporate contraction and the
surrender of shares would be meaningless because
the distribution is pro rata. Rev. Rul. 90–13. *See*
Fowler Hosiery Co. (7th Cir.1962). If no shares are
surrendered, the number of shares treated as redeemed is "that number of shares the total fair
market value of which equals the amount of the
distribution." Rev. Rul. 77–245, clarifying Rev.
Rul. 56–513. Exchange treatment for distributions
in partial liquidation is expressly limited to noncorporate shareholders. Stock held by "pass-thru entities" (*i.e.,* a partnership, estate or trust) is treated
as if actually held by the entity's partners or beneficiaries. § 302(e)(5).

(d) *Corporate Distributees.* A distribution in partial liquidation to a corporate shareholder will be
treated as a dividend eligible for the dividends-
received deduction, if the distributing corporation

has sufficient e & p. This seemingly preferential treatment of corporate distributees was, in fact, originally intended to prevent corporate distributees from obtaining a stepped-up basis for selected assets without a corporate-level tax under prior law. The repeal of the *General Utilities* doctrine eliminated the underlying abuse in both liquidating and nonliquidating distributions, so that the original reason for special treatment of corporate distributees is no longer relevant. The apparent advantage of dividend treatment for corporate distributees is negated in effect, however, by the special basis reduction rules of § 1059 for redemptions in partial liquidation. *See* § 13 below. *See also* Chapter 4.

## § 7.  Redemptions to Pay Death Taxes: § 303

Section 303 permits exchange treatment for a redemption of stock that is included in a decedent's gross estate, subject to certain limitations. Congress was concerned that it might be necessary to sell or liquidate a family-held business to pay death taxes and related expenses at the death of a major shareholder. Thus, § 303 offers a one-time opportunity to redeem closely held stock with little or no tax cost, since the basis of any stock included in the decedent's gross estate will be stepped up (or down) to fair market value. Exchange treatment is available, independently of the provisions of § 302(b), up to the amount of specified death taxes and related expenses, regardless of whether the estate is illiquid or whether the proceeds of the redemption are actually used to pay such taxes and expenses.

In order to qualify under § 303, the redeemed stock must be included in the deceased shareholder's gross estate for federal estate tax purposes. Thus, the stock must be owned by the decedent at the time of his death or have been transferred during life in a manner that causes it to be includible in his gross estate. In addition, the value of the stock included in the decedent's gross estate must be at least 35% of his adjusted gross estate, *i.e.,* the value of the gross estate reduced by deductions allowable under §§ 2053 and 2054 (funeral and administration expenses, debts and losses). § 303(b)(2)(A). A special rule permits the stock of two or more corporations to be aggregated for purposes of the 35% rule, if at least 20% of the value of the total outstanding stock of each corporation is includible in the decedent's gross estate. § 302(b)(2)(B).

The amount of the distribution eligible for exchange treatment under § 303 is limited to the sum of death taxes imposed because of the decedent's death and funeral and administration expenses allowable as deductions for federal estate tax purposes. § 303(a). Moreover, § 303 treatment is generally available only for amounts distributed within 4 years (or longer, in certain cases), after the decedent's death, § 303(b)(1), and only to the extent that the interest of the shareholder receiving the distribution is reduced by payment of death taxes and funeral and administration expenses. § 303(b)(3). Thus, although the stock must be included in the decedent's gross estate to be eligible for § 303 treatment, it may be redeemed from a beneficiary who bears at least some of the burden of death taxes and funeral and administration expenses.

Section 303(c) also permits a redemption of stock ("new stock") whose basis is determined by reference to the basis of stock actually included in the decedent's gross estate ("old stock"), such as stock issued as a tax-free stock dividend or in a recapitalization. *See* Rev. Rul. 87-132 (distribution of nonvoting common stock to estate was a tax-free dividend under § 305(a); subsequent redemption qualified under § 303).

## § 8.  Redemptions Through Related Corporations: § 304

(a) *General*. Section 304 is intended to prevent a shareholder from selling stock of one corporation to another related corporation in order to bail out corporate e & p at capital gain rates. Despite the intricacy of its provisions, the purpose of § 304 can be demonstrated simply. For example, assume that A, an individual shareholder, owns all of the stock of two corporations, X and Y, each having ample e & p. If X redeems some of A's stock, the distribution will be treated as a dividend under *Davis*. If A instead sells some of his X stock to Y, sale treatment should not be available because A continues, directly or constructively, to own all of the X stock. In essence, the purported sale resembles a dividend. Section 304 recasts the sale as a hypothetical distribution of cash in redemption of Y shares; dividend equivalency is determined under § 302(b), however, by reference to A's stock ownership of X.

(b) *Application of § 304.* Section 304 applies to a transfer of stock in one corporation (the "issuing corporation") to another corporation (the "acquiring corporation") in exchange for property, if one or more persons are in "control" of both the issuing corporation and the acquiring corporation (*i.e.*, own stock possessing at least 50% of total voting power or total value). *See* Rev. Rul. 89–57 (value test applied to aggregate value of all classes of stock). For purposes of determining control, the attribution rules of § 318(a), with certain modifications, are applicable. The 50% stock ownership requirement for corporation-to-shareholder attribution and shareholder-to-corporation attribution is reduced to 5% in each case, and the amount of stock attributed to a corporation from a less-than-50% shareholder is limited to such shareholder's proportionate ownership. § 304(c)(3). If the two corporations are "brother-sister" corporations, the transaction is governed by § 304(a)(1); if the issuing corporation is in control of the acquiring corporation (a "parent-subsidiary" relationship), the transaction is governed by § 304(a)(2).

(c) *Brother-Sister Relationship.* If a brother-sister relationship exists, § 304(a)(1) treats the shareholder as receiving a distribution in redemption of his stock of the acquiring corporation (Y); the § 302(b) test for dividend equivalency, however, is applied by reference to the stock of the issuing corporation (X), *i.e.*, the corporation whose stock is sold. The attribution rules of § 318(a)(without regard to the 50% stock ownership requirement for corporation-to-shareholder attribution or shareholder-to-corporation attribution) are applicable in testing for dividend equivalency. § 304(b)(1). For purposes of determining the amount of the distribution that is a dividend, the e & p of both corporations are taken into account. § 304(b)(2). To the extent that the redemption is treated as a § 301 distribution, the sale of stock of the issuing corporation (X) to the acquiring corporation (Y) is treated as a contribution to Y's capital.

*Example:* Shareholder A owns 50 of the 100 outstanding shares of the stock of X Corp. and 50 of the 100 outstanding shares of the stock of Y Corp.; the remaining shareholders are unrelated to A and each other. If X redeemed half of A's X stock, A would reduce her percentage interest from $^{50}/_{100}$ to $^{25}/_{75}$, or from 50% to 33⅓%. The redemption qualifies as "substantially disproportionate" under § 302(b)(2). If A instead sells half of her X shares to Y, § 304(a)(1) applies. The transaction is treated as a redemption of A's Y stock, but the "substantially disproportionate test" is applied by looking at the percentage reduction in A's ownership of X stock. After the transaction, A owns 25 shares of X stock directly and 12.5 shares of X stock (50% of the 25 shares of X stock sold to Y) constructively. Since X's total outstanding stock is still 100 shares, A owns a total of 37.5% of X's stock, actually or constructively. Since the percentage reduction in A's ownership of X stock is still greater than 20%, the sale of X stock to Y is treated as an exchange under § 302(b)(2).

A sale of the issuing corporation's stock is treated as a contribution to capital of the acquiring corporation only to the extent that the distribution is subject to § 301. § 304(a)(1). If § 301 dividend treatment applies, the shareholder's basis in the stock transferred is added to the basis of his stock in the acquiring corporation, and the acquiring corporation takes a basis in the transferred stock equal to its basis in the shareholder's hands. If § 302(b)(2) exchange treatment applies, however, the acquiring corporation is treated as purchasing the stock transferred, and receives a cost basis in such stock. If exchange treatment applies, the shareholder will recover his basis in computing gain or loss on the transferred stock. The transaction is treated as a redemption of fictional stock of the acquiring corporation having a basis equal to the basis of the transferred stock. The shareholder's basis in the acquiring corporation's stock will apparently be unaffected by the exchange.

(d) *Parent-Subsidiary Relationship.* Under § 304(a)(2), similar principles apply if a subsidiary acquires stock of its parent from a controlling shareholder. If § 304(a)(2) applies, the transaction is recharacterized as a redemption of the parent's stock for purposes of the § 302(b) dividend equivalency test, and earnings of both corporations are taken into account in determining the amount of any dividend.

The basis consequences of a deemed § 301 distribution are less clear in the parent-subsidiary context than in the brother-sister context; apparently, the shareholder's basis in the transferred parent stock will be added to his basis in his remaining stock of the parent. It should be noted that a brother-sister relationship could be converted into a parent-subsidiary relationship, by virtue of the attribution rules. The Regulations implicitly adopt the position, however, that an actual brother-sister relationship will prevail over a constructive parent-subsidiary relationship.

(e) *Definition of Property*. Section 304 applies only if stock is transferred to a related corporation in exchange for "property." Section 317(a) defines property as money, securities or other property, except stock (or stock rights) of the distributing corporation. In *Bhada* (Tax Ct.1987), the Tax Court considered the applicability of § 304(a)(2) to a transaction in which a subsidiary transferred cash and issued its own stock to shareholders of its parent corporation in exchange for stock of the parent. The cash concededly represented property, as defined in § 317(a). The court held, however, that the subsidiary stock received by the parent's shareholders was not property because it was "stock in the corporation making the distribution," which is expressly excepted from the definition of property in § 317(a). As a result, the court concluded that § 304(a)(2) did not apply to the receipt of subsidiary stock by the parent's shareholders, and held that the exchange of parent stock for subsidiary stock was eligible for exchange treatment under § 1001. The court acknowledged that its analysis might permit a bailout at capital gains rates if the subsidiary transferred preferred stock to the parent's shareholders in exchange for their common stock. The parent's shareholders could then sell the preferred stock without surrendering control of the combined corporate enterprise.

(f) *Overlap With § 351.* Section 304 may overlap with § 351. For example, a shareholder may transfer stock of a brother corporation to a sister corporation in exchange for stock of the sister corporation plus cash. If the shareholder owns 80% of the sister corporation after the transfer, § 351 could apply with the result that the boot would be taxed only to the extent of the shareholder's realized gain. In 1982, Congress amended § 304 to provide that § 304 will generally prevail over § 351. § 304(b)(3)(A). Thus, in the example, the cash boot would be tested for dividend equivalency under the rules of § 302(b); the stock of the sister corporation would be received tax free, however, since it would not constitute property under § 317(a) and § 304(a)(1). In addition, § 304(b)(3)(B) contains special rules concerning assumption of liabilities if §§ 304 and 351 overlap.

(g) *Transfers of Stock Within an Affiliated Group.* The application of § 304 to corporate sellers offers unintended opportunities to exploit dividend characterization of the sale proceeds. In response to perceived abuses, Congress enacted § 304(b)(4) which is aimed at stock transfers among members of an affiliated group. Instead of prescribing detailed new rules in this area, however, the Treasury exercised its regulatory authority to provide that § 304 does not apply to stock sales within an affiliated group that files a consolidated return. Reg. § 1.1502–80(b). Given its primary purpose of preventing conversion of dividend income into capital gain, perhaps § 304 should be restricted to individual sellers.

## § 9.  Redemptions in Connection with Sale of a Corporation

(a) *Bootstrap Acquisitions.* Redemptions are frequently used to withdraw nonessential liquid assets from a closely held corporation and permit a purchaser to acquire the remaining stock of the corporation at a reduced price. In this type of "bootstrap" acquisition, the seller may sell part of his stock to the purchaser and arrange for the corporation to redeem the remainder of his stock. Regardless whether the redemption occurs before or after the sale, the seller will be entitled to exchange treatment on the redemption if the redemption and sale are part of an integrated plan to dispose of the seller's entire interest. *See* Zenz v. Quinlivan (6th Cir.1954). Similarly, the Service has ruled that a sale and redemption may be combined in order to qualify the redemption under the "substantially disproportionate" test of § 302(b)(2). Rev. Rul. 75–447.

In *Durkin* (Tax Ct.1992), the taxpayer purchased assets at a bargain price from his 50%-owned corporation and simultaneously sold his stock in the corporation to the other 50% shareholder. The government argued successfully that the bargain purchase resulted in a constructive dividend to the taxpayer. Belatedly, the taxpayer argued that the bargain purchase and sale of stock should be treated as part of an integrated plan to dispose of his entire stock interest. The court refused, however, to permit the taxpayer to disavow the form of the transaction, which was intentionally structured to conceal the bargain purchase. Notwithstanding *Durkin*, it seems clear that an arm's-length redemption of a portion of a shareholder's stock in exchange for appreciated corporate assets, coupled with a sale of the remainder of the shareholder's stock, should qualify as a complete redemption. In an arm's-length transaction, the corporation would recognize gain on the deemed sale of appreciated property for its fair market value, and the redeemed shareholder would recover his basis and treat any excess amount as capital gain.

If a corporate seller is involved, dividend treatment may be more favorable than exchange treatment. In such cases, however, the Service is likely to recast the dividend to the seller as part of the purchase price, eliminating the possibility of a dividends-received deduction. *See* Waterman Steamship Corp. (5th Cir.1970). In *Waterman Steamship,* the purported dividend was distributed in the form of a note which was subsequently paid with funds supplied by the corporate purchaser; this offered the government a favorable opportunity to treat the dividend as part of the purchase price.

In a recent case, the Tax Court distinguished *Waterman Steamship,* and held that a subsidiary's pre-sale dividend to one of its corporate parents was not part of the purchase price for the subsidiary's stock. Uniroyal, Inc. (Tax Ct.1993). In *Uniroyal,* the taxpayer and another unrelated corporation each owned 50% of a subsidiary; they agreed to rearrange their interests by having the subsidiary

distribute cash to the taxpayer, followed by a sale of
the taxpayer's stock in the subsidiary to the other
shareholder. The government argued that the cash
distribution and stock sale should be treated as part
of an integrated transaction. The court refused to
apply the step-transaction doctrine, however, noting
that the taxpayer was unable unilaterally to alter
the form of the transaction. It also noted that
dividend treatment of the distribution was consistent with the rationale for the intercorporate dividends-received deduction, namely, to prevent multiple taxation of income at the corporate level. *See
also* Litton Industries, Inc. (Tax Ct.1987)(absence of
a prearranged plan to sell subsidiary's stock at the
time of the dividend distribution).

A purported sale of stock by a controlling shareholder to employees may be recharacterized as a
redemption, coupled with transfer of the stock as a
bonus to the employees. Estate of Schneider (7th
Cir.1988). In *Schneider*, the transferred stock became subject to the terms of the employer's stock
bonus plan in the employees' hands. Because the
redemption was equivalent to a dividend, the controlling shareholder realized ordinary income rather
than capital gain from a sale or exchange.

(b) *Buy-Sell Agreements and Redemptions.* A
purchaser who has entered into a binding obligation
to purchase stock from an existing shareholder may
arrange for the corporation to assume the obligation and redeem the shareholder's stock. The
use of corporate funds to discharge the purchaser's
obligation will be treated as a dividend to the pur-

chaser. *See* Wall (4th Cir.1947); Sullivan (8th Cir. 1966). If the purchaser has only an option to acquire the shareholder's stock, rather than an unconditional obligation, the purchaser does not have a dividend if he assigns the option to the corporation and the corporation redeems the seller's stock. *See* Holsey (3d Cir.1958). *See also* Rev. Rul. 69–608. In *Citizens Bank & Trust Co.* (Ct.Cl.1978), the court did not find a constructive dividend where a corporation purchased property (stock of another corporation) at fair market value that its controlling shareholder was obligated to purchase. The court distinguished *Wall* and *Sullivan* by noting that the corporation did not purchase its own shares, but rather shares of another corporation; there was no constructive dividend because the corporation received property equal to the value of the consideration paid by it.

The *Wall* and *Sullivan* issues may also arise in connection with a redemption incident to a divorce. In *Arnes* (9th Cir.1992), the Ninth Circuit considered a divorce settlement that provided for a redemption of stock which was owned jointly by the taxpayer and her husband. The court viewed the taxpayer as having initially transferred her half of the stock to her husband in a nontaxable § 1041 transfer. The subsequent redemption constituted a dividend to the husband because it discharged his obligation to purchase the redeemed stock. *See also* Hayes (Tax Ct.1993)(constructive dividend to husband); *but see* Blatt (Tax Ct.1994)(wife taxable on redemption because husband had no primary obligation to purchase her stock). Where the divorcing spouses take inconsistent positions in separate proceedings, the government faces a potential "whipsaw" problem. For example, in the sequel to *Arnes,* the Tax Court held that the husband received no constructive divided because he lacked a primary obligation to purchase the redeemed stock. Arnes (Tax Ct.1994)(refusing to treat the Ninth Circuit's findings as controlling with respect to the husband). Thus, neither spouse was taxed on the redemption. Given the uncertainty in this area, formal guidance may be necessary to ensure consistent treatment of redemptions incident to divorce settlements.

Buy-sell agreements may play a useful role in estate planning by providing for liquidity and orderly transfer of family-held businesses. Under § 2703(a), enacted in 1990, buy-sell agreements are generally disregarded in valuing property for gift and estate tax purposes. Nevertheless, § 2703(b) provides an exception for certain bona fide business arrangements that have terms "comparable to similar arrangements" entered into in arm's-length transactions. The nature and scope of the exception for comparable arrangements remains unclear.

## § 10.  Consequences to the Distributing Corporation

If a corporation distributes property (other than cash) in redemption of stock, the distributing corporation recognizes gain (but not loss), whether the shareholder receives dividend treatment under § 301 or exchange treatment under § 302(a) or

§ 303. Under § 312(b), the corporation's e & p will be increased by the excess (if any) of the fair market value of the distributed property over its basis in the corporation's hands. If the redemption is treated as a distribution under § 301(a), § 312(a) requires that the corporation's e & p be reduced by the adjusted basis of the distributed property (or fair market value, under § 312(b), if the property is appreciated).

If the distribution is treated as an exchange under § 302(a) or § 303, the adjustment to e & p is further limited by § 312(n)(7). Under § 312(n)(7), the part of the distribution which is properly chargeable to the corporation's e & p cannot exceed the ratable share of accumulated e & p attributable to the redeemed stock. This treatment reflects the fact that the value of the redeemed shares includes unrealized appreciation (or depreciation) in the value of corporate assets which is not reflected in e & p and therefore should not be taken into account for purposes of the § 312(a) adjustment to e & p. Furthermore, the value of the redeemed shares includes a share of accumulated profits which reduces e & p (even though the shareholder is not taxed as if he received a dividend).

*Example:* Assume that 50% of the stock of X Corp. is redeemed for $250,000 at a time when X's balance sheet shows a capital account of $100,000 (the amount of cash originally contributed by X's shareholders) and accumulated e & p of $225,000. If the total net fair market value of all of X's assets is $500,000, X's assets must have unrealized appreciation of $175,000, *i.e.,* the excess of net asset value ($500,000) over the sum of paid-in capital ($100,-000) and accumulated e & p ($225,000). Under § 312(n)(7), the amount of the distribution charged to X's e & p is $112,500 (50% of $225,000). The remaining $137,500 of the distribution is treated as attributable to the shareholder's paid-in capital ($50,000) and unrealized appreciation ($87,500).

It may be more difficult to determine the proper charge to e & p if the corporation has more than one class of stock. Legal priorities between the different classes of stock must be taken into account in allocating e & p among classes of stock. Presumably, a redemption of preferred stock should not reduce e & p at all, except for any accumulated dividends, since a preferred stockholder is generally entitled only to a return of capital on liquidation.

*Example:* X Corp. has two classes of common stock, Class A and B, which are identical except that Class A has a preference over Class B in dividends and liquidating distributions in the ratio of 2:1. X has net assets worth $210,000, and accumulated e & p of $120,000. If X distributes $140,-000 (⅔ of $210,000) in redemption of all of the Class A stock, § 312(n)(7) requires that X's e & p be reduced by $80,000 (⅔ of $120,000).

## § 11. Computation of Shareholder's Gain (or Loss) in Exchange

If a distribution is treated as an exchange under § 302(a) or § 303, the shareholder recognizes gain or loss on the difference between the amount of the distribution and his basis in the redeemed stock. The basis of the distributed property in the shareholder's hands will be its cost, which is equal to fair market value as a result of the taxable exchange. If the shareholder does not actually surrender any stock (as in the case of a pro-rata distribution in partial liquidation), an appropriate number of shares will be deemed to be surrendered for purposes of determining gain or loss. On an actual surrender of shares, the shareholder may be able to manipulate the amount of gain or loss by selecting shares with a high or low basis.

*Example:* X Corp. redeems 100 shares of its stock from shareholder A for $25,000, their fair market value. A's basis in the redeemed stock is $26,000, and she retains an additional 100 shares of stock which also have an adjusted basis of $26,000 before the redemption. If the redemption qualifies as an exchange under § 302(a), A will report a $1,000 capital loss.

## § 12. Redemptions Treated as § 301 Distributions: § 302(d)

If a redemption does not qualify for exchange treatment under § 302(a) or § 303, the shareholder's surrender of shares is ignored and he will be treated as receiving a § 301 distribution. The shareholder receives a basis in the distributed property equal to its fair market value, under the general rule of § 301(d). Under § 301(c), the distribution will be treated as a dividend to the extent of e & p, and any remaining amounts will be treated as recovery of basis or capital gain. If a distribution is treated as a dividend, the Regulations provide that "proper adjustment of the basis of the remaining stock will be made with respect to the stock redeemed." Reg. § 1.302–2(c). Thus, the shareholder's basis in the redeemed shares is added to his basis in the remaining shares.

*Example:* X Corp., which has ample e & p, redeems 2 out of 10 shares held by shareholder A for $30. A had an adjusted basis of $10 per share in her X stock ($100 aggregate basis) before the redemption. The entire amount received ($30) is treated as a § 301 distribution, resulting in $30 of dividend income to A since X has sufficient e & p to cover the distribution. A's adjusted basis in the 2 redeemed shares will be reallocated among the remaining 8 shares, resulting in a new basis of $12.50 per share and an unchanged aggregate basis of $100.

If the corporation lacks e & p, § 301 may still apply to a distribution in redemption of stock which is made under circumstances that would otherwise render it essentially equivalent to a dividend. Although the law is not entirely clear, the statutory language supports the view that the shareholder may apply the amount of the distribution against the basis of all of his stock (not merely the redeemed shares) and treat as capital gain only the amount in excess of his aggregate basis.

A problem of "disappearing basis" may arise if the shareholder retains no stock but the redemption is nevertheless treated as a § 301 distribution, *e.g.*, because of the constructive ownership rules. In this situation, the Regulations permit the shareholder's basis in the redeemed shares to be added to the basis of the related party. Reg. § 1.302–2(c), Example (2). *See also* Levin (2d Cir.1967)(basis of taxpayer's redeemed shares added to basis of shares owned by his son). In Revenue Ruling 70–496, however, the Service held on the particular facts of the transaction that the shareholder's basis was simply "lost" in a § 304/§ 301 distribution. The problem of disappearing basis does not arise with respect to a redemption treated as an exchange, since the shareholder recovers the basis of the redeemed stock in computing gain or loss.

## § 13.  Special Treatment of Corporate Shareholders: § 1059

Ordinarily, a corporate shareholder prefers that a redemption be treated as a § 301 distribution because of the dividends-received deduction of § 243. If the distribution constitutes an "extraordinary dividend" under § 1059, however, the corporate distributee's basis in its remaining stock must be reduced by the amount of the dividend excluded under § 243. *See* Chapter 4. Section 1059 eliminates an abuse that arose under prior law where a corporate shareholder might withdraw the value of preferred stock from the distributing corporation in the form of a dividend and then sell the preferred stock at a loss. *See* Rev. Rul. 77–226 (recasting the purported dividend as part of the sale price and treating such a transaction as a complete termination under *Zenz*). If the corporate shareholder does not intend to dispose of its remaining stock immediately, however, the impact of the basis reduction rules of § 1059 will be deferred and will be correspondingly less burdensome.

# CHAPTER 6
# STOCK DIVIDENDS

## § 1. General

A stock dividend is a distribution by a corporation of its own stock to shareholders. Under § 305(a), a stock dividend is generally tax free to the recipient, unless the distribution falls within one of the exceptions in § 305(b). If § 305(b) applies, the distribution is taxed under the rules of § 301 for nonliquidating distributions discussed in Chapter 4.

In *Eisner v. Macomber* (S.Ct.1920), the Supreme Court held that a taxpayer did not recognize income on receipt of a common stock dividend, when the only class of stock outstanding was common stock. This result, while probably not constitutionally required, is reflected in the general rule under § 305(a) for distributions of common stock with respect to common stock. For many years after the *Macomber* decision, a stock dividend was taxable only if it increased the recipient's proportionate interest in the corporation. To provide greater certainty in applying the proportionate interest test, Congress in 1969 enacted the statutory rules of § 305(b); it also added § 305(c) to ensure that § 305(b) would not be circumvented by transactions having an effect similar to taxable stock dividends.

144

If a stock dividend is nontaxable under § 305(a), it may nevertheless be classified as "§ 306 stock." The principal purpose of § 306 is to prevent a "preferred stock bailout," *i.e.*, a tax-free distribution of preferred stock to a shareholder who then sells the stock to a third party at capital gain rates. When applicable, § 306 treats some or all of the gain recognized on a sale or other disposition of § 306 stock as ordinary income.

## § 2. Basis of Tax–Free Stock Dividends: § 307

A tax-free stock dividend typically represents a reallocation of the shareholders' preexisting investment among an increased number of shares; the aggregate value of the shareholders' investment does not change, but the value of each share decreases to reflect the increased number of outstanding shares. Accordingly, when a shareholder who already owns stock ("old stock") receives a distribution of additional stock ("new stock") as a tax-free § 305(a) dividend, § 307(a) requires that the shareholder allocate his aggregate adjusted basis in the old stock (determined immediately before the distribution) among the old stock and the new stock. The Regulations require that the shareholder's basis be allocated in proportion to the respective fair market values of the old and new stock on the date of the distribution. Reg. § 1.307–1(a).

*Example:* Assume that A owns 50 shares of common stock of X Corp., with an adjusted basis of $24 per share. If A receives 10 additional shares of common stock as a tax-free stock dividend, her aggregate $1,200 basis in the old stock must be reallocated among the 60 shares of X stock owned by A after the distribution. Assuming that each share of X stock is of equal value, A will have a basis of $20 per share of X stock (both old and new) immediately after the distribution.

If different classes of stock are involved, basis is allocated in proportion to the fair market value of each class. In the example above, assume that the fair market value of A's common stock is $10,000 immediately before the distribution and A receives 10 shares of a new class of preferred stock with a fair market value of $1,000; the distribution leaves A's common stock with a value of $9,000. Of A's $1,200 aggregate basis in the old stock, 10% ($120) will be allocated to the preferred stock and 90% ($1,080) to the common stock in proportion to their respective fair market values ($1,000 and $9,000).

The holding period of new stock received tax free under § 305(a) "tacks" onto the holding period of the old stock. § 1223(5). Thus, any gain will be long or short-term capital gain, depending on the shareholder's holding period for the original shares. In keeping with the tax-free nature of the distribution, the corporation's e & p is not reduced by a § 305(a) stock dividend. § 312(d)(1)(B).

### § 3. Taxable Stock Dividends: § 305(b)

(a) *General*. A distribution of stock (or stock rights) is taxable as a § 301 distribution if, but only if, it falls within one of the exceptions of § 305(b).

Under § 301(b), the amount of the distribution is the fair market value of the distributed stock. The shareholder recognizes ordinary income if the corporation has sufficient e & p to cover the distribution; the remainder is treated as basis recovery and any excess as capital gain. § 301(c). The shareholder takes a basis in the distributed stock equal to its fair market value under § 301(d); there is no tacking of holding periods. At the corporate level, a taxable stock dividend may be viewed as a distribution of cash equal to the fair market value of the distributed stock: the corporation recognizes no gain under § 311, and the corporation's e & p is reduced (but not below zero) by the fair market value of the distributed property. *See* § 312(a); Reg. § 1.312–1(d).

(b) *Optional Distributions: § 305(b)(1)*. If any shareholder can elect to receive a cash distribution in lieu of a stock dividend, the distribution is taxable to all of the shareholders under § 305(b)(1), even if the shareholder actually elects to receive only stock. In the case of a § 305(b)(1) taxable stock dividend, a shareholder who receives cash is taxed directly under § 301, and a shareholder who receives stock is taxed under §§ 305(b)(1) and 301 as if he had received cash and used it to purchase additional shares. The amount of the § 301 distribution to shareholders receiving stock is the greater of the fair market value of the stock or the amount of cash which they might have received. Rev. Rul. 76–53.

Under § 305(b)(1), it does not matter whether the election to receive stock or cash is exercisable before or after the declaration of the stock dividend.

Section 305(b)(1) also applies to "dividend reinvestment plans" which permit a shareholder to elect to receive stock of a greater value than the cash dividend or to purchase additional shares at a discount. Rev. Rul. 78–375. Similarly, the Service has held that a pro-rata distribution of preferred stock that is immediately redeemable at the shareholder's option is taxable under § 305(b)(1). Rev. Rul. 76–258; Rev. Rul. 83–68. *But see* Colonial Sav. Ass'n (7th Cir.1988)(§ 305(b)(1) inapplicable because Federal Home Loan Bank had discretion to redeem); *accord* Western Fed. Sav. Ass'n (8th Cir.1989).

(c) *Disproportionate Distributions: § 305(b)(2).* Under § 305(b)(2) tax-free treatment is denied in the case of a distribution that increases the proportionate interests of some shareholders in the assets or earnings of the corporation, while other shareholders receive cash (or other property). The Regulations provide that the requirement of an accompanying distribution may be met regardless of whether "the stock distributions and cash distributions are steps in an overall plan or are independent and unrelated." Reg. § 1.305–3(b)(2). If the distribution of cash or other property occurs more than 36 months before or after the stock distribution, however, the Regulations presume that the distributions are outside § 305(b)(2), unless the distributions are part of an integrated plan. Reg. § 1.305–3(b)(4).

*Example (1):* X Corp. has two classes of common stock outstanding, Class A and Class B, which are identical except that X pays stock dividends on Class A and cash dividends on Class B. The distributions of cash to the Class B shareholders are taxed under § 301. The distributions of stock to the Class A shareholders are taxed under §§ 305(b)(2) and 301, because the interest of the Class A shareholders in the assets and earnings of X has increased while the Class B shareholders have received property. Reg. 1.305–3(e), Example (1).

*Example (2):* X Corp. has two classes of stock outstanding, Class A common stock and Class B nonconvertible preferred stock. X pays stock dividends on Class A and cash dividends on Class B. The Class B shareholders receiving cash are taxed under § 301. The distribution of common stock on common stock to the Class A shareholders, however, is tax free under § 305(a). Since the Class A common stockholders have the entire right to the residual assets and earnings of X both before and after the distribution, there has been no increase in their proportionate interests. Reg. § 1.305–3(e), Example (2).

The outcome would be different, however, if the Class B stock were convertible preferred stock, *e.g.,* if each share of Class B preferred were convertible into one share of Class A common. In that case, the stock dividend to the Class A shareholders would increase the total number of outstanding Class A shares; unless the conversion ratio were adjusted, however, the interests of the existing Class A shareholders (who receive additional Class A shares) in X's residual earnings and assets would be increased relative to the interests of the Class B shareholders (who do not receive a right to additional Class A shares). Accordingly, if the Class B stock is convertible preferred stock with a fixed conversion ratio, the Class A shareholders should be taxed under §§ 305(b)(2) and 301 on the distribution of additional shares of common stock. Reg. § 1.305–3(e), Example (4).

*Example (3):* X Corp. has two classes of stock outstanding, Class A common stock and Class B nonconvertible preferred stock. X declares a stock dividend on the Class A stock, payable in Class B stock, and declares a cash dividend on the Class B stock. The distribution of cash to the Class B shareholders is taxed under § 301. The Class A shareholders have increased their proportionate interest in the assets and earnings of X, because they are now entitled to share in any future dividends and liquidating proceeds allocable to the preferred stock. Accordingly, the distribution of preferred stock to the Class A shareholders is taxed under §§ 305(b)(2) and 301.

The Regulations provide an exception to § 305(b)(2) if the corporation declares a dividend payable in stock and distributes cash in lieu of fractional shares. The stock distribution is not taxable under § 305(b)(2), provided that the purpose for the cash payment is to save the corporation the "trouble, expense, and inconvenience" of issuing fractional shares. Reg. § 1.305–3(c).

(d) *Distributions of Common and Preferred: § 305(b)(3).* A distribution of common stock to some common stockholders and preferred stock to other common stockholders is taxable under

§ 305(b)(3). A § 305(b)(3) distribution, like a § 305(b)(2) distribution, alters the proportionate interests within the class of common stockholders. Technically, a § 305(b)(3) distribution might fail to meet the accompanying distribution test of § 305(b)(2), however, because the definition of "property" under § 317(a) excludes stock of the distributing corporation. Section 305(b)(3) overcomes this technical difficulty by providing specifically for the taxability of such distributions.

(e) *Distributions on Preferred: § 305(b)(4).* Any distribution on preferred stock (other than certain adjustments in conversion ratios) is taxable under § 305(b)(4). The Regulations define preferred stock generally as any stock which has "limited rights and privileges (generally associated with specified dividend and liquidation priorities) but does not participate in corporate growth to any significant extent." Reg. § 1.305–5(a). Thus, stock which has a fixed priority as to dividends and liquidations will generally be preferred stock. If stock has both priority as to dividends and liquidations and, in addition, a meaningful right to participate in corporate growth, it is not preferred stock.

*Example:* X Corp. has two classes of stock outstanding, Class A common stock and Class B preferred stock. X distributes preferred stock to the Class A stockholders and common stock to the Class B stockholders. The distribution of common stock on the preferred stock held by the Class B stockholders is taxable under § 305(b)(4). The distribution of common stock to the Class B stockholders is therefore treated as a distribution of "property" for purposes of § 305(b), and the distribution of preferred stock on the Class A common stock increases the proportionate interest of the Class A stockholders in the assets and earnings of X. § 305(b)(2). Accordingly, the distribution to the Class A shareholders is taxed under § 305(b)(2).

The exception under § 305(b)(4) for certain adjustments in the conversion ratio of convertible preferred stock permits tax-free adjustment of conversion ratios in order to avoid dilution of the preferred stockholders' proportionate interests. The Service has held that the anti-dilution exception is limited to changes in conversion ratios, and does not apply to an actual distribution on preferred stock. Thus, if a corporation distributes common stock to holders of its convertible preferred stock to compensate for a stock dividend on common stock into which the preferred stock is convertible, the Service has ruled that the preferred stockholders are taxed under § 305(b)(4), even if the distribution has the same effect as a change in conversion ratios (which could be accomplished tax free). Rev. Rul. 83–42.

(f) *Distributions of Convertible Preferred: § 305(b)(5).* Distributions of convertible preferred stock are taxable under § 305(b)(5) unless the corporation can establish that they will not result in a disproportionate distribution within the meaning of § 305(b)(2). The Regulations provide further that a distribution of convertible preferred is ordinarily not taxable if the conversion rights may be exercised over a long period (*e.g.,* 20 years) and the dividend rate is consistent with market rates at the time of distribution. Reg. § 1.305–6. Conversely, a distribution of convertible preferred is taxable if the conversion period is relatively short and it may be anticipated that some shareholders will exercise their conversion rights while others will not. The likelihood that some (but not all) shareholders will exercise their conversion rights indicates that the end result will be a disproportionate distribution within the meaning of § 305(b)(2).

## § 4. Deemed Distributions: § 305(c)

Under § 305(c), certain transactions are treated as distributions of property to shareholders, even in the absence of an actual stock dividend, if they increase the proportionate interest of any share-holder in earnings or assets of the corporation. The transactions covered by § 305(c) include: a change in conversion ratio or redemption price, a difference between redemption price and issue price, a redemption treated as a § 301 distribution, and any transaction (including a recapitalization) having a similar effect on the interest of any stock-holder. A "deemed distribution" is taxable under § 305(c) if it has a result described in § 305(b)(2)–(5). Reg. § 1.305–7(a).

*Example:* X Corp. has two shareholders, A and B, who each own 50 shares of X stock. If X redeems 20 of A's shares for cash, A's proportionate interest will decrease from 50% to 37.5% (satisfying the "substantially disproportionate" requirement of § 302(b)(2)), and the redemption will be treated as an exchange under § 302(a) rather than a distribution under § 301. If only 10 of A's shares were redeemed, however, the "substantially disproportionate" requirement would not be met, and the redemption would be treated as a § 301 distribution. The deemed distribution rules of § 305 would then apply, and B (the non-redeeming shareholder) would be treated as receiving a constructive dividend due to the increase in her proportionate interest (from 50% to 55.56%). Thus, any redemption to which § 301 applies could potentially trigger a deemed § 305(c) distribution to the shareholders whose stock is not redeemed.

Fortunately, the Regulations provide relief from § 305(c) treatment in this situation, restricting such treatment to transactions that are part of a "plan to periodically increase a shareholder's proportionate interest" in the corporation's assets or earnings. Reg. § 1.305–7(c). The Regulations confirm that an isolated redemption is not taxable under § 305(c), regardless of whether the redemption is treated as a § 301 distribution or a § 302 exchange. Reg. §§ 1.305–3(b)(3)(last sentence) and 1.305–3(e), Example (10). The result is the same even if a stock dividend is distributed at the same time as the isolated redemption. Reg. § 1.305–3(e), Example (11). Similarly, typical recapitalizations involving a transfer of control from one generation to another are exempted from § 305(c) treatment. Reg. § 1.305–3(e), Example (12). *See* Chapter 9.

If a corporation offers to redeem a certain percentage of its stock annually, however, the transaction may fall under § 305(c) as part of a plan for periodic increases in the proportionate interests of some shareholders. The Service has held, for example, that periodic redemptions taxable as § 301 distributions to the shareholders whose stock was redeemed also triggered § 305(c) constructive dividends taxable to the other shareholders under §§ 305(b)(2) and 301. Rev. Rul. 78–60. If the redemptions had qualified for exchange treatment under § 302, however, § 305(c) would not have applied.

If a corporation issues preferred stock which may be redeemed after a specified period of time at a price higher than the issue price, the excess of the redemption price over the issue price may be treated as a constructive dividend under § 305(c). Reg. § 1.305–5(b). As amended in 1990, § 305(c) requires that the amount of a constructive dividend be determined annually in the same manner as original issue discount (OID) on a bond. § 305(c)(3). The Regulations provide an exception, however, for "reasonable redemption premiums"; a redemption premium not in excess of 10% of the issue price of stock which is not redeemable for 5 years from the date of issuance will be considered reasonable. *Id.;* Reg. § 1.305–5(d), Example (4). If preferred stock is required to be redeemed or the holder has the right to put the stock to the issuer, more stringent rules apply. A redemption premium on such preferred stock is treated as unreasonable if it exceeds a de minimis OID threshold; moreover, if the redemption premium is unreasonable, the entire amount of the premium must be amortized under

OID principles.   §§ 305(c)(1) and 305(c)(3).   The Regulations extend these rules to preferred stock that is callable by the issuer if a redemption is "more likely than not to occur."   Reg. § 1.305–5(b)(3).

In 1993, Congress enacted § 305(e) to deal with "stripped preferred stock," *i.e.*, a debt-like instrument created by separating the underlying stock ownership from the right to future dividends.   Generally, the holder of the stripped stock must include in income annually an amount determined as if he had purchased an OID bond.   § 305(e)(1).

## § 5.   Distribution of Stock Rights

For purposes of § 305(a), rights to acquire stock are treated as stock, and an owner of such rights is treated as a shareholder.   § 305(d).   The basis of stock rights, if received tax free, is determined under § 307.   If the rights are exercised or sold, basis is allocated between the old stock and the new rights in accordance with their respective fair market values.   Reg. § 1.307–1(a)(last sentence).   If the rights expire or lapse in the shareholder's hands, no deduction is allowed and the basis of the old stock is unaffected.   If the value of the rights is less than 15% of the fair market value of the stock with respect to which the rights are distributed, the shareholder takes a zero basis in the rights unless he elects to allocate basis under § 307.   § 307(b).   If the shareholder later exercises a right to acquire stock, his basis in the acquired stock will be the exercise price plus any basis originally allocated to the right.  The holding period of the acquired stock begins on the date of exercise.  § 1223(6).

## § 6.  Non–Pro–Rata Stock Surrenders

A non-pro-rata surrender of stock does not fit easily within any of the Code provisions.  It may resemble a stock dividend to the non-surrendering shareholders whose proportionate interests are increased or a contribution to capital by the surrendering shareholder.  In *Fink* (S.Ct.1987), the Supreme Court held that no deductible loss arises when a dominant shareholder surrenders some stock non pro rata but retains voting control over the corporation after the surrender.  *See also* Schleppy (5th Cir.1979) and Frantz (2d Cir. 1986)(both disallowing losses on non-pro-rata surrenders).  The Supreme Court treated the surrender as a nontaxable contribution to capital, even though there was no increase in the corporation's net worth.  Thus, the shareholder's basis in the surrendered shares was shifted to his basis in the remaining stock, and the determination of the shareholder's economic loss was postponed until later sale or disposition.

The Supreme Court's decision in *Fink,* however, leaves open several questions of interpretation.  Instead of adopting a bright-line rule that non-pro-rata stock surrenders do not give rise to a deductible loss, the Supreme Court limited its holding to surrenders by "dominant" shareholders who retain "control."   A concurring opinion would have reached the same result even if the surrendering shareholder had not retained control. Moreover, the majority's opinion suggests that § 302(b)(2) may provide an appropriate analogy in determining whether the reduction in the shareholder's interest after the surrender is sufficiently substantial to warrant loss recognition.

## § 7.  Preferred Stock Bailouts: § 306

(a) *General*.  Section 306 is intended to prevent a preferred stock bailout in which shareholders receive a tax-free distribution of preferred stock on their common stock and then sell the preferred stock to a third party.  A typical bailout transaction is illustrated by the facts of *Chamberlin* (6th Cir. 1953), in which a corporation distributed a new class of preferred stock tax free to its common shareholders; the shareholders then sold the new preferred stock to an outside investor, with the expectation that the preferred stock would be redeemed over a period of several years.  The end result was that the old shareholders received cash on the sale of the preferred stock, recovered their allocable basis in the preferred stock tax free while reporting capital gain on the sale proceeds in excess of basis, and retained undiminished control over the corporation.  Congress responded to *Chamberlin* by enacting § 306, which characterizes certain tax-free stock dividends as "§ 306 stock" and taxes as ordinary income some or all of the proceeds received on a sale or other disposition of § 306 stock.  Under current law, § 306 remains important because of the preferential capital gains rate and limitations on the deductibility of capital losses.  Furthermore, § 306 serves to prevent shareholders from exploiting the *Chamberlin* technique to accelerate tax-free recovery of a portion of their basis.

(b) *Definition of § 306 Stock*.  Section 306 operates by "tainting" preferred stock received as a tax-free stock dividend.  Under § 306(c)(1)(A), § 306 stock is defined to include any stock (other than common stock issued with respect to common stock) which is received wholly or partially tax free under § 305(a).  Section 306 stock also includes stock (other than common stock) received in a tax-free reorganization or § 355 exchange if receipt of the stock is essentially equivalent to a stock dividend. § 306(c)(1)(B).  It also generally includes stock having a basis determined by reference to the basis of § 306 stock, *e.g.*, stock received as a gift under § 1015 or in exchange for § 306 stock under § 351. § 306(c)(1)(C).  *See* Reg. § 1.306–3(e).  Stock having a basis stepped up (or down) under § 1014 (relating to property acquired from a decedent), however, is not § 306 stock in the hands of the transferee.

Section 306 stock does not include any stock received tax free if the distributing corporation had no earnings and profits at the time of the distribution.  § 306(c)(2); Reg. § 1.306–3(a).  The applicability of this exception depends essentially on whether a distribution of cash in lieu of stock would have been a dividend at the time of distribution.  If the corporation lacked e & p, a cash distribution would not have been treated as a dividend, and the rationale for tainting the stock received in lieu of cash does not apply.  If the corporation had *any* e &

p, however, all (not merely a portion) of the stock received is treated as § 306 stock.

The definition of § 306 stock means that a distribution of common stock on common stock can never be § 306 stock; thus, § 306 applies essentially to preferred stock. For this purpose, preferred stock is stock which does not participate to a significant extent in corporate growth. *See, e.g.,* Rev. Rul. 82–191. A distribution of common stock is not viewed as offering the same bailout potential because a subsequent sale of the common stock would diminish the shareholder's interest in the corporation.

In 1982, Congress added § 306(c)(3), which treats stock (other than common stock) acquired in a § 351 transaction as § 306 stock if a distribution of cash (in lieu of stock) would have been taxable as a dividend. In determining dividend equivalency, rules similar to those of § 304(b)(2) apply. *See* Chapter 5. This provision prevents taxpayers from avoiding a § 306 taint by transferring common stock of one corporation (X) to a newly-formed, commonly-controlled corporation (Y) with no earnings and profits, in exchange for Y preferred stock. Under § 306(c)(3), the transfer will be tested to determine whether the shareholders would have had a dividend on a distribution of cash in lieu of the Y preferred stock. Although Y has no e & p, § 304(b)(2) requires that X's e & p be taken into account. If X has any e & p, the Y preferred stock will be tainted § 306 stock because a cash distribution would have resulted in a dividend under § 304.

## § 8.  Operation of § 306

On redemption or other disposition of § 306 stock, the tax consequences are determined under § 306(a), subject to exceptions under § 306(b).

(a) *Redemptions: § 306(a)(2)*.  If § 306 stock is redeemed, the entire amount realized is treated as a § 301 distribution.  § 306(a)(2).  The amount received is taxable as ordinary income to the extent of e & p at the time of the redemption, and any excess is treated as basis recovery or capital gain under § 301(c).  Presumably, basis recovery is allowed against the shareholder's aggregate basis, not merely the basis allocated to the redeemed § 306 stock.

(b) *Other Dispositions: § 306(a)(1)*.  If § 306 stock is disposed of other than by redemption, the amount realized is treated as ordinary income to the extent of the shareholder's ratable share of e & p as of the time of the distribution of the § 306 stock.  § 306(a)(1)(A).  The remainder of the amount realized is treated as basis recovery or capital gain.  § 306(a)(1)(B).  For this purpose, basis recovery is limited to the adjusted basis of the stock actually sold or otherwise disposed of.  If the shareholder does not recover his entire basis in the stock sold (*e.g.*, because the entire amount realized is a dividend), then the unrecovered portion of his basis is added back to the basis of his remaining stock.  Under § 306(a)(1)(C), no loss is recognized to the shareholder.

It is important to note that redemptions of § 306 stock are treated differently from other dispositions.  In a disposition other than a redemption, dividend treatment is determined by reference to

the corporation's e & p at the time the § 306 stock
was originally distributed to the shareholders; by
contrast, in a redemption it is necessary to look at
the corporation's e & p at the time of the redemption.    Moreover, § 306(a)(1)(dispositions other
than redemptions) limits the amount of ordinary
income to the shareholder's ratable share of e & p,
but § 306(a)(2)(redemptions) contains no similar
limitation.    Thus, a redemption results in ordinary
income to the full extent (not merely a ratable portion) of the corporation's e & p.    Since a redemption is treated as a § 301 distribution, it reduces
corporate e & p by the amount of the distribution.
§ 312(a).    By contrast, in the case of a disposition
other than a redemption, there is no distribution
from the corporation and e & p is unchanged.

*Example (1):* X Corp. issues a new class of preferred stock as a tax-free stock dividend with respect to common stock, at a time when X has
$100,000 e & p.    The preferred stock is § 306 stock.
Shareholder A, who owns 10% of X's stock, receives
100 shares of new preferred stock; her allocable
basis in the preferred stock is $90,000.    A sells the
preferred stock two years later for $92,000.    Under
§ 306(a)(1)(A), A recognizes ordinary income on the
sale to the extent of her ratable share of X's e & p
as of the time when the preferred stock was distributed ($10,000).    The remainder of the sales price
($82,000) is treated as basis recovery, leaving A
with $8,000 of unrecovered basis in the stock sold.
A's $8,000 unrecovered basis is added back to the
basis of her remaining common stock.    Reg.

§ 1.306–1(b)(2), Example (2). If A instead sold the preferred stock for $102,000, A would still have $10,000 ordinary income. Since the remainder of the sales price ($92,000) exceeds A's $90,000 basis in the stock sold, A would treat the amount in excess of basis ($2,000) as capital gain.

*Example (2):* The facts are the same as in Example (1), except that X redeems A's preferred stock for $100,000 at a time when X has e & p of $150,000. Under § 306(a)(2), the entire amount realized ($100,000) is treated as a § 301 distribution. Since the amount of the distribution does not exceed X's e & p at the time of the redemption, A must report $100,000 ordinary income. It is unclear whether A's unrecovered basis of $90,000 in the redeemed stock may be added back to the basis of A's remaining common stock or whether this basis simply disappears. Under the general rule for redemptions treated as § 301 distributions, reallocation of the unrecovered basis may be permitted. *See* Reg. § 1.302–2(c).

## § 9. Exceptions: § 306(b)

Section 306(b) provides four exceptions to the application of § 306(a). The first three exceptions are mechanical safe-harbor rules, and the fourth is a subjective test.

(a) *Termination of Shareholder Interest.* If a shareholder disposes of all of his common and preferred stock in a transaction (other than a redemption) that terminates the shareholder's interest (actual and constructive) in the corporation, § 306(a)

does not apply. § 306(b)(1)(A). If the shareholder
completely terminates his interest, there is no bailout potential. Similarly, if the shareholder's § 306
stock is redeemed in a transaction that qualifies for
exchange treatment under § 302(b)(3) or (4)(complete termination or partial liquidation), § 306(a)
does not apply. § 306(b)(1)(B). In the case of a
redemption in complete termination of the shareholder's interest, the shareholder may waive the
family attribution rules under § 302(c)(2) to facilitate safe-harbor treatment. The family attribution
rules may not be waived, however, in a non-redemp-
tion transaction that completely terminates the
shareholder's actual (but not constructive) ownership, *e.g.*, a sale to a related family member. In
this situation, the shareholder would have to rely
on the subjective test of § 306(b)(4).

(b) *Liquidation*. Section 306(a) does not apply if
the shareholder's § 306 stock is redeemed in a
complete liquidation. § 306(b)(2). Since § 331 allows capital gain treatment to shareholders whose
stock is redeemed in a complete liquidation, there is
no reason to treat § 306 stock differently in this
context.

(c) *Nonrecognition Transactions*. If a shareholder transfers his § 306 stock in a nonrecognition
transaction, § 306(a) does not apply to the transfer.
§ 306(b)(3). The § 306 taint, however, carries over
to any stock acquired in the nonrecognition transaction. § 306(c)(1)(C). Thus, if a transferor gives
§ 306 stock to his children, the transferor is not
taxed under § 306(a) but the stock remains tainted
§ 306 stock in the children's hands. Similarly, if a
shareholder transfers § 306 stock to a controlled

corporation in exchange for common stock, in a § 351 transaction, the common stock will be § 306 stock in the shareholder's hands. *But see* § 306(e)(common stock is not § 306 stock if exchanged tax free for § 306 stock of the same corporation).

(d) *Transactions Not in Avoidance*. Under the subjective test of § 306(b)(4), § 306(a) does not apply if the taxpayer satisfies the Service that the transaction was not part of a plan having tax avoidance as "one of its principal purposes." The shareholder must demonstrate a non-tax-avoidance purpose both for the distribution and for the disposition; however, only the disposition is considered if the shareholder, in a prior or simultaneous transaction, disposes of the underlying stock with respect to which the § 306 stock was issued.

In *Fireoved* (3d Cir.1972), the court addressed the question of whether a prior sale of a portion of the taxpayer's underlying common stock removed the § 306 taint from an equivalent portion of the taxpayer's § 306 stock, in the context of a redemption. The court held that § 306(b)(4) was inapplicable, in part because the taxpayer retained effective control of the corporation despite the prior sale of common stock. *Fireoved* leaves open the question whether a combined redemption of common and preferred stock that is not substantially equivalent to a dividend under the tests of § 302(b)(1) or (2) might be sufficient to meet the requirements of § 306(b)(4).

In *Pescosolido* (1st Cir.1988), the court rejected the argument that § 306(b)(4) applies only to minority shareholders who are not in control of the distributing corporation. Nevertheless, the taxpayer failed to establish the absence of a tax-avoidance purpose for the distribution and disposition of preferred stock that was contributed to charitable organizations. Because § 306 applied, the taxpayer's charitable deduction was limited to the fair market value of the § 306 stock reduced by the amount of gain that would not have been long-term capital gain on a taxable sale. *See* § 170(e)(1)(A). Thus, § 306 backstops the § 170(e) limitation on deductions for certain charitable contributions of ordinary-income property.

It may be difficult for the taxpayer to demonstrate the absence of a tax-avoidance purpose for a distribution of the § 306 stock. The Service has ruled that even if a valid business purpose exists, the distribution may still be considered part of a tax-avoidance plan if the corporation could have achieved the same business result by some other means. *See, e.g.,* Rev. Rul. 80–33 (taxable distribution of corporate debt would have accomplished same business result as distribution of preferred stock).

The Service has ruled that § 306 may apply to preferred stock of a widely held corporation unless the shareholder disposing of such stock establishes the absence of a tax-avoidance purpose. Rev. Rul. 89–63. The Service had formerly granted almost automatic relief from § 306 in the case of widely held preferred stock where there was no intention to redeem such stock in the near future. Ironically, the Service's reversal of its earlier position coincided with the Supreme Court's *Clark* decision; under *Clark*, preferred stock issued in acquisitive reorganizations involving widely held corporations is extremely unlikely to be § 306 stock. *See* Chapter 9. Thus, a subsequent disposition of such stock should result in capital gain because there is no § 306 taint.

## § 10.  Uses of § 306 Stock

Despite the § 306 taint, a distribution of § 306 stock may still be useful for tax planning purposes. For example, an older-generation family member may receive common and preferred stock in exchange for common stock in a tax-free recapitalization. If the older-generation family member retains the preferred stock until death, the § 306 taint will be removed when the basis is stepped up (or down) in the recipient's hands under § 1014. This type of recapitalization might also be useful in limiting the value of the older-generation family member's interest in the corporation, for estate tax purposes, while providing fixed dividend income. The 1990 Act substantially reduced the attractiveness of such an "estate freeze," however, by enacting special gift tax valuation rules. *See* § 2701; *see also* Chapter 9.

# CHAPTER 7

# COMPLETE LIQUIDATIONS; COLLAPSIBLE CORPORATIONS

## § 1. Introduction

When a corporation distributes its assets to shareholders in complete liquidation, the transaction is generally treated as an exchange of the distributed assets for the shareholders' stock. At the shareholder level, § 331 expressly precludes § 301 dividend treatment and provides instead that amounts received by shareholders in complete liquidation are treated as "full payment in exchange for the stock." Under the general sale or exchange rules, a shareholder determines gain or loss by subtracting his adjusted basis in the stock from the amount realized on the liquidating distribution. §§ 1001(a) and 1001(b). If the stock is a capital asset in the shareholder's hands (as is normally the case), such gain or loss will be capital in nature.

At the corporate level, § 336(a) states the general rule that a corporation recognizes gain or loss on a distribution in complete liquidation as if the distributed property were sold at fair market value. Congress amended § 336 in 1986 to provide for recognition of gain or loss at the corporate level, abandoning the rule of nonrecognition formerly codified, subject to numerous exceptions, in § 336. Prior to the 1986 Act, a corporation could distribute its assets in complete liquidation at the cost of a nominal "toll charge" tax at the corporate level; shareholders were taxed on the distribution at favorable capital gains rates and received a stepped-up basis in the distributed property equal to its fair market value. Thus, unrealized corporate gains, having escaped tax at the corporate level, were taxed only at the shareholder level, while realized corporate gains were generally subject to tax at both levels. The 1986 Act eliminated this disparity by treating a distribution to shareholders in complete liquidation as a deemed sale. Under present law, a liquidating distribution of corporate assets produces substantially the same tax consequences as an actual sale of corporate assets followed by a liquidating distribution of the after-tax sale proceeds. *See* Chapter 8.

The following discussion of complete liquidations covers the tax consequences to shareholders and to the liquidating corporation. The special rules applicable to subsidiary liquidations are considered separately. This Chapter concludes with an overview of the "collapsible corporation" provisions of § 341.

## § 2. Tax Treatment of Shareholders

(a) *Recognition of Gain or Loss and Basis*. Typically, in a complete liquidation, each shareholder recognizes capital gain or loss on the difference between the amount realized on surrender of his stock and the adjusted basis of his stock. §§ 331 and 1001. Each shareholder to whom property is distributed in a complete liquidation takes the property with a basis equal to its fair market value. § 334(a). In comparison to a nonliquidating distribution under § 301, a liquidating distribution under § 331 is generally taxed at lower capital gains rates. In addition, a liquidating distribution is advantageous because the shareholder can recover his basis and offset capital gains against capital losses subject to the limitations of § 1211.

*Example:* An individual, A, recently inherited all of the stock of X Corp., which has a basis in A's hands of $500,000, the fair market value of the stock at the date of the previous owner's death. § 1014(a). The fair market value of X's assets is presently also $500,000. X distributes $200,000 to A as a dividend and A then sells the stock for $300,000, the net value of X's remaining assets after paying the dividend. A will have ordinary income of $200,000 (assuming X has sufficient e & p) and a capital loss of $200,000, which can be used to offset only $3,000 of ordinary income for the current year. By contrast, if X had distributed all $500,000 of its assets to A in complete liquidation, A would have had no gain or loss on surrendering her stock.

The Regulations require that the amount and character of gain or loss on a liquidating distribution be calculated separately for each block of stock. Reg. § 1.331–1(e). Thus, if a shareholder has one block of stock with a high basis and another with a low basis, he may recognize a loss on the high-basis stock and gain on the low-basis stock.

*Example:* In December 1996, X Corp. makes a cash distribution of $1,000 per share in complete liquidation; the shareholders surrender all of their stock for cancellation. Shareholder A surrenders 50 shares which she purchased at $200 per share 2 years ago, and 40 shares which she purchased at $1,500 per share 11 months ago. A recognizes long-term capital gain of $40,000 ($50,000 amount realized less $10,000 adjusted basis) on the 2–year–old block of stock, and short-term capital loss of $20,-000 ($60,000 adjusted basis less $40,000 amount realized) on the 11–month–old block.

If the corporation makes a series of distributions to shareholders pursuant to a plan of complete liquidation, the series is treated as a single liquidating distribution under § 346(a) and shareholders are permitted to recover basis before recognizing gain or loss. *See* Rev. Rul. 85–48, amplifying Rev. Rul. 68–348. For example, assume that shareholder A owns stock with a basis of $3,000 and receives liquidating distributions of $2,000 in Year 10 and $2,500 in Year 11. A reports gain of $1,500 in Year 11. If A's basis were instead $6,000, A would report a loss of $1,500 in Year 11.

A liquidating corporation may distribute assets (*e.g.*, disputed claims or contingent contract rights) that are difficult to value with reasonable accuracy. Although the assets normally must be valued at the time of distribution, the transaction may be held "open" in "rare and extraordinary" circumstances. Reg. § 1.1001–1(a). *See* Burnet v. Logan (S.Ct. 1931). The effect of open transaction treatment is to defer the reporting of all or part of the stockholder's gain or loss. In an open liquidation, any gain or loss ultimately realized when the value of the assets becomes ascertainable will be treated as part of the capital gain or loss on the liquidation; if the transaction is treated as a closed transaction, however, any subsequent gain may be ordinary in character in the absence of a sale or exchange. *See* Waring (3rd Cir.1969).

The Installment Sales Revision Act of 1980 was intended to foreclose open transaction reporting even when the selling price could not be readily ascertained. *See* § 453(j). Implementing § 453(j)(2), the Regulations drastically curtail open transaction treatment of contingent payment obligations. *See* Reg. § 15a.453–1(d)(2)(iii). *See also* § 453(g) (denying use of open transaction treatment in installment sales of depreciable property between related parties). If § 453 applies to a series of liquidating distributions, shareholders should be required to allocate each distribution ratably between basis recovery and taxable gain. The fair market value of any contingent payment obligations would be deemed to be not less than the fair market value of the property exchanged (less any other consideration received in the exchange).

Installment sale treatment is not available if the liquidating corporation's stock is traded on an established securities market. § 453(k)(2). *See also*

§ 453(h)(1)(C)(related-party sales). Section 453A, enacted in 1988, further curtails the advantages of installment sale treatment by (i) imposing an interest charge on the seller's deferred tax liability arising from installment obligations in excess of $5 million and (ii) requiring immediate gain recognition if the seller pledges the installment obligation to secure any indebtedness.

(b) *Special Treatment of Liabilities*. If a shareholder assumes (or takes property subject to) liabilities in connection with a liquidating distribution, the liabilities reduce the amount realized on the distribution. Contingent liabilities that cannot be valued are not taken into account; a shareholder may have a capital, rather than an ordinary loss, if he pays the contingent liability in a subsequent year, on the theory that the later payment "relates back" to the original liquidation. *See* Arrowsmith (S.Ct.1952).

*Example:* X Corp. makes a liquidating distribution to shareholder A of property with a gross value of $10,000, subject to a liability of $4,000. A has an adjusted basis of $2,000 in her stock. A will realize $6,000 (the net value of the property taking the liability into account) on the distribution, and will report a gain of $4,000 (amount realized less basis in the X stock). A's basis in the property will be $10,000, its fair market value. If the liability were contingent and could not be reasonably valued, it would be disregarded in determining the amount initially realized by A, leaving A with a recognized gain of $8,000 ($10,000 gross value less $2,000 stock basis). If A subsequently paid $4,000 in satisfaction of the liability, she would realize a capital loss of $4,000.

(c) *Distribution of Installment Obligations*. Under § 453B, a corporation recognizes gain on distribution of an installment obligation if the fair market value of the installment obligation exceeds its adjusted basis. No gain is recognized, however, if the distributee is an 80%-owned subsidiary or the distributing corporation is an S corporation. § 453B(d) and (h). If installment obligations are distributed to shareholders (in exchange for their stock) in a § 331 liquidation, the shareholder-level gain may be deferred under § 453(h). The shareholders are not taxed upon receipt of the obligation, but instead report payments received under the obligation as received in exchange for their stock. The installment obligation must arise from sales or exchanges by the corporation during the 12–month period beginning on the date of adoption of a plan of complete liquidation and the liquidation must be completed within such 12–month period. § 453(h)(1)(A). An installment sale of inventory does not qualify for this special rule, unless it constitutes a sale of substantially all of the corporation's inventory to one person in one transaction. § 453(h)(1)(B).

## § 3.  Tax Treatment of the Liquidating Corporation

(a) *Recognition of Gain or Loss*.  Under § 336(a), a corporation is generally taxed on a liquidating distribution of property as if the property had been sold to the shareholders at fair market value. A corporation generally recognizes losses as well as gains on a liquidating distribution; this treatment is distinctly more favorable than the treatment of nonliquidating distributions under § 311(a), which disallows losses while requiring recognition of gains. *See* Chapter 4. The purpose of disallowing losses on nonliquidating distributions is apparently to prevent corporations from selectively distributing loss property. In a complete liquidation, however, there is no problem of selective distribution, since the corporation must distribute all its assets. Nevertheless, § 336(d) limits losses in certain situations perceived by Congress as potentially abusive. In addition, § 336(c) provides an exception for distributions governed by the reorganization provisions. *See* Chapter 9. Finally, § 337 provides for nonrecognition of gain or loss on certain liquidating distributions from a subsidiary corporation to an 80% parent corporation.

Because § 336(a) treats a distribution in complete liquidation as a deemed sale of the corporation's assets, gains and losses are apparently computed separately for each asset. *See* Williams v. McGowan (2d Cir.1945). Thus, a liquidating corporation may realize capital losses from certain assets that cannot be used to offset ordinary income from other assets. This result is generally less advantageous to the corporation than if it were permitted to report its aggregate gain or loss. Indeed, the corporation may be unable either to deduct its capital losses currently or to carry them back to previous taxable years (if there were no capital gains in such years). *See* § 1212(a)(1).

(b) *Loss Limitations*. Section 336(d) contains two separate loss limitation rules. Section 336(d)(1) absolutely disallows losses on certain liquidating distributions to a "related person." Section 336(d)(2) applies to so-called "built-in" losses (*i.e.,* losses accrued before property was transferred to the corporation) on distributions to any shareholder (whether or not a related person) as well as built-in losses on sales and exchanges.

(c) *Losses on Distributions to Related Parties: § 336(d)(1)*. Section § 336(d)(1) denies recognition of losses to a corporation on certain liquidating distributions to a "related person" (within the meaning of § 267). Typically, the related person referred to in § 336(d)(1) is a shareholder who owns, directly or indirectly, more than 50% of the stock of the liquidating corporation. Although the relationship between the corporation and the distributee is determined by reference to § 267, the treatment of losses at the corporate level is governed exclusively by § 336(d)(1). Unlike § 267(a)(1)(which by its terms does not apply to liquidating distributions), § 336(d)(1) permanently disallows recognition of the corporation's loss and makes no provision for deferred loss recognition to the distributee. Section 336(d)(1) applies if: (i) the distribution is not pro rata or (ii) the distributed property is "disqualified property," defined as property acquired by the corporation in a § 351 transaction (or as a contribution to capital) during the 5–year period ending on the date of the distribution.

*Example:* X Corp. has two shareholders, A and B; A owns 75% of the stock and B owns 25%. X has only two assets, both of which were contributed to

X more than 5 years ago. Each asset has a fair market value of $500. Asset # 1 has a basis of $450 and Asset # 2 has a basis of $550. If X distributes a 75% interest in each asset to A and the remaining 25% to B in complete liquidation, the distribution will be pro rata. Because the distribution is pro rata and the distributed property was contributed more than 5 years ago, § 336(d)(1) does not apply, and X recognizes a $50 gain on Asset # 1 and a $50 loss on Asset # 2.

In the above example, assume instead that X distributes equal undivided interests in Asset # 1 to A and B, and distributes Asset # 2 entirely to A. (Note that A and B still receive distributions corresponding in value to their respective proportionate stock ownership.) X will recognize the $50 gain on Asset # 1, but not the $50 loss on Asset # 2 because Asset # 2 was not distributed pro rata and A is a related person. Thus, it appears that the only way that a corporation may recognize a loss on property distributed to a related shareholder in complete liquidation is to allocate the loss property ratably among all shareholders, in proportion to their respective percentages of stock ownership.

If the property is "disqualified property" within the meaning of § 336(d)(1)(B)(*i.e.,* property contributed within the 5–year period ending of the date of distribution), the loss is disallowed at the corporate level regardless of whether the property is distributed pro rata. § 336(d)(1)(A)(ii). This prohibition on loss recognition was aimed at the potential double counting of losses when property

with a basis exceeding its fair market value is
contributed to a corporation during the tainted 5–
year period preceding the distribution. Both the
corporation's basis in the contributed property and
the shareholder's basis in his stock will preserve
the pre-contribution loss under the rules relating
to § 351 exchanges and capital contributions. *See*
Chapter 3. But for § 336(d)(1), the pre-contribution loss might thus be recognized at both the
corporate and shareholder level. Section 336(d)(1)
denies recognition of the corporation's loss, however, even if the property has a fair market value
exceeding its basis at the time of contribution but
subsequently declines in value. This result may
seem anomalous particularly since § 336 provides
no parallel nonrecognition treatment for pre-contribution appreciation.

*Example:* A is the sole shareholder of X Corp.
X's assets consist exclusively of two parcels of land:
Parcel # 1, which X bought 3 years ago, has a fair
market value of $10,000 and a basis of $5,000;
Parcel # 2, which A contributed 6 months ago, has
a fair market value of $5,000 and a basis of $10,000.
X distributes both parcels to A in complete liquidation. But for § 336(d)(1), X would have no net
gain or loss on the distribution because the $5,000
loss on Parcel # 2 would offset the $5,000 gain on
Parcel # 1. Section 336(d)(1) disallows X's $5,000
loss on Parcel # 2 because it is "disqualified property," *i.e.,* property contributed within the 5–year
period preceding the distribution. X must recognize the $5,000 gain on Parcel # 1. The result

would be the same even if Parcel # 2 had a fair market value of $15,000 and a basis of $10,000 at the time of the contribution, and subsequently declined in value to $5,000. Section 336(d)(1) would deny recognition of the post-incorporation loss in X's hands even though there was no tax-avoidance purpose for the contribution.

(d) *Losses With Tax–Avoidance Purpose:* *§ 336(d)(2)*. Section 336(d)(2) imposes a separate limitation on loss recognition if the distributed property was acquired in a § 351 transaction (or as a contribution to capital) as "part of a plan a principal purpose of which was to recognize loss by the liquidating corporation with respect to such property in connection with the liquidation." Section 336(d)(2) denies recognition only of the amount of the built-in loss (determined as the excess of the adjusted basis of the property over its fair market value immediately after the contribution). Thus, if the contributed property has built-in gain at the time of contribution, § 336(d)(2) will not apply, but § 336(d)(1) may nevertheless apply if the distribution is to a related shareholder.

Unlike § 336(d)(1)(B), which applies only to property distributed within 5 years after contribution, § 336(d)(2) potentially applies no matter how long the corporation has held the property. Except as otherwise provided in Regulations, any acquisition of built-in loss property after the date 2 years before the corporation adopts a plan of complete liquidation (including acquisitions after adoption of the plan) is presumed to be for a tax-avoidance purpose. The legislative history contemplates that the Regu-

lations will limit the statutory tax-avoidance presumption to situations in which "there is no clear
and substantial relationship" between the contributed property and the corporation's business (e.g.,
unimproved real estate in the southwest is contributed to a manufacturing company operating exclusively in the northeast). The legislative history also
indicates that a tax-avoidance purpose will be found
only in rare and exceptional circumstances if the
contribution occurs more than 2 years before adoption of the plan of complete liquidation.

In any sale, exchange or distribution to which
§ 336(d)(2) applies, the liquidating corporation is
required to reduce its adjusted basis in the property, for purposes of determining the amount of loss
recognized, by the amount of the built-in loss at the
time of contribution. § 336(d)(2)(A). The corporation's basis for purposes of computing depreciation
and gain, however, is not affected by the downward
basis adjustment. If the corporation's adjusted basis in the loss property has not changed since the
time of contribution, the § 336(d)(2)(A) adjustment
will produce a stepped-down basis equal to the
property's fair market value at the time of contribution for purposes of determining the corporation's
loss.

*Example:* On September 1, 1996, X Corp. acquires property in a § 351 transfer with a fair
market value of $150 and a substituted basis of
$500. On August 31, 1997, X adopts a plan of
complete liquidation and distributes the property
which is then worth $50. If § 336(d)(2) applies, X's

adjusted basis in the property for loss purposes will be reduced from $500 to $150 (the $350 difference being equal to the built-in loss at the time of contribution). Accordingly, X's recognized loss will be $100 ($150 adjusted basis less $50 fair market value). If X instead sold the property in 1997 for $50 and distributed the proceeds in liquidation, X's recognized loss would still be limited to $100 because § 336(d)(2) applies to sales and exchanges as well as distributions.

If a corporation adopts a plan of complete liquidation which causes § 336(d)(2) to become applicable to a loss on a transaction reported in an earlier taxable year, § 336(d)(2)(C) permits the Service to "recapture" the disallowed portion of the loss in lieu of reopening the corporation's return for the earlier year. In the above example, assume that X sells the property for $50 on December 1, 1996, and reports a loss of $450. If X then adopts a plan of complete liquidation in 1997, the $350 portion of the $450 loss reported in 1996 is retroactively subject to disallowance under § 336(d)(2). Instead of reopening X's 1996 return, the Service may require X to report an additional $350 of gross income in 1997.

(e) *Application of Both Loss Disallowance Rules.* If § 336(d)(1) and (2) both apply to the same transaction, the harsher provisions of § 336(d)(1) will prevail.

*Example:* Shareholders A and B own 70% and 30%, respectively, of the stock of X Corp. X's only assets consist of two separate parcels of real property: Parcel # 1 with a fair market value of $15,000 and a basis of $30,000, and Parcel # 2 with a fair market value of $7,500 and a basis of $3,000. Parcel # 1 was contributed to X on January 1, 1996, with a fair market value of $27,000 and a basis of $30,000. On December 31, 1997, X adopts a plan of complete liquidation and distributes a 70% undivided interest in each parcel to A and the remaining 30% to B. X will recognize a $4,500 gain on Parcel # 2 ($7,500 fair market value less $3,000 basis). Under § 336(d)(1), X's loss on the 70% share of Parcel # 1 distributed to A will be disallowed because A is a related person and Parcel # 1 is "disqualified property." In addition, § 336(d)(2) may limit the remaining loss on the 30% of Parcel # 1 distributed to B, an unrelated shareholder, because Parcel # 1 is built-in loss property acquired within 2 years. Thus, X's adjusted basis in Parcel # 1, for loss purposes, will be $27,000 ($30,000 substituted basis less $3,000 built-in loss at the time of contribution). X will recognize a $3,600 loss on distributing 30% of Parcel # 1 to B ($12,000 loss × 30%). If § 336(d)(2) did not apply, X would recognize a $4,500 loss on distributing 30% of Parcel # 1 to B ($15,000 loss × 30%).

(f) *Liabilities in Excess of Basis.* Under § 336(b), the value of property distributed in complete liquidation is treated as not less than the amount of any liability to which the property is subject or which is assumed by shareholders in connection with the liquidation. The treatment of excess liabilities in connection with a liquidating distribution is the same as the treatment, discussed in Chapter 4, in the context of nonliquidating distributions. Read literally, § 336(b) requires the liquidating corporation to recognize gain to the extent of any liability in excess of basis. If the shareholder's assumption of the liability is treated as an additional capital contribution followed by the corporation's payment of the liability, however, there would be no excess liabilities to trigger recognition of gain at the corporate level.

*Example:* X Corp. purchases an asset for $500 with borrowed funds, and gives the lender a security interest in the asset. X claims $200 of depreciation deductions on the asset, reducing its adjusted basis to $300, and distributes the asset in liquidation to a shareholder. If the shareholder assumes the $500 liability, X must apparently recognize $200 gain under § 336(b). Alternatively, the shareholder could have contributed $200 to X to pay off the excess liability, and X could then have distributed the property without recognizing gain. The difference between the two situations is that in one case the shareholder has actually paid $200 out of pocket (as a capital contribution) while in the other he has merely assumed an additional liability of $200. If the liabilities are nonrecourse, it seems appropriate to require the corporation to recognize gain to the extent that nonrecourse liabilities exceed the corporation's adjusted basis in the distributed property, since neither the corporation nor the shareholder may ultimately pay the excess liabilities.

## § 4.  Ancillary Issues

(a) *Liquidation-Reincorporation Problems*.  A complete liquidation contemplates a termination of the corporation as an entity and a winding-up of its affairs.  Liquidation-reincorporation problems may arise if the corporation's assets are distributed to shareholders who then form a new corporation to carry on the old business, or if some shareholders are shareholders of another corporation which acquires the liquidating corporation's operating assets.  Under prior law, the benefits of liquidation treatment consisted of a step-up in the basis of the corporate assets, the elimination of accumulated e & p, and distribution of unwanted nonoperating assets without dividend treatment.  Since the liquidating corporation escaped gain on unrealized appreciation of its assets, the tax cost of a successful liquidation-reincorporation was limited to a single capital gains tax at the shareholder level.  The Service employed a variety of weapons to defeat liquidation-reincorporation plans.  A "failed" liquidation-reincorporation might be reclassified as a § 368 reorganization, with gain to the continuing shareholders taxable as a § 301 distribution to the extent of any "boot" received.  In 1984, Congress also amended § 368 to facilitate treatment as a D-reorganization.  *See* Chapter 9.

The liquidation-reincorporation issue is not entirely dead, although the 1986 Act's imposition of a corporate-level tax on unrealized appreciation has significantly diminished its importance.  A liquidation-reincorporation may still be attractive in some circumstances, *e.g.*, if the liquidating corporation has sufficient losses to offset unrealized appreciation inherent in its assets or if shareholders have a relatively high basis in their stock. The Service will continue to attack liquidation-reincorporations to the extent this technique remains viable.

(b) *Assignment of Income and Related Problems*. The hypothetical sale requirement of § 336 eliminates the need in most cases for the government to invoke judicially-developed doctrines to ensure that a liquidating corporation does not avoid recognizing income. Under prior law, the Supreme Court applied the tax-benefit doctrine to require a liquidating corporation to recognize gain on an in-kind distribution of supplies where the corporation had already deducted the cost of the supplies in an earlier taxable year. Hillsboro Nat. Bank (S.Ct. 1983). *But see* Rojas (Tax Ct.1990)(tax-benefit doctrine does not apply to expenses deducted for materials and services which were used and consumed prior to the liquidation). Since § 336 now generally reaches this result more directly, the tax-benefit doctrine is less significant after the 1986 Act. Assignment-of-income problems may still arise, however, if a corporation has potential income that is contingent or not yet reflected under its method of accounting.

The *Court Holding* issue is unlikely to arise in connection with a complete liquidation. *See* Chapter 4. Conceivably, the Service might seek to attribute to the liquidating corporation a shareholder-level sale of distributed property if the amount realized exceeds the fair market value for purposes of determining gain under § 336(a). Alternatively, the Service might seek to disregard the form of a corporate-level sale to the extent that the loss limitation rules of § 336(d)(1) would have applied to a distribution followed by a shareholder-level sale. Thus, the identity of the seller continues to be significant in these limited circumstances.

If a shareholder gives his stock to a donee (*e.g.*, a charity or a lower-bracket family member) during the liquidating process, any gain on the transferred stock will most likely be taxed to the donor on assignment-of-income principles. *See, e.g.*, Jones (6th Cir.1976); Hudspeth (8th Cir.1972). By contrast, a gift of stock prior to formal adoption of the plan of liquidation is usually effective in shifting the gain to the donee. *See* Caruth (5th Cir.1989)(preferred stock donated to charity shortly after dividend declared but before dividend record date).

(c) *Liquidating Corporation's Deductions.* The costs of liquidating a corporation may be deductible as ordinary and necessary business expenses. A liquidation represents the last chance for the corporation to claim a deduction for accrued but unpaid liabilities. In the case of a cash-method taxpayer, where payment of the liabilities would have generated a deduction at the corporate level, the question is whether a deduction should be allowed to the corporation on liquidation when its shareholders assume the liabilities. In the context of an actual sale, one court held that the transferor corporation, a cash-method taxpayer, was entitled to a deduction for accrued liabilities assumed by the purchaser of its assets. Commercial Sec. Bank (Tax Ct.1981). Since § 336 analogizes a liquidation to an actual sale, the liquidating corporation should thus be able to deduct liabilities for ordinary and necessary business expenses when such liabilities are assumed by shareholders.

## § 5.  Liquidation of a Subsidiary

(a) *Stock Ownership*.  When a subsidiary corporation distributes property in complete liquidation to a parent corporation, if the requirements of § 332(b) are met, §§ 332 and 337 provide that no gain or loss is recognized to the parent or the subsidiary.  In order to qualify for nonrecognition treatment, § 332(b) requires that the parent corporation own a specified amount of the subsidiary's stock and that the liquidating distributions occur within a specified time period.  The first requirement is met if the parent owns stock that (i) possesses at least 80% of the total voting power of the outstanding stock of the subsidiary and (ii) has a value equal to at least 80% of the total value of the stock of the subsidiary (without regard to certain nonvoting stock that is limited and preferred as to dividends).  §§ 332(b)(1) and 1504(a)(2).  The 80%-stock-ownership test must be met "on the date of adoption of the plan of liquidation" and continuously thereafter until the final liquidating distribution. § 332(b)(1).

Often, a subsidiary liquidation can be structured intentionally in a way that meets (or fails to meet) the stock ownership test, thereby making nonrecognition treatment optional to a certain extent, despite the mandatory language of § 332.  Riggs, Inc. (Tax Ct.1975).  Thus, for example, a parent corporation having a basis in subsidiary stock exceeding the value of the subsidiary's assets may be able to recognize a loss on liquidation of the subsidiary by selling sufficient stock to reduce its ownership below the 80% requirement. Conversely, a corporation that lacks 80% ownership may be able to obtain § 332 nonrecognition treatment by acquiring additional stock (or by arranging for the redemption of stock held by others) immediately before the liquidation. In such a case, however, the government might argue that the plan of liquidation was "adopted" informally before the additional shares were acquired and that the requisite 80% stock ownership therefore did not exist on the date the plan of liquidation was adopted.

In *Associated Wholesale Grocers* (10th Cir.1991), the court held that § 332 applied to a purported sale of a subsidiary's assets, followed promptly by the parent's repurchase of nearly all of the subsidiary's assets. Applying the step-transaction doctrine, the court found that the substance of the transaction was a nontaxable liquidation of the subsidiary rather than a taxable sale of the subsidiary's assets. Accordingly, the subsidiary's loss on the asset sale was disallowed, and the parent's potential loss in the subsidiary's stock was eliminated. Although *Associated Wholesale Grocers* indicates that taxpayers' ability to avoid § 332 is not unlimited, the court's decision was strongly influenced by the transitory nature of the asset disposition.

*Example:* X Corp. owns all of the stock of Y Corp., which operates two divisions, T1 and T2. X's basis in the Y stock is $450. T1's assets have a basis of $400 and a fair market value of $320. T2's

assets have a basis of $50 and a fair market value of
$80. Y sells T1 and T2 to P Corp. for $80 cash and
P's note for $320. Shortly thereafter, Y is liqui-
dated under § 332 and X purchases the T1 assets
for an amount equal to P's note. If the transaction
is respected, Y recognizes a loss of $80 on the sale of
T1, which offsets Y's gain of $30 on the sale of T2.
If the transaction is recast as a nontaxable § 332
liquidation, followed by X's sale of T2 to P, the loss
inherent in T1 is not recognized. X takes the T1
assets with a substituted basis of $400, and X's loss
of $50 inherent in the Y stock disappears. §§ 332
and 334(b).

(b) *Timing of Distributions*. Section 332(b) also
requires that the liquidating distributions occur either (i) within a single taxable year, or (ii) within a
3–year period from the close of the taxable year in
which the first distribution occurs. The term "taxable year" refers to the taxable year of the subsidiary. Rev. Rul. 76–317. The single-taxable-year
rule is satisfied if all liquidating distributions are
completed within a single taxable year (which need
not be the taxable year in which the plan of liquidation is adopted). Rev. Rul. 71–326. For purposes of the single-taxable-year rule, a resolution of
the subsidiary's shareholders authorizing the distributions is treated as adoption of a plan of liquidation. Under the 3–year rule, by contrast, the
plan of liquidation must specifically provide that all
liquidating distributions are to be completed within
the statutory period (3 years from the close of the
taxable year in which the first distribution occurs),
and the distributions must actually be completed
within this period. It has been held, however, that

the 3–year rule may be satisfied if the liquidation is completed within the statutory period, even if the plan of liquidation fails to limit the time for distribution. Burnside Veneer Co. (6th Cir.1948). Under the 3–year rule, the parent must file a waiver of the statute of limitations (to permit retroactive taxation of earlier distributions if the liquidating distributions are not completed within the statutory period) and may be required to post a bond. § 332(b). *See also* Reg. §§ 1.332–4(a)(2) and 1.332–4(a)(3).

(c) *Treatment of Parent.* If the requirements of § 332(b) are met, § 332(a) provides that the parent corporation recognizes no gain or loss on receipt of property distributed in complete liquidation of the subsidiary. Under § 334(b), the property distributed to the parent in a § 332 liquidation has a substituted basis in the parent's hands equal to its basis in the subsidiary's hands. In effect, the parent steps into the subsidiary's shoes, and will recognize gain or loss (including built-in gain or loss at the time of the liquidating distribution) on subsequent disposition of the distributed property. The parent's basis in the stock of the subsidiary (which may be higher or lower than the subsidiary's basis in its assets) is not taken into account, and any gain or loss inherent in the parent's subsidiary stock is eliminated. The nonrecognition and substituted basis provisions of §§ 332(a) and 334(b) apply only to property distributed to the parent; in the case of property distributed to any other shareholder, the general rules of § 331 (taxable exchange) and § 334(a)(basis stepped up to fair market value) are applicable.

The operation of §§ 332 and 334 has the effect of eliminating the parent's gain or loss on an investment in a subsidiary, as illustrated by the following alternatives:

| Subsidiary Stock and Assets | A | B |
|---|---|---|
| Basis of Parent's Subsidiary Stock | $9,000 | $ 5,000 |
| Basis of Subsidiary's Assets | $6,000 | $18,000 |
| Fair market value of Subsidiary's Assets (and Parent's Subsidiary Stock) | $7,000 | $15,000 |

In alternative A, the parent has a potential loss of $2,000 in its subsidiary stock, *i.e.*, the excess of the parent's basis in its subsidiary stock over fair market value. In the case of a § 332 liquidation, the parent will take a substituted basis of $6,000 in the subsidiary's assets and recognize a gain of $1,000 if the assets are sold immediately. By contrast, in alternative B, the parent's potential gain of $10,000 in its subsidiary stock will disappear when the subsidiary is liquidated under § 332. If the assets are sold immediately, the parent will recognize a loss of $3,000 ($18,000 substituted basis less $15,-000 fair market value).

(d) *Treatment of the Subsidiary*. In a subsidiary liquidation to which § 332 applies, the subsidiary recognizes no gain or loss on distributions to an "80% distributee" (*i.e.*, the parent corporation meeting the 80% stock ownership requirements of § 332(b)). § 337(a). Section 337 in its present form should not be confused with the provisions of prior law bearing the same section number but relating to entirely different subject matter, which were repealed by the 1986 Act. Section 337 nonrecognition treatment also applies to distributions of property to the parent in satisfaction of the subsidiary's preexisting debts owed to the parent. § 337(b). Special rules are provided to ensure that § 337 nonrecognition cannot be converted into a permanent exclusion, in the case of certain tax-exempt organizations and foreign corporations. §§ 337(b)(2) and 337(d). *See also* § 367(e)(2). If the distributing corporation recognizes gain under these special rules, the distributee corporation takes a basis in the distributed property equal to its fair market value. *See* § 334(b)(1).

Section 337 nonrecognition treatment applies only to the subsidiary's gain or loss on the property actually distributed to the parent, as distinguished from a ratable share of the subsidiary's aggregate gain or loss. The subsidiary must recognize gain on any appreciated property distributed to shareholders other than the parent, under the general provisions of § 336. Losses, however, are subject to a special rule disallowing recognition of the subsidiary's loss on any distribution in the case of "any liquidation to which § 332 applies." § 336(d)(3). Congress may have been concerned that the liquidating subsidiary might distribute disproportionate amounts of appreciated property to a parent without recognizing gain, while recognizing loss on disproportionate distributions of loss property to other shareholders. Section § 336(d)(3) in effect prevents a subsidiary from recognizing losses on distributions to minority shareholders in a § 332 liquidation. The special loss disallowance provision of § 336(d)(3) only applies to distributions to an 80% distributee if the distributing corporation is entitled to nonrecognition treatment under the general rule of § 337.

*Example:* X Corp. owns 80% of the voting stock of Y Corp., and individual A owns the remaining 20% of Y's voting stock. X has a basis of $6,000 in its Y stock, and A has a basis of $1,000 in her Y stock. Y owns only two assets: Asset # 1 with a fair market value of $8,000 and a basis of $5,000, and Asset # 2 with a fair market value of $2,000 and a basis of $4,000. Pursuant to a plan of liquidation, Y distributes the gain property (Asset # 1) to X and the loss property (Asset # 2) to A. Under § 337(a), Y will not recognize any gain on distributing Asset # 1 to X because X is an 80% distributee. X will receive a substituted basis of $5,000 in Asset # 1. X's basis in its Y stock disappears as a result of Y's liquidation. Section 336(d)(3) prevents Y from recognizing its $2,000 loss on the distribution of Asset # 2 to A. A will realize $2,000 (the fair market value of Asset # 2) on the deemed exchange for her Y stock, producing a taxable gain of $1,000 on the liquidation ($2,000 amount realized less $1,000 basis in Y stock). §§ 331 and 334(a).

Section 337(c) provides that the 80% ownership requirement of § 332 must be met by direct ownership, without regard to certain provisions in the consolidated return regulations. This provision is intended to eliminate so-called "mirror transactions," a technique for disposing of unwanted assets at the cost of a single-level corporate tax. As illustrated below, one remaining variant of the mirror pattern involves acquisition of a target corporation's stock 80% by the acquiring corporation and 20% by its subsidiary. The basic mirror pattern is likely to reemerge in other guises.

*Example:* A purchasing corporation (P) desires to acquire all of the stock of a target corporation (T) for $100. T operates two divisions, T1 and T2, with appreciated assets worth $80 and $20, respectively. P forms a subsidiary, S, capitalized with $20 to "mirror" the fair market value of the unwanted T2 assets. P and S each acquire 80% and 20%, respectively, of the T stock; T then liquidates, distributing the T1 assets to P and the T2 assets to S. Since P acquired 80% of T's stock directly and S the remainder, P (but not S) qualifies as an 80% distributee, and T's gain on the T1 assets (but not on the T2 assets) is entitled to nonrecognition under § 337. If P had acquired only 79% of T's stock directly, § 337 would not apply to the liquidation of T and all of T's gain on the T1 and T2 assets would be recognized under § 336.

## § 6. Techniques for Avoiding Repeal of *General Utilities*

The repeal of the *General Utilities* doctrine leaves several unanswered questions concerning when a corporation can or should be able to avoid gain on a transfer of appreciated property. Congress failed to provide clear guidance on whether the repeal of *General Utilities* was intended to require recognition of corporate-level gain when appreciated assets are transferred out of an economic unit but nevertheless remain in corporate solution and retain their historic basis. Under an expansive view of the *General Utilities* repeal, it might be argued that it is necessary to tax corporate-level gain in such transactions, which combine elements both of stock sales and asset sales, in order to prevent circumvention of the general rule of gain recognition. Under a more restrictive view, however, it might be argued that corporate-level gain should be taxed only when the assets receive a stepped-up basis as a result of a transfer. *See* Chapter 10.

Section 337(d) gives the Treasury broad authority to issue regulations to prevent circumvention of the *General Utilities* repeal. Proposed Regulations require a corporate partner to recognize gain when it contributes appreciated property to a partnership which owns or acquires the corporate partner's stock. *See* Prop. Reg. § 1.337–3(h). The Proposed Regulations, which are aimed at so-called partnership "mixing bowl" transactions, are intended to prevent use of a partnership to avoid gain recognition under §§ 311(b) and 336. For example, assume that a corporate partner (C) contributes a division with a basis of $0 and a fair market value of $100 to a partnership (PS), and an individual partner (A) contributes C stock with a basis and fair market value of $100. Assuming each partner has an equal 50% partnership interest, the economic effect is the same as if C transferred 50% of the appreciated division in exchange for 50% of the C

stock held by PS. Accordingly, under § 311(b), C
must recognize gain of $50 on the deemed distribu-
tion of appreciated property (the division) in partial
redemption of its stock. A corporate partner may
also recognize gain if it receives a disproportionate
distribution of its own stock.

The Service has indicated that it will issue regulations on the tax consequences of so-called "corporate inversion transactions," *i.e.*, transactions that
invert the positions of related corporations. *See*
Notice 94–93; *see also* Rev. Proc. 94–76. The Notice is aimed primarily at inversion transactions
that result in excessive dilution of the former parent corporation's interest in subsidiary stock, thereby eliminating potential gain inherent in such
stock. To the extent necessary to prevent tax
avoidance, the Regulations will (i) require recognition of income or gain at the time of the inversion
transaction or (ii) reduce the basis of the stock of
the corporations involved in the inversion transaction. Notice 94–93.

## § 7. Collapsible Corporations: § 341

(a) *Overview.* Section 341 is intended to prevent
a taxpayer from converting unrealized ordinary
gain at the corporate level into capital gain at the
shareholder level by means of a "collapsible corporation." Although the collapsible-corporation problem arose under pre–1986 law and is effectively
eliminated by other provisions of present law, § 341
survived the 1986 Act virtually intact. In a typical
§ 341 situation, an individual forms a corporation
to build an apartment building, intending to liqui-

date the corporation (or sell his stock) upon completion of the construction. Under prior law (other than § 341), if the corporation distributed the improved property in liquidation, the corporation would recognize no gain on the distribution and the shareholder would be taxed on the appreciation at favorable capital gains rates. Alternatively, if the shareholder merely sold his stock without liquidating the corporation, the shareholder would also be taxed at capital gains rates. In either case, a shareholder who was a real estate dealer would avoid being taxed on the appreciation at the ordinary income rates imposed on a direct sale of the improved property.

Section 341 requires that the shareholder's gain on liquidation of a collapsible corporation (or a sale of collapsible-corporation stock) be taxed as ordinary income rather than capital gain. By repealing the preferential capital gain rates of prior law, the 1986 Act effectively neutralized the § 341 penalty (although shareholders with large capital losses may still prefer capital gain treatment in order to offset the losses currently). Even if preferential capital gains rates are reintroduced, however, the repeal of the *General Utilities* doctrine has further reduced the attractiveness of collapsible corporations: distributions of appreciated property are now subject to tax at the corporate level. Although a shareholder might nevertheless sell his stock, the purchase price would probably be reduced to reflect the built-in corporate-level tax liability. Given the diminished importance of § 341 after the 1986 Act, its provisions are discussed only briefly here.

(b) *Definition of Collapsible Corporation.* A collapsible corporation is any corporation "formed or availed of principally for the manufacture, construction or production of property" (or purchase of property under certain circumstances), "with a view to" sale, liquidation or distribution before the corporation realizes ⅔ of the taxable income to be derived from the property (and realization by shareholders of gain attributable to the property). § 341(b). If these requirements are met, shareholders must generally report as ordinary income any gain from a sale or exchange of stock, a distribution in partial or complete liquidation, or a non-liquidating distribution that would otherwise be treated as long-term capital gain. § 341(a). *See also* Reg. § 1.341–4(a). Since many corporations are concededly organized and operated to manufacture, construct or produce property, the crucial issue is usually whether the corporation is formed or availed of with a view to sale, liquidation or distribution. The Regulations provide that the requisite view is present if such action was "contemplated, unconditionally, conditionally or as a recognized possibility," by those in a position to determine the policies of the corporation at any time during the manufacture, construction or production of the property. Reg. § 1.341–2(a)(2). Section 341 generally does not apply, however, if the requisite view is formed subsequently as a result of circumstances that could not reasonably have been foreseen at the time of manufacture, construction or production of the property (*e.g.,* ill health of a major shareholder arising after production of property). Reg. § 1.341–2(a)(3). *See* Computer Sciences Corp. (Tax Ct.1974).

A corporation will also be collapsible if it is formed or availed of to purchase "§ 341 assets" with the requisite view to sale, exchange or distribution. "Section 341 assets" are defined in § 341(b)(3) to include inventory, property held for sale to customers, unrealized receivables and certain § 1231 property. The inclusion of § 1231 property is intended to prevent real estate dealers from converting ordinary income into capital gain by forming a separate corporation for each venture. Even if the shareholders are not dealers and would otherwise be entitled to capital gain, however, § 341(b)(3)(D) imposes § 341 treatment on the typical real estate holding company, subject to the "escape-hatch" provisions of § 341(e), discussed below. Regardless of the type of property involved, § 341 assets are limited to assets held for less than 3 years by the corporation. The 3–year holding period only begins to run, however, after completion of manufacture, construction, production or purchase. § 341(b)(3)(last sentence).

(c) *Presumption of Collapsibility.* Collapsibility is presumed if the fair market value of the corporation's § 341 assets is (i) 50% or more of the fair market value of total assets and (ii) 120% or more of the adjusted basis of such § 341 assets. § 341(c). To prevent circumvention of these tests, § 341(c) provides that cash, stock and certain securities may not be taken into account in determining the fair market value of the corporation's total assets.

(d) *Limitations of § 341(d).* Even if a corporation is determined to be collapsible under § 341(b), § 341(d) provides three limitations on ordinary income treatment, applied on a shareholder-by-share-holder basis. First, ordinary income treatment applies only to a shareholder who has at some time owned (actually or constructively) more than 5% in value of the corporation's stock. § 341(d)(1). Second, ordinary income treatment applies only if more than 70% of a shareholder's gain on sale, liquidation or distribution in a taxable year is attributable to collapsible property. § 341(d)(2). This rule is important if the corporation owns two or more separate properties, and has realized ⅔ of the taxable income attributable to at least one of the properties. If 30% of the shareholder's total gain is attributable to property on which there has been adequate realization (i.e., noncollapsible property), then none of the shareholder's gain will subject to § 341(a), even if the remaining 70% is attributable to collapsible property. In order to prevent manipulation of this rule, Congress amended § 341(d) in 1984 to permit the Treasury to aggregate all of the corporation's inventory assets in applying the 70% test. § 341(d)(last sentence). Finally, ordinary income treatment does not apply to a shareholder's gain realized more than 3 years after the corporation completes manufacture, construction, production or purchase of the property. § 341(d)(3). This provision is potentially risky, however, since the 3–year holding period begins to run only upon completion and it may be unclear whether particular property comprises a single completed project or a series of ongoing projects. Any portion of the shareholder's gain attributable to property completed more than 3 years earlier should be treated as capital gain, even if the shareholder's remaining gain is taxed as ordinary income.

(e) *Escape Hatch of § 341(e)*. Section 341(e) is intended to permit a shareholder to receive capital gain treatment on a sale of stock of a collapsible corporation if the gain is attributable to property which would be capital gain property in the hands of the shareholder. This "escape hatch" is necessary to mitigate the broad definition of § 341 assets in § 341(b)(3)(D), which includes certain § 1231 assets (*e.g.*, rental apartment buildings). Section 341(e) operates by reference to the net unrealized appreciation in the corporation's "subsection (e) assets" (roughly speaking, those assets which would produce ordinary income in the hands of the corporation or in the hands of any shareholder owning more than 20% of the corporation's stock).

If the net unrealized appreciation in the corporation's "subsection (e) assets" does not exceed 15% of the corporation's net worth, a sale of stock will result in capital gain treatment to any shareholder who owns 5% or less of the corporation's stock. If the shareholder owns more than 5% of the corporation's stock, he must take into account both the corporation's "subsection (e) assets" plus any corporate assets that would be ordinary income assets in his hands (if owned directly) in applying the 15% test. If the shareholder owns more than 20% of the corporation's stock, he must also take into account any corporate assets that would be ordinary income assets (if owned directly), assuming that he held in his individual capacity the property of certain other corporations in which he was a more-than–20% shareholder during the preceding 3 years. Moreover, if a more-than–20% shareholder would be classified as a dealer in the property in question, the character of the property in the corporation's hands will be tainted, adversely affecting all of the shareholders (regardless of their percentage of stock ownership) for purposes of § 341(e).

*Example:* A (an investor) and B (a real estate dealer) form X Corp. which holds an appreciated apartment building as its sole asset. If B owns 20% or less of X's stock, B's status as a dealer will not be imputed to X. The apartment building will not be a "subsection (e) asset" in X's hands, and the net unrealized appreciation under § 341(e)(1) will be zero (assuming X is not a dealer). Thus, A will receive capital gain treatment if she sells her stock; and so will B if she owns 5% or less of X's stock. If B owns more than 5% of X's stock, B will recognize ordinary income if the net unrealized appreciation in the apartment building exceeds 15% of X's net worth. If B owns more than 20% of the stock, B's status as a dealer will be attributed to the corporation and the apartment building will be treated as a "subsection (e) asset" in X's hands; both shareholders will receive ordinary income treatment, therefore, if the net unrealized appreciation in the apartment building exceeds 15% of X's net worth. (If A owns 5% or less of X's stock, she may nevertheless escape ordinary income treatment under the alternative route of § 341(d), which makes § 341(a) inapplicable to 5%-or-less shareholders.)

(f) *Amnesty of § 341(f).* Section 341(f) provides an additional escape hatch from ordinary income treatment on a sale of stock of a collapsible corporation if the corporation consents to recognize its gain on "subsection (f) assets" (primarily real estate, unrealized receivables and non-capital assets) when it disposes of them in certain transactions that would otherwise qualify for nonrecognition treatment. When § 341(f) was enacted, a corporation could escape gain by distributing its assets in complete liquidation. Because a liquidating corporation must recognize gain in any event under present law, the additional burden imposed by a § 341(f) consent is negligible. Although a § 341(f) consent thus imposes no additional burden on the corporation, it also offers less benefit than under prior law because of the reduced advantages of capital gain treatment.

# CHAPTER 8

# TAXABLE ACQUISITIONS

## § 1. Introduction

Ownership of a corporate business may be sold either in the form of the shareholders' stock or in the form of the corporation's assets. A sale of corporate assets followed by a liquidating distribution to shareholders will generate gain both at the corporate level and at the shareholder level. The purchaser, of course, will have a cost basis in the assets equal to their fair market value. Alternatively, the shareholders may sell their stock at the cost of only a shareholder-level tax. The basis of the corporate assets will not be stepped up, however, and any unrealized appreciation in the assets will be preserved. From the shareholders' standpoint, a stock sale may be preferable because any contingent liabilities will become the responsibility of the purchaser. On the other hand, the purchaser may seek to shift the risk of contingent liabilities back to the selling shareholders by demanding warranties as to the corporation's financial condition or by depositing part of the purchase price in escrow pending resolution of the contingent liabilities.

Prior to the repeal of the *General Utilities* doctrine in the 1986 Act, an acquisition of a corporate business preceded or followed by a complete liquidation offered significant advantages. Section 338, originally enacted in 1982, is intended to permit equal treatment for a purchase of corporate stock and a purchase of corporate assets. Section 338 was drastically revised in 1986 to reflect the repeal of the *General Utilities* doctrine, and its attractiveness is greatly reduced under present law. Generally, the future tax benefits from a § 338 election (*e.g.*, higher depreciation deductions) will not fully compensate for the cost of an immediate corporate-level tax. A § 338 election may nevertheless be advantageous if the acquired corporation has net operating losses sufficient to offset the gain on the deemed sale of its assets. *See* Chapter 11. Section 338 may also be useful for a corporation that sells an 80%-owned subsidiary and makes a § 338(h)(10) election.

This Chapter first considers taxable asset acquisitions, including allocation of purchase price and amortization of acquired intangibles, and then describes the operation of § 338 in connection with taxable stock acquisitions. Various limitations on the deductibility of corporate takeover expenses are discussed separately.

## § 2. Asset Acquisitions

A taxable asset acquisition may be structured as a purchase of the target corporation's assets, followed or preceded by a liquidation of the target. These alternative methods of acquiring the target's assets generally have equivalent tax consequences, as the following example illustrates. Assume that a target corporation (T) holds Blackacre with a basis of $400 and a fair market value of $600, as well as $50 cash; T's sole shareholder (A) has a basis of $100 in his T stock. A purchasing corporation (P) purchases Blackacre from T for $600 and T is liquidated. For purposes of simplicity, assume T and A are taxed at flat rates of 25% and 40%, respectively.

On a sale of Blackacre to P, T incurs a tax liability of $50 ($200 gain × 25%), which T pays from its cash; T then distributes the $600 sales proceeds to A in complete liquidation. Under § 331(a), A recognizes gain of $500 (the excess of the $600 liquidating distribution over A's $100 basis in his stock). After paying tax of $200 ($500 × 40%), A is left with net proceeds of $400. Under § 1012, P takes a cost basis in Blackacre.

The result is identical if T liquidates and A then sells Blackacre to P. Upon a liquidating distribution of Blackacre, T recognizes gain of $200 and uses its cash to pay the tax liability of $50. § 336(a). A recognizes gain of $500 on the liquidating distribution, incurs a tax liability of $200, and takes Blackacre with a basis equal to its fair market value. §§ 331(a) and 334(a). On the subsequent sale of Blackacre, A recognizes no gain and retains $400 of sale proceeds net of taxes. Under § 1012, P takes a cost basis of $600 in Blackacre. A would retain the same after-tax proceeds if T instead distributed all of its assets in liquidation, subject to the $50 tax liability.

An asset acquisition may also be accomplished by a state law merger of the target corporation (T) into the purchasing corporation (P) or its subsidiary. Pursuant to the merger, T's shareholders receive cash (or a combination of cash and P notes) in exchange for their P stock. For tax purposes, such a "cash merger" is treated as a taxable sale of T's assets followed by a liquidation of T. *See* Rev. Rul. 69–6; West Shore Fuel, Inc. (2d Cir.1979). Alternatively, an asset acquisition may be structured as a tax-free reorganization if certain requirements are satisfied. *See* Chapter 9. If reorganization treatment applies, both the corporate-level and shareholder-level taxes may be deferred, but the basis of the acquired assets is not stepped up.

## § 3. Allocation of Purchase Price

(a) *Section 1060.* Prior to 1986, the Service generally respected an allocation of purchase price in a taxable acquisition of a business to the extent that the allocation reflected an arm's-length agreement between the parties. The diminution of a capital gains preference greatly reduced the likelihood that the buyer and seller would have adverse tax interests. Sellers had little incentive to allocate purchase price to capital assets rather than ordinary-income assets. At the same time, buyers sought to avoid an allocation of purchase price (prior to the 1993 enactment of § 197) to nonamortizable goodwill and going concern value.

In response, Congress enacted § 1060 which governs the allocation of a lump-sum purchase price among multiple assets. Section 1060 applies to any acquisition of assets which constitute a trade or business in a cost-basis transaction, *i.e.*, any transaction in which the transferee's basis in the assets is determined wholly by reference to the consideration paid for the assets. If § 1060 applies, the prescribed allocation method will affect both the transferor's gain or loss on the transfer and the transferee's basis for the assets. The Regulations provide that the "residual method" of valuing goodwill and going concern value must be applied in any direct or indirect asset purchase described in § 1060. *See* Reg. § 1.1060–1T(d). The residual method is intended to assign a higher basis to goodwill and going concern value than if a lumpsum purchase price were allocated among assets in proportion to their respective fair market values.

Specifically, the § 1060 Regulations allocate purchase price among four classes of assets: (i) Class I assets, including cash and cash equivalents, (ii) Class II assets, including certificates of deposit, U.S. government securities, and readily marketable stock or securities, (iii) Class III assets, consisting of all other assets except goodwill and going concern value, and (iv) Class IV assets, comprising goodwill and going concern value. Within each class, the purchase price is allocated among assets based on the value of assets within the class. Any "excess" purchase price, *e.g.*, premiums paid by the purchaser in excess of the fair market value of tangible and intangible assets other than goodwill and going concern value, is allocated to Class IV assets. As amended in 1990, § 1060 provides that a written agreement allocating the purchase price is generally binding on the parties (but not the Service) unless the agreement is unenforceable because of mistake, undue influence, fraud or similar circumstances. *See* Danielson (3d Cir.1967).

(b) *Section 197 Intangibles.* The 1993 Act created a new category of intangible assets ("§ 197 intangibles") which must generally be amortized over a 15–year period using the straight-line method. The legislative history indicates that the § 1060 allocation rules will be modified to treat all amortizable § 197 intangibles as Class IV assets. The enactment of § 197 represents a compromise intended to eliminate disputes between taxpayers and the Service over amortization of particular intangibles purchased as part of a business.

In a controversial decision, the Supreme Court held that a purchaser was entitled to amortize customer lists with a useful life and an ascertainable value. Newark Morning Ledger Co. (S.Ct. 1993). The Court rejected the government's argument that customer lists and similar intangibles reflect merely "the expectancy of continued patronage" and thus are inseparable from goodwill and going concern value. *See also* Citizens & Southern Corp. (Tax Ct.1988)(permitting amortization of purchased bank core deposits). In another case, the Fourth Circuit treated an "assembled workforce" as amortizable, but denied a deduction because the taxpayer failed to provide a reliable estimate of useful life. Ithaca Indus., Inc. (4th Cir.1994).

Although § 197 provides more certainty than under prior law, allocation disputes are likely to persist. In the case of previously nonamortizable intangibles, such as goodwill and going concern value, § 197 offers a significant benefit to purchasers. By contrast, § 197 extends the recovery period for other intangibles that were formerly amortizable over a shorter life, *e.g.*, most covenants not to compete. Generally, amortizable § 197 intangibles include goodwill and going concern value, workforce in place, customers and suppliers, business information base, know-how, government licenses, franchises, trademarks, computer software and covenants not to compete. *See* § 197(d). Certain intangibles such as "off-the-shelf" computer software and fees for professional services are specifically excluded from the definition of § 197 intangibles. *See* § 197(e)(3) and (8). Goodwill and going concern value are always treated as amortizable § 197 intangibles. Other intangibles are covered by § 197 only if there is a related acquisition of a business by a purchase of assets or, in some cases, stock. No loss is allowed upon disposition of a § 197 intangible if the purchaser continues to hold other § 197 intangibles acquired in the same or a related transaction; any unrecovered basis is added to the basis of the retained § 197 intangibles. *See* § 197(f)(1).

After the enactment of § 197, taxable asset acquisitions (or stock acquisitions followed by a § 338 election) may be more attractive when goodwill or going concern value represents a significant portion of the purchase price. Under prior law, the parties had an incentive to allocate the purchase price to a covenant not to compete (amortizable over the life of the agreement) rather than nonamortizable goodwill. Although § 197 allows amortization of both types of intangibles over 15 years, it may now be more advantageous to allocate purchase price to goodwill. From an individual seller's perspective, a sale of goodwill generally results in capital gain taxable at a maximum rate of 28%, while noncompete payments are treated as ordinary income taxable at a maximum rate of 39.6%. From the buyer's perspective, an allocation of purchase price to goodwill may be advantageous for financial reporting purposes. Under generally accepted accounting principles, goodwill may be amortized over as long as 40 years, whereas a covenant not to compete must be amortized over the life of the agreement. Thus, the purchasing corporation's earnings ratio generally will be higher in earlier years if purchase price is allocated to goodwill.

In the case of a corporate seller, it may be advantageous to structure a portion of the purchase price as a shareholder-level payment for a covenant not to compete. Although noncompete payments to controlling shareholders will be taxable as ordinary income, they will escape tax at the corporate level, producing an overall tax saving. Of course, the Service may challenge an allocation of purchase price to a covenant not to compete as unreasonable or excessive, particularly if the parties do not have adverse interests. Section 1060(e) authorizes reporting requirements whenever a 10%-owner of a business transfers a portion of his interest in the business and simultaneously enters into an employment agreement or covenant not to compete.

## § 4. Stock Sales Treated as Asset Transfers: § 336(e)

Section 336(e) authorizes the Treasury to issue Regulations that will permit a parent corporation to elect to treat a sale (or distribution) of subsidiary stock as a sale of the subsidiary's assets. A parent corporation is defined by reference to the same 80% stock ownership requirements referred to in § 332(b). If the parent elects to treat the stock sale as an asset transfer under § 336(e), the parent's gain or loss on the actual stock sale is simply ignored. Instead, gain or loss is determined solely by reference to the gain or loss that the subsidiary would have recognized on a direct sale of its assets for the amount paid for the parent's stock. The subsidiary receives a corresponding step-up in its basis for the assets. The purpose of § 336(e) is to put the parent and the subsidiary in the same position as if the subsidiary had sold its assets in a taxable transaction and then distributed the sale proceeds tax free to the parent in a § 332 liquidation.

*Example:* X Corp. originally contributed $500 to its subsidiary, Y Corp., in exchange for all of Y's stock. Y used the $500 to purchase property that subsequently appreciated to $1,000. X then sold the Y stock to P Corp. for $1,000, the fair market value of Y's assets. If X elects under § 336(e) to treat the stock sale as an asset transfer, the deemed asset sale will trigger a $500 gain ($1,000 amount realized less Y's $500 basis in its assets). X will recognize no gain or loss on the actual sale of its Y stock. The new basis of Y's assets will be $1,000 (the fair market value). If Y immediately sells its assets for $1,000, no further gain or loss will be recognized. This result is proper because the gain inherent in Y's assets has already been taxed to X, and there is no reason to impose an additional tax at the corporate level unless Y's assets appreciate further in value.

If X did not make a § 336(e) election, X would recognize $500 gain on the sale of its Y stock ($1,000 amount realized less $500 stock basis), but Y's basis in its assets would still be $500. Thus, Y would recognize a $500 gain on an actual sale of its assets for $1,000. The same $500 of economic gain would hence be taxed twice at the corporate level, once to X on the sale of X's Y stock and again to Y on Y's sale of its assets. Section 336(e) offers relief from this potential multiple taxation of the same economic gain by providing a corresponding step-up in the basis of the subsidiary's assets when appreciated subsidiary stock is sold.

## § 5. Stock Acquisitions: § 338

(a) *Overview.* In a taxable stock acquisition, the purchaser (P) acquires stock of the target corporation (T) from T's shareholders for cash (or a combination of cash and other consideration). If P is an individual, P must liquidate T in order to obtain a stepped-up basis in T's assets, and T will recognize gain on the liquidating distribution. §§ 334(a) and 336. Since P has a cost basis in T's stock, P will recognize no gain on the liquidating distribution. § 331. If P is a corporation, § 338 allows P to obtain a stepped-up basis in T's assets without an actual liquidation of T, at the cost of a corporate-level tax on the unrealized appreciation in T's assets.

After the repeal of the *General Utilities* doctrine, a stock purchase (without a § 338 election) is usually more attractive than an asset acquisition. As a matter of tax policy, there is no reason to treat stock purchases more favorably than asset purchases. One proposal would impose a mandatory § 338 election in order to restore parity between the treatment of asset and stock sales. Alternatively, elective treatment of an asset acquisition as a carryover basis transaction would achieve neutrality by eliminating corporate-level tax on the asset sale. It seems unlikely, however, that either proposal will be adopted in the near future.

In enacting § 338, Congress intended to repeal the nonstatutory treatment of a stock purchase followed by a liquidation as a taxable purchase of assets. *See* Kimbell–Diamond Milling Co. (5th Cir. 1951). The Service has confirmed that where a § 338 qualified stock purchase is followed by a subsequent liquidation of the target corporation, the stock purchase will be accorded "independent significance" regardless of whether a § 338 election is made. Rev. Rul. 90–95. The subsequent liquidation is tax free under §§ 332 and 337, and § 338 is the exclusive method of obtaining a stepped-up basis in the target corporation's assets. Accordingly, a stock purchase followed by a liquidation will not be treated as a taxable asset purchase under the step-transaction doctrine.

Where the target corporation is liquidated following a qualified stock purchase but no § 338 election is made, and the purchasing corporation may succeed to the target's net operating losses and other tax attributes. If the principal purpose for the liquidation is tax avoidance, § 269(b) authorizes the Service to disallow deductions and other tax benefits. Section 269(b) has been rendered largely obsolete, however, by the repeal of the *General Utilities* doctrine and tightening of the § 382 limits on losses. *See* Reg. § 1.269–7; *see also* Chapter 11.

(b) *Mechanics of § 338.* To be eligible to make a § 338 election, a purchasing corporation (P) must make a "qualified stock purchase," *i.e.,* P must purchase at least 80% of the total voting power and at least 80% of the total value of the stock of the target corporation (T) during a 12–month acquisition period. § 338(d)(3). The term "purchase" is generally defined as any acquisition of stock (other than from certain related parties) in a taxable transaction. § 338(h)(3). The 12–month acquisition period begins to run on the date of the first purchase of stock included in a qualified stock purchase. Under § 338(g), P must make the election no later than the 15th day of the ninth month beginning after the month which includes the acquisition date (*i.e.,* the date on which the 80% stock purchase requirement is met). If P makes a § 338 election, the original target corporation (old T) is deemed to sell its assets to a new corporation (new T) at fair market value. § 338(a). The deemed sale is treated as occurring at the close of the acquisition date. § 338(a)(1). New T takes a basis in the assets of old T determined by reference to the purchase price for old T's stock, appropriately adjusted for liabilities and other items. § 338(b).

*Example:* Assume that T owns a single asset with a basis of $500 and a fair market value of $1,000, and that T's only liability is a potential tax of $75 that would be imposed on a sale of its asset. P buys all of T's stock for $925 ($1,000 fair market value of T's asset less potential tax liability of $75). If P makes a § 338 election, T will be treated as selling its asset to new T for $1,000, triggering $500 of gain. New T will receive the asset with a basis of $1,000 ($925 stock purchase price plus the $75 tax liability on the deemed sale of the asset). Since T has only a single asset, the entire $1,000 would be allocated to the basis of that asset. The tax consequences would be identical if T actually sold its asset to P for $1,000, paid $75 tax on the asset sale, and distributed $925 ($1,000 less $75 tax) to T's former shareholders in complete liquidation.

Section 338 quickly becomes more complex if P acquires less than all of T's stock, or if P acquired some T stock before the 12–month acquisition period. In either situation, old T will still be treated as selling its assets to new T at fair market value, triggering taxable gain to old T. New T's basis in old T's assets will be determined by what the Regulations refer to as "adjusted grossed-up basis" (AGUB). This amount depends on four factors: (i) the grossed-up basis of the P's "recently purchased stock" (*i.e.*, stock purchased within the 12–month acquisition period); (ii) the basis of P's "nonrecently purchased stock" (*i.e.*, stock, other than recently purchased stock, held on the acquisition date); (iii) T's liabilities, and (iv) certain other items. Reg. § 1.338(b)–1(c)(1).

*Example (1):* In the previous example, assume that P purchases 80% of T's stock for $740 (80% of $925). Old T will still be treated as selling its asset to new T for $1,000 (fair market value), triggering a $75 tax. The basis of the asset in new T's hands will be the "grossed-up basis" of P's recently purchased stock (as defined by § 338(b)(4)) plus the $75 tax liability. Under § 338(b)(4), the grossed-up basis of P's recently purchased stock will be its basis in P's hands ($740) multiplied by 100%/80%. The grossed-up basis, $925, is the amount that P would have had to pay to acquire 100% of the T stock, assuming that the 20% minority shareholders had sold their stock for the same average price as P paid for the rest of the T stock. In effect, new T is given a basis increase equal to P's purchase price for 80% of the T stock plus the fair market value of the remaining 20% of the T stock held by minority shareholders. Thus, new T's asset basis will be $1,000 ($925 grossed-up basis plus $75 tax liability), even though minority shareholders are not taxed on the unrealized appreciation in their stock. The result is less than a full double tax because new T's asset basis is stepped up to fair market value but minority shareholders are not taxed as if T actually liquidated.

*Example (2):* In the previous example, assume that P purchased 20% of T's stock 5 years ago for $100 and then acquired an additional 80% in a qualified stock purchase. The grossed-up basis of P's recently purchased stock, under § 338(b)(4), will be $740 multiplied by 80%/80%. The adjusted grossed-up basis will be the sum of $740 (the grossed-up basis of P's recently purchased stock) plus $100 (the basis of P's nonrecently purchased stock) plus the $75 tax liability. This amount ($915) is less than the fair market value of T's assets ($1,000). Under § 338(b)(3), new T can obtain a $1,000 basis in its assets only if P elects to recognize gain on a hypothetical sale of its nonrecently purchased stock for the average price of the recently purchased stock. The hypothetical sale price would be $185 ($740 times 20%/80%), resulting in an $85 gain to P ($185 less P's stock basis of $100). If P recognizes the $85 gain on the hypothetical sale of its nonrecently purchased T stock, new T can obtain an additional $85 basis in its asset. If P does not elect to recognize this gain, new T's asset basis will be the fair market value of old T's asset ($1,000) less the unrealized appreciation in P's nonrecently purchased stock ($85) or $915. Assuming that new T then distributes its property to P in a § 332 liquidation, P will receive a substituted basis of $915 in the distributed asset, thus preserving the unrealized appreciation inherent in P's T stock. The result is two levels of corporate tax on the same $85 of gain, taxed once to old T on the deemed § 338 sale and then again to new T (or P) on a subsequent sale of the asset.

New T's adjusted grossed-up basis is increased to reflect old T's liabilities, including any tax liability resulting from the deemed sale of assets. Reg. § 1.338(b)–1(f)(1); 1.338–3(d)(3). The upward adjustment is necessary because the amount paid for the stock presumably will be discounted to reflect the net value of the target corporation. For example, assume that T Corp. (T) has assets worth $800,000, subject to a liability of $300,000. Although P would normally be willing to pay only approximately $500,000 for T's stock (ignoring any corporate-level tax liability), new T's basis in old T's assets should be $800,000, *i.e.*, the same basis that new T would receive if it purchased the assets from an unrelated party and assumed (or took the property subject to) $300,000 of liabilities. Contingent or speculative liabilities are not initially included in basis, but may be taken into account when they become fixed and determinable. Reg. §§ 1.338(b)–1(f)(2); 1.338(b)–3T(c)(1).

(c) *Consistency Requirements*. When § 338 was originally enacted in 1982, a major concern was that an acquiring corporation should not be permitted to exploit the *General Utilities* doctrine selectively to obtain a stepped-up basis in some, but not all, of the acquired assets. In addressing this problem of selectivity, § 338 took an all-or-nothing approach and imposed an exceedingly complex set of asset and stock consistency rules which survived the 1986 Act. *See* §§ 338(e)(1) and 338(f). Repeal of the *General Utilities* doctrine eliminated the conceptual underpinning of the consistency rules, however, and significantly reduced the potential for abuse. Accordingly, in 1994, the Service issued Regulations under § 338 that drastically narrow the scope of the consistency rules. *See* Reg. § 1.338–4. The revised Regulations also eliminate the concept of a "deemed" § 338 election, *i.e.*, a mandatory § 338 election in the absence of an express election. Thus, a violation of the consistency rules will generally result in a carryover basis for any purchased assets. *See* Reg. § 1.338–4(d).

The Regulations retain the asset consistency rules mainly to deal with tax-avoidance opportunities related to (i) the investment basis adjustment rules under the consolidated return provisions and (ii) the 100% dividends-received deduction under § 243 for certain affiliated but nonconsolidated corporations. Reg. § 1.338–4(a). The asset consistency rules are intended to preserve two levels of corporate tax when a target corporation sells an asset to a purchasing corporation and the target's parent then sells the target's stock to the purchasing corporation. In the absence of anti-abuse rules, the target would be taxed on the gain from the asset sale, but the parent's gain from the stock sale might escape taxation as an unintended consequence of the investment basis adjustment rules (or 100% dividends-received deduction). The asset consistency rules impose a carryover basis on the purchased asset in the purchaser's hands, thereby preserving a potential second level of corporate tax. Since the tax at the individual shareholder level is not affected, the asset consistency rules in effect preserve triple-level taxation.

*Example*: X Corp. owns all of the stock of Y Corp., with an adjusted basis of $90 and a fair market value of $100; X and Y file a consolidated return. On January 1, 1997, Y recognizes a $10 gain from the sale of an asset to P Corp.; under the investment basis adjustment rules, X's basis in the Y stock is increased from $90 to $100. *See* Reg. § 1.1502–32. If X subsequently sells the Y stock to P for $100, X recognizes no gain or loss. Absent the asset consistency rules, P would take a cost basis in the purchased asset even though the investment basis adjustment rules eliminate X's gain on the stock sale. By contrast, if P had acquired only Y stock, X would have recognized $10 of gain on the stock sale and Y's basis in its assets would have remained unchanged. To preserve Y's built-in gain of $10, the Regulations impose a carryover basis on the purchased asset in P's hands.

The Regulations virtually eliminate the stock consistency rules, except as a backstop to the asset consistency rules. Reg. § 1.338–4(a)(6). Accordingly, a § 338 election with respect to a target corporation no longer triggers a deemed election with respect to all target affiliates. The Regulations also provide relief from potential multiple taxation when a purchasing corporation (P) makes a qualified stock purchase of a target corporation

(T) which owns at least 80% of a subsidiary (S). If P makes a § 338 election with respect to T only, T must recognize gain on the deemed sale of its assets, including the S stock. T's gain on the S stock is disregarded, however, if P makes a § 338 election with respect to both corporations. *See* Reg. § 1.338–3(c). The rationale is that S could have sold its assets and distributed the proceeds tax free to T in a § 332 liquidation, eliminating any potential gain inherent in the S stock.

(d) *Section 338(h)(10) Election.* If an acquiring corporation purchases stock of a target corporation from the target's parent, a § 338(h)(10) election will often be desirable. If § 338(h)(10) is elected, the parent will not recognize gain or loss on the sale of the target's stock, and the target will recognize gain or loss as if it sold its assets. The treatment of the parent's stock sale as an asset sale produces the same results as a § 336(e) election, permitting the parent to dispose of the subsidiary with only one tax at the corporate level even though the purchaser obtains a stepped-up basis in the assets. This election is also advantageous if the unrealized appreciation in the subsidiary's assets is less than the unrealized appreciation in the parent's stock. A § 338(h)(10) election will be especially attractive if the purchase price is allocable to depreciable assets or amortizable § 197 intangibles.

Prior to issuance of the current Regulations, a § 338(h)(10) election was available only if the target was a member of a "selling consolidated group," *i.e.*, a group of corporations filing a consolidated return. The Regulations extend the § 338(h)(10) election to certain nonconsolidated affiliated corporations and S corporations. Reg. § 1.338(h)(10)–1(a). In the case of an S corporation, the § 338(h)(10) election must be made jointly by the purchasing corporation and the S corporation shareholders. Reg. § 1.338(h)(10)–1(d). If the election is made, any gain (or loss) recognized by the S corporation on the deemed sale of its assets passes through to its shareholders and increases the basis of their stock. See §§ 1366 and 1367; see also Chapter 12. The S corporation is deemed to distribute the sale proceeds to its shareholders in a complete liquidation governed by § 331. See Reg. § 1.338(h)(10)–1(e). In general, S shareholders recognize no gain on the deemed liquidation because their stock basis reflects previously taxed corporate-level gain. Although the overall result is a single-level tax, the consequences at the shareholder level depend on each shareholder's basis in his stock. For example, a shareholder whose stock basis is especially high (e.g., due to a § 1014 step-up) may recognize ordinary income on the asset sale and a capital loss on liquidation.

(e) *Allocation of Basis.* The Regulations provide detailed rules for allocating the acquiring corporation's basis among the target's assets. Reg. § 1.338(b)–2T. These rules parallel the residual allocation method mandated by the § 1060 Regulations. Before any basis is allocated, the adjusted grossed-up basis (AGUB) is first reduced by the amount of cash and similar items to which no basis is allocated. The remaining AGUB is then allocated among all other assets (except goodwill and going concern value) in proportion to their respective fair market values; the amount of AGUB allocated to any asset may not exceed the asset's fair market value. Any residual basis is then allocated to goodwill and going concern value. The § 338 Regulations have not yet been amended to reflect the 1993 enactment of § 197. Presumably, the revised allocation rules will place all amortizable § 197 intangibles in the same residual category as goodwill and going concern value.

*Example:* On January 1, 1997, P Corp. purchases all of the stock of T Corp. for $100,000 and makes a § 338 election. T's assets consist of $10,000 cash, a building with a fair market value of $100,000, machinery with a fair market value of $20,000 and goodwill. T's assets are subject to liabilities of $40,000. P incurs $3,000 of expenses in acquiring T's stock and new T incurs a tax liability of $7,000 on the deemed sale of old T's assets. New T's adjusted grossed-up basis in the assets acquired from old T is $150,000, consisting of $100,000 purchase price for T's stock, $40,000 of old T's liabilities, $3,000 of acquisition expenses, and $7,000 of tax liability.

The AGUB would first be reduced to $140,000 by excluding the $10,000 cash. Of this amount, $100,-000 would be allocated to the building and $20,000 to the machinery (100% of their respective fair market values); the excess, $20,000, would be assigned to goodwill. If the AGUB were only $100,-000, the $90,000 remaining after excluding the cash would be allocated entirely to the building and the machinery in proportion to their respective fair market values: $75,000 to the building ($100,000/$120,000 times $90,000), and $15,000 to the machinery ($20,000/$120,000 times $90,000). The goodwill would have a basis of zero because there is no residual basis in excess of the fair market value of the other assets.

Because most intangible assets are now amortizable, § 197 reduces but does not eliminate the significance of the residual method. Assume that a purchasing corporation (P) purchases all of the stock of a target (T), and that P enters into a non-compete agreement with T's sole shareholder (A). As long as there is a related acquisition of a business (by a purchase of assets or stock), a covenant not to compete is treated as an amortizable § 197 intangible. Accordingly, P must amortize any non-compete payments to A over a 15–year period. If P makes a § 338 election, new T will be deemed to have purchased old T's assets, and any portion of the purchase price allocated to goodwill will be amortizable under § 197. In the absence of a § 338 election, the basis of T's assets will not be stepped up and no amortization deduction will be allowed for goodwill.

## § 6.  Corporate Takeover Expenses

(a) *Redemption Expenses*. Section 162(k) denies a deduction for any amount paid or incurred by a corporation "in connection with the redemption of its stock." The legislative history indicates that the phrase "in connection with" should be construed broadly to include legal expenses, accounting and brokerage fees, and payments under so-called "standstill" agreements which obligate a redeemed shareholder not to purchase additional stock. Section 162(k)(2) specifically excludes interest (otherwise deductible under § 163) from the general disallowance rule. The Service will scrutinize closely transactions which are not directly related to a redemption but are proximate in time, such as a non-compete payment to a redeemed shareholder.

Although the costs of arranging a loan to finance a redemption would normally be amortizable over the life of the loan, the Service has invoked § 162(k) to disallow such expenses. In *Kroy (Europe) Ltd.* (9th Cir.1994), the Ninth Circuit concluded that loan fees to finance a redemption were amortizable because they were incurred "in a separate and independent borrowing transaction"; it distinguished the loan fees from nondeductible expenses which have their "origin" in a stock redemption transaction. In *Fort Howard Corp.* (Tax Ct.1994), the Tax Court rejected the "origin" test and instead focused on whether the loan fees constituted amounts paid "in connection with" a redemption. Based on the "clear and logical relation" between the redemption and the borrowing costs, it held that the loan fees were nonamortizable. To the extent that loan fees do not represent payments for professional services, such fees may be economically indistinguishable from additional interest paid to the lender (for which a § 163 deduction is allowed).

(b) *INDOPCO-Type Expenses*. General principles may also require capitalization of expenses that provide a long-term benefit to a corporation in connection with changes in its capital structure. In INDOPCO (S.Ct.1992), a target corporation was required to capitalize expenses incurred in a friendly takeover, including investment banking fees and legal fees. The Supreme Court found that the expenses provided a significant future benefit and that creation of a "separate and distinct additional asset" was sufficient, but not necessary, to require capitalization. The future benefits to the target corporation included (i) significant synergies between the target's and the acquiring corporation's businesses, (ii) access to the "enormous resources" of the acquiring corporation, (iii) reduced shareholder-related expenses through elimination of the target's public shareholders and (iv) administrative simplification.

Although the scope of INDOPCO remains unclear, an "incidental" future benefit should not be sufficient to require capitalization. One court has allowed a deduction for expenses incurred in unsuccessfully resisting a hostile takeover on the ground that the expenses did not provide any long-term benefit. *See* Federated Dep't Stores (S.D.Ohio 1994). The acquiring corporation lacked experience in the acquired corporation's business, and the highly-leveraged acquisition eventually led to bankruptcy proceedings. If a hostile takeover turns friendly as a result of subsequent negotiations, INDOPCO may require capitalization of the target's expenses. *See* Victory Markets (Tax Ct.1992); A.E.

Staley Manufacturing Co. (Tax Ct.1995) (no distinction between hostile and friendly takeovers). Outside the acquisition context, the Service has adopted a relatively narrow interpretation of INDOPCO. *See, e.g.*, Rev. Rul. 94–38 (environmental cleanup costs).

(c) *Other Acquisition Expenses.* Section 279, enacted in 1969, disallows a deduction for corporate interest in excess of $5 million per year on certain "corporate acquisition indebtedness," which is defined to include certain convertible subordinated debt. The limitations of § 279 were circumvented relatively easily during the acquisition activities of the early 1980s. More recently, Congress enacted § 163(e)(5) which denies or limits the corporate interest deduction for any "applicable high yield discount obligation" (AHYDO). This provision is aimed at debt obligations with an issue price significantly lower than the stated redemption price and related "payment-in-kind" (PIK) bonds which call for payments in debt or stock of the issuer rather than cash.

An AHYDO is defined as a debt instrument that has (i) a more than 5–year maturity, (ii) a yield to maturity that exceeds a designated federal rate by at least 5 percentage points, and (iii) "significant original issue discount." *See* § 163(i). If § 163(e) applies, the original issue discount (OID) is divided between a portion which is deductible as interest when actually paid and a nondeductible portion which may be eligible for a dividends-received deduction in the case of a corporate lender. This approach represents a compromise between treating the instrument entirely as equity (for which no interest deduction would be allowed) or entirely as debt. In addition, § 163(j) defers the deduction for interest paid to certain related persons (such as foreign affiliates) who are exempt from U.S. tax on the interest received. *See* § 163(j).

Congress was also concerned that an acquiring corporation might inflate its net operating loss carrybacks through interest deductions attributable to debt-financed acquisitions, thereby generating a tax refund. Accordingly, in 1989, Congress amended § 172 to limit NOL carrybacks if the losses are created by interest deductions attributable to a "corporate equity reduction transaction" (CERT). *See* § 172(h). A CERT is defined as a "major stock acquisition" (an acquisition of 50% or more of the vote or value of another corporation's stock within a 2–year period) or an "excess distribution" (current distributions in excess of a base amount determined by reference to the distributing corporation's prior three years' average distributions or the value of its stock). § 172(h)(3)(B) and (C). A de minimis rule provides that the carryback limitation applies only if the interest expense exceeds $1 million. § 172(h)(2)(D). The carryback limitation has no effect on a profitable corporation that engages in a CERT if its current profits are sufficient to absorb the additional interest expense without generating an NOL.

Section 280G disallows deductions for certain "golden parachute" payments designed to cushion the departure of management from corporations subject to hostile takeovers. This provision disal-

lows a deduction for payments to a "disqualified
individual" (officer, shareholder or other highly
compensated individual), if the payment is contingent on a change in ownership or control of a
company and the present value of the payments
exceeds 3 times a defined base amount. The base
amount is determined by reference to the individual's annual average compensation for the 5–year
period preceding the change of ownership or control, with certain adjustments. In addition, § 280G
disallows any amounts paid under an agreement in
violation of generally enforced securities laws or
regulations. A companion provision, § 4999, imposes an excise tax of 20% on the recipient of a
golden parachute payment.

Section 5881 imposes an excise tax of 50% on any
gain realized (whether or not recognized) by a person who receives greenmail. "Greenmail" is defined as any consideration paid by a corporation in
redemption of its stock if the shareholder has held
such stock for less than 2 years before agreeing to
transfer the stock to the corporation, provided that
the shareholder (or any person acting in concert
with the shareholder or a related person) "made or
threatened to make a public tender offer for stock"
of the corporation during the 2–year period.
§ 5881(b). The excise tax does not apply, however,
if the redemption is pursuant to an offer which is
available to all other shareholders on the same
terms.

# CHAPTER 9

## REORGANIZATIONS

### § 1. Introduction

If a transaction qualifies as a "reorganization" within the meaning of § 368, the Code provides generally for nonrecognition of gain or loss at both the shareholder level (§§ 354 and 356) and the corporate level (§ 361); any unrecognized gain or loss is reflected in the substituted basis of qualifying property received by a shareholder (§ 358) or a corporation (§ 362), and is preserved for recognition in a subsequent taxable disposition.

Tax-free treatment of reorganizations is premised on the notion of "continuity of investment": investors are viewed as preserving their interest in a business enterprise through continuing stock ownership, notwithstanding the change in corporate form. In order to qualify as a reorganization, a transaction must fall within one of the categories defined in § 368(a)(1). In addition, the Regulations require continuity of proprietary interest, business purpose and continuity of business enterprise.

This Chapter discusses amalgamating reorganizations ("A," "B," "C," and some "D" reorganizations) and single-corporation reorganizations ("E" and "F" reorganizations). Divisive "D" reorganizations are discussed separately in Chapter 10.

## § 2. "A" Reorganizations

(a) *General.* An "A" reorganization, as defined in § 368(a)(1)(A), is a merger (or consolidation) under state law. In a typical statutory merger, one corporation (the "acquiring corporation") acquires the assets of another corporation (the "acquired corporation"), in exchange for assumption of the acquired corporation's liabilities (by operation of law) and for stock of the acquiring corporation; the shareholders of the acquired corporation may also receive additional consideration. The acquired corporation disappears as a legal entity, and its shareholders and creditors become shareholders and creditors of the acquiring corporation.

(b) *Continuity of Proprietary Interest.* Although § 368 contains no express restriction on the type of consideration that may be received in an A reorganization, a transaction will be treated as a taxable sale rather than a tax-free reorganization unless the shareholders of the acquired corporation maintain sufficient continuity of proprietary interest. Generally, for advance ruling purposes, the Service requires at least 50% continuity of interest by value, *i.e.*, shareholders of the acquired corporation in the aggregate must receive stock of the acquiring corporation equal in value to at least 50% of the acquired corporation's stock. Sales or redemptions made pursuant to a plan of reorganization are considered in determining whether the 50% continuity-of-interest requirement is met. Rev. Proc. 77-37. Courts have found continuity of interest where shareholders of the acquired corporation received less than 50% in value of the acquired corporation's stock. *See, e.g.,* John A. Nelson Co. (S.Ct.1935)(38% continuity sufficient). Although there is no fixed minimum required percentage of continuing stock ownership, less than 20% continuity is likely to preclude reorganization treatment. *See, e.g.,* May B. Kass (Tax Ct.1973)(16% insufficient); Yoc Heating Corp. (Tax Ct.1973)(15% insufficient). The continuity-of-interest test applies to the shareholders in the aggregate rather than to each separate shareholder of the acquired corporation. If some shareholders receive cash while others receive stock, the transaction as a whole may still qualify as a reorganization; only the shareholders who receive stock, however, will be entitled to nonrecognition treatment. *See* § 9 below.

In order to establish continuity of proprietary interest, the shareholders of the acquired corporation must receive an equity interest in the acquiring corporation. Thus, stock of any class (common or preferred, voting or nonvoting) counts toward continuity; cash and cash equivalents (*e.g.,* short-term notes) do not count toward continuity of interest. An early line of cases established that consideration consisting of debt securities does not count toward continuity, because shareholders receiving such consideration are viewed as terminating their investment as shareholders to become creditors. Pinellas Ice & Cold Storage Co. (S.Ct.1933); Le Tulle v. Scofield (S.Ct.1940). These cases indicate that stock is the only type of consideration embodying a proprietary interest, even though the economic position of a preferred shareholder may be closer to that of a creditor than that of a common shareholder.

The Supreme Court held that continuity of interest was lacking in a merger of two savings and loan associations (one authorized to issue "guaranty stock" to its shareholders and the other having no capital stock), where shareholders of the acquired corporation gave up their guaranty stock in exchange for passbook accounts and certificates of deposit in the surviving corporation. Paulsen (S.Ct. 1985). The passbook accounts and certificates of deposit had several equity characteristics (including the right to vote on association matters and participate in liquidation proceeds), but the debt characteristics were predominant. The result was perhaps not surprising, since the consideration could be viewed as essentially a cash equivalent without significant equity features. The taxpayer argued, however, that the continuity-of-interest test should focus on the nature of the consideration received rather than the relative change in proprietary interest. If this is the appropriate test, it is difficult to distinguish the *Paulsen* situation from a merger of two non-stock savings and loan associations, which has been held to constitute a tax-free reorganization. Rev. Rul. 69–3. Although the Supreme Court sought to distinguish Revenue Ruling 69–3, the *Paulsen* decision leaves some uncertainty concerning the appropriate standard.

Continuity of interest must also be maintained for a sufficient period to show a definite and substantial ownership interest. Rev. Rul. 66–23 (5 years unrestricted ownership sufficient). A prearranged plan to sell stock received in the reorganization may render the entire transaction taxable. *See* McDonald's Restaurants of Illinois, Inc. (7th Cir. 1982) (step-transaction doctrine applied to post-merger sales; transaction treated as a taxable sale rather than a tax-free reorganization). If the subsequent sales are not contemplated as part of the plan of reorganization, however, continuity of interest is not broken. *See* Penrod (Tax Ct.1987); Estate of Christian (Tax Ct.1989).

Recently, the Tax Court held that the continuity-of-interest requirement was satisfied, even though approximately 78% of the acquired corporation's stock was sold for cash after the date on which competing tender offers were announced and before completion of a second-step merger. Seagram Corp. (Tax Ct.1995). In *Seagram*, the taxpayer acquired 32% of the acquired corporation's stock for cash pursuant an abortive tender offer and subsequently exchanged such stock for stock of the acquiring corporation. The court concluded that the two-step acquisition (the acquiring corporation's successful tender offer and subsequent merger) constituted a valid reorganization and thus disallowed the taxpayer's claimed loss on the exchange. Notwithstanding the pre-merger sales, approximately 54% of the consideration received by the acquired corporation's shareholders in the merger was stock of the acquiring corporation. For continuity purposes, the court indicated that the existence of a continuing equity interest, not the identity of the "historic" shareholders, is determinative. Since the taxpayer's stock interest was deemed to represent a continuation of the historic shareholders' interest, the requirement of continuity was met. The court noted that a shareholder-tracking requirement would jeopardize tax-free treatment of any acquisition involving a target whose stock is actively traded. Thus, pre-acquisition sales are apparently less likely to trigger continuity problems than are post-acquisition sales.

(c) *Continuity of Business Enterprise.* The Regulations also require continuity of business enterprise at the corporate level. Under Reg. § 1.368–1(d), the acquiring corporation must either continue the acquired corporation's "historic business" or use a significant portion of the acquired corporation's "historic business assets" in another business. If an acquired corporation has more than one line of business, continuity of business enterprise requires only that the acquiring corporation continue a significant line of business. Reg. § 1.368–1(d)(3)(ii). The Regulations warn, however, that a corporation's historic business is "not one the corporation enters into as part of a plan of reorganization." Reg. § 1.368–1(d)(3)(iii). Thus, the continuity-of-business-enterprise requirement is not met if the acquired corporation sells all of its historic business assets and reinvests the proceeds in a new business immediately prior to the reorganization, even though the acquiring corporation continues to conduct the new business. See Rev. Rul. 87–76 (continuity not satisfied where acquired corporation sold its historic business assets, consisting of investment portfolio of corporate stocks and bonds, and bought municipal bonds).

## § 3. "B" Reorganizations

(a) *General*. A "B" reorganization is defined in § 368(a)(1)(B) as the acquisition of stock of one corporation in exchange solely for voting stock of the acquiring corporation (or its parent), provided that the acquiring corporation has control of the acquired corporation immediately after the transaction. "Control" means ownership of at least 80% of the total combined voting power of voting stock and at least 80% of the total number of shares of all other classes of stock. § 368(c). Although the acquiring corporation must have control immediately after the transaction, it does not matter whether the acquiring corporation gains control in the reorganization exchange or in a previous transaction (or series of transactions). Thus, an acquiring corporation owning 79% of the acquired corporation may acquire an additional 1% in a "creeping B" reorganization.

(b) *Solely for Voting Stock*. The requirement that the acquiring corporation use solely voting stock means that there will generally be continuity of interest in a B reorganization. Redemptions and other dispositions pursuant to the plan of reorganization must be considered in applying the 50% continuity-of-interest test. Permissible consideration includes voting stock of either the acquiring corporation or (under the parenthetical provisions of § 368(a)(1)(B)) its parent, but not a combination thereof. A reorganization in which the acquiring corporation uses its parent's stock as consideration (often referred to as a "parenthetical B") is considered below with triangular reorganizations.

The term "solely" has been strictly interpreted to preclude the use of any amount of consideration other than voting stock in a B reorganization. *See, e.g.,* Turnbow (9th Cir.1960). This restriction does not prevent the acquiring corporation from paying cash in lieu of issuing fractional shares, provided that such cash is incidental to the exchange and not separately bargained for. Rev. Rul. 66–365, amplified by Rev. Rul. 81–81. In addition, the acquiring corporation may pay cash to the acquired corporation's shareholders (other than in their capacity as shareholders) in a separate transaction without disqualifying the stock-for-stock exchange as a B reorganization. For example, simultaneously with a B reorganization, the acquiring corporation may pay cash to a majority shareholder for entering into a non-compete agreement in a separate transaction, provided that the cash is not in reality paid as additional consideration for the stock acquired in the B reorganization.

The receipt of anti-takeover "poison pill rights" by shareholders of the acquired corporation does not violate the "solely" requirement in a B reorganization. Typically, a poison pill gives shareholders a right to acquire additional stock of the issuing corporation (or any acquiring corporation) at a bargain price, in the event of a hostile takeover. In Rev. Rul. 90–11, the Service held that adoption of a poison pill plan did not constitute a taxable event because of the contingent nature and nominal value of the rights involved. It did not address the income tax consequences upon exercise of the rights.

(c) *Series of Transactions*. The requirement that the acquiring corporation use solely voting stock may cause problems if a series of transactions are collapsed into a single transaction for tax purposes. The Regulations indicate that a series of transactions taking place over a relatively short period of time (*e.g.*, 12 months) may qualify as a B reorganization. Reg. § 1.368–2(c). For example, if the acquiring corporation acquires 20% of the acquired corporation's stock and then acquires an additional 60% six months later solely for its voting stock, the exchanges will be viewed together as a single B reorganization.

Acquisition of 80% control solely for voting stock may qualify as a B reorganization even if the acquiring corporation purchased some stock in an earlier, unrelated taxable transaction. *See* Chapman (1st Cir.1980). In *Chapman,* the acquiring corporation purchased 8% of the acquired corporation's stock for cash, and then exchanged its voting stock for the remaining voting stock of the acquired corporation. For purposes of the summary judgment motion at issue in *Chapman,* the taxpayer conceded that the initial cash purchases were intended to further its acquisition of the acquired corporation. The court held that if the 8% stock purchase and the later stock-for-stock exchange were viewed as part of a single transaction, the cash boot would disqualify the entire transaction as a B reorganization. This would be so even if the acquiring corporation acquired 80% of the acquired corporation's stock solely for voting stock, since the "solely" requirement applies to the total consideration received in the exchange. If the 8% stock purchase were unrelated or sufficiently remote in time ("old and cold"), however, it would not violate the "solely" requirement of § 368(a)(1)(B).

## § 4. "C" Reorganizations

(a) *General*. In a "C" reorganization, as defined in § 368(a)(1)(C), one corporation acquires "substantially all" of the assets of another corporation in exchange for voting stock of the acquiring corporation (or its parent). For advance ruling purposes, the requirement that the acquired corporation transfer "substantially all" of its assets is deemed to be satisfied only if the transferred assets constitute at least 90% of the fair market value of the net assets and at least 70% of the gross assets held by the acquired corporation immediately before the transfer. Rev. Proc. 77–37. Threshold redemptions, extraordinary dividends and payments to dissenters made pursuant to the plan of reorganization are taken into account.

The purpose of the "substantially all" requirement is to ensure that a transaction which is divisive in nature will not qualify as a C reorganization, but instead will be subject to the rules for divisive D reorganizations. *See* Rev. Rul. 57–518; *see also* Chapter 10. If an acquired corporation sells 50% of its business assets and immediately thereafter transfers all of its assets (including the cash from the sale) to the acquiring corporation, the Service has held that the "substantially all" requirement is

satisfied. Rev. Rul. 88–48. The Service emphasized that the transaction was not divisive in nature
because the former business was sold to an unrelated party and the sale proceeds were not retained by
the acquired corporation or its shareholders. Under prior law, a transferor corporation might retain
operating assets for the purpose of continuing in
business after the reorganization. Under present
law, however, if the transferor corporation continues in existence, the transaction will fail to qualify
as a C reorganization, as discussed below. Thus,
the Service may be inclined to interpret the "substantially all" requirement less restrictively than
under prior law.

(b) *Liabilities;*     *Boot*     *Relaxation.*     Section
368(a)(1)(C) requires that the consideration for the
acquired corporation's assets consist "solely" of voting stock of the acquiring corporation (or its parent). "Triangular" reorganizations are discussed
in § 5 below. As in a B reorganization, the requirement that voting stock be used generally ensures
that there will be continuity of interest; in a C
reorganization, however, the "solely" requirement
is subject to two important exceptions. First,
§ 368(a)(1)(C) permits the acquiring corporation to
assume liabilities of the acquired corporation (or
acquire property subject to liabilities) in any
amount if the other consideration consists exclusively of voting stock of the acquiring corporation.
Second, the boot relaxation rules of § 368(a)(2)(B)
permit the use of cash or other boot (*i.e.*, property
other than voting stock of the acquiring corporation), provided that at least 80% of the acquired

corporation's assets (by gross fair market value) are acquired solely for voting stock.

For the limited purpose of applying the 80% requirement of § 368(a)(2)(B)(iii), liabilities assumed (or taken subject to) are treated as cash. Under § 368(a)(2)(B), the sum of (i) any liabilities assumed (or taken subject to), (ii) the fair market value of other boot consideration, and (iii) the fair market value of any assets retained by the acquired corporation may not exceed 20% of the gross fair market value of the acquired corporation's assets. Thus, if no liabilities are assumed and the acquired corporation transfers all of its assets, up to 20% of the consideration for the assets may consist of cash or other boot. The amount of permissible boot will be reduced, however, to the extent that liabilities are assumed or less than all of the acquired corporation's assets are transferred. For purposes of § 368(a)(2)(B), if voting stock of both the acquiring corporation and its parent is used as consideration, the parent stock is treated as boot.

A liability created in the reorganization and assumed by the acquiring corporation (*e.g.*, an obligation to pay cash to dissenting shareholders of the acquired corporation) may be treated as boot for purposes of § 368(a)(2)(B). Rev. Rul. 73–102. The payment by the acquiring corporation of the acquired corporation's share of reorganization expenses (*e.g.*, legal and accounting fees) is not considered boot if such expenses were directly and solely related to the reorganization; but the payment of unrelated expenses (*e.g.*, investment and estate planning advice to shareholders) is treated as boot. Rev. Rul. 73–54.

*Example (1):* X Corp. has assets with a fair market value of $100,000 and liabilities of $25,000. Y Corp. may acquire all of X's assets in a C reorganization by issuing solely Y voting stock worth $75,-000 and assuming X's liabilities of $25,000. The assumption of liabilities is disregarded for purposes of § 368(a)(1)(C) because the other consideration consists solely of voting stock.

*Example (2):* The facts are the same as in the preceding example, except that X has only $15,000 of liabilities. Under § 368(a)(2)(B), Y may issue $80,000 of its voting stock, assume the $15,000 liabilities, and pay up to $5,000 cash without disqualifying the transaction as a C reorganization. If X retains an additional $1,000 of assets (or Y pays an additional $1,000 cash) and Y issues only $79,-000 of voting stock, however, the transaction will fail as a C reorganization, because the sum of the liabilities ($15,000) and the cash paid and assets retained ($6,000) exceeds 20% of the fair market value of X's assets ($20,000). The provision of § 368(a)(1)(C) permitting liabilities to be disregarded does not apply if any cash or other boot is paid.

(c) *Liquidation of Transferor.* A corporation that transfers its assets in a C reorganization (the "transferor corporation") must distribute all of the stock, securities and other property received in the reorganization, as well as any retained assets, pursuant to the reorganization plan. § 368(a)(2)(G)(i). This provision furthers the underlying objective of preventing a divisive C reorganization. If the transferor corporation fails to make the required distributions, the transaction will be treated as a taxable exchange. The Service will not waive the liquidation requirement unless the parties agree to treat the transferor as if liquidated within one year after the reorganization. Rev. Proc. 89–50.

(d) *Overlapping Provisions.* Except for the requirement that the consideration consist of voting stock, a C reorganization resembles an A reorganization. In addition, a transaction that would otherwise qualify as a B reorganization will be treated instead as a C reorganization if the stock-for-stock exchange is followed promptly by a prearranged liquidation of the acquired corporation. *See* Rev. Rul. 67–274. A failed B reorganization (*e.g.*, in which a limited amount of boot is paid by the acquiring corporation) may still qualify as a Type C reorganization if the asset transfer and liquidation requirements are complied with.

## § 5. Triangular Reorganizations

A "triangular" reorganization generally refers to an A, B, or C reorganization in which the consideration for the stock or assets of the acquired corporation includes stock of a parent corporation (the "controlling corporation") in control of the acquiring corporation. The transaction could be structured as a normal A, B, or C reorganization in which the controlling corporation acquired the stock or assets of the acquired corporation in exchange for its own stock followed by a distribution of the stock or assets to the controlling corporation's subsidiary, under the "drop down" provisions of § 368(a)(2)(C). A triangular reorganization achieves the same end result in a single step.

Sections 368(a)(1)(B) and 368(a)(1)(C) expressly permit a B or C reorganization, respectively, to be structured as a direct acquisition of the acquired corporation's stock or assets in exchange for voting stock of the acquiring corporation's parent. In an A reorganization, two types of triangular structures are permitted under § 368(a)(2)(D)("forward subsidiary merger") and § 368(a)(2)(E)("reverse subsidiary merger"), respectively.

A forward subsidiary merger is an A reorganization in which the acquired corporation merges into the acquiring corporation and the former shareholders of the acquired corporation receive stock of the controlling corporation; additional consideration may also be used, subject to the continuity-of-interest requirement, but no stock of the acquiring corporation may be used. § 368(a)(2)(D)(i). A further provision of § 368(a)(2)(D) which distinguishes forward subsidiary mergers from normal A reorganizations requires that the acquiring corporation receive "substantially all" of the acquired corporation's assets. This requirement is analogous to the corresponding requirement for C reorganizations.

A reverse subsidiary merger is an A reorganization in which the acquiring corporation's controlled subsidiary merges into the acquired corporation; the acquired corporation survives, and its shareholders exchange controlling stock of the acquired corporation for voting stock of the acquiring corporation (*i.e.*, the merged subsidiary's parent). For this purpose, controlling stock means 80% of the voting power of the voting stock, and 80% of the total number of shares of all other classes of stock, of the acquired corporation. Although up to 20% boot consideration may be used in a reverse subsidiary merger, the requirement that the acquiring parent obtain control of the acquired corporation in the transaction generally precludes the possibility of a "creeping" reverse subsidiary merger.

## § 6. Non-divisive "D" Reorganizations

A "D" reorganization, as defined in § 368(a)(1)(D), requires that one corporation (the "transferor") transfer all or part of its assets to another "controlled" corporation (the "transferee"), and that the transferor then distribute stock or securities of the controlled corporation either in a non-divisive § 354 transaction or in a "divisive" § 355 transaction. The present discussion focuses on non-divisive D reorganizations; divisive transactions are dealt with in Chapter 10.

The "control" requirement of § 368(a)(1)(D) is satisfied if, immediately after the transfer, the transferee corporation is controlled by the transferor or by one or more of its shareholders (including persons who were shareholders immediately before the transfer). For purposes of non-divisive D reorganizations, control is defined in the same manner as under § 304(c), *i.e.*, 50% of the voting stock or 50% of the fair market value of all classes of stock (applying modified § 318 attribution rules). § 368(a)(2)(H).

A transaction will qualify as a non-divisive D reorganization only if (i) the transferee corporation acquires "substantially all" of the assets of the transferor corporation and (ii) the transferor distributes any retained assets, as well as the stock and securities (and other consideration, if any) received from the transferee, pursuant to the plan of reorganization. § 354(b)(1). If these requirements are met, the transferor corporation disappears, leaving some or all of its shareholders in control of the transferee corporation. Thus, in a non-divisive D reorganization, the assets of the transferor and transferee are combined in the hands of the transferee; in this respect, a non-divisive D reorganization resembles a C reorganization. Under § 368(a)(2)(A), however, a transaction described in both § 368(a)(1)(C) and § 368(a)(1)(D) is treated exclusively as a D reorganization.

*Example:* A transferor corporation (T) transfers all of its assets (with a fair market value of $1,000,-000) to its newly-formed subsidiary (S) in exchange for all of the S stock (with a fair market value of $700,000) and $300,000 of S bonds; T then liquidates and distributes the S stock and bonds to its shareholders; some T shareholders receive exclusively S stock, while others receive a combination of stock and bonds. The end result at the corporate level is that S takes over T's continuing business enterprise; at the shareholder level, there is continuity, but not identity, of stock ownership. Any assets retained by T could be used to satisfy preexisting liabilities without violating the "substantially all" requirement. *See* Reg. § 1.354–1(a)(2)(second sentence); *see also* Rev. Proc. 77–37 (retention of 30% of gross assets violates "substantially all" requirement). T must distribute any retained assets, together with all of the property received from S, to its shareholders in complete liquidation. The tax treatment of T's shareholders is determined under §§ 354 and 356, discussed in § 9 below.

## § 7. "E" Reorganizations

(a) *General.* Section 368(a)(1)(E) defines an "E" reorganization simply as a "recapitalization." The Supreme Court has described a recapitalization as a "reshuffling of a capital structure within the framework of an existing corporation." Southwest Consol. Corp. (S.Ct.1942). The Regulations offer several examples of "recapitalizations." Reg. § 1.368–2(e).

(b) *Exchanges of Stock for New Stock.* An exchange of stock for stock (preferred for common or common for preferred) qualifies as an E reorganization. Reg. §§ 1.368–2(e)(3) and 1.368–2(e)(4). In addition, an exchange of common for common or preferred for preferred would also be tax free under § 1036 even if it occurred directly between two shareholders.

If a corporation issues new preferred stock in exchange for its outstanding common stock, the new preferred stock may be § 306 stock. § 306(c)(1)(B). The Regulations employ a cash-substitution test to determine whether the transaction is substantially equivalent to receipt of a stock dividend, *i.e.*, whether cash received in lieu of the preferred stock would have been treated as a dividend under § 356(a)(2). Reg. § 1.306–3(d). Thus, if shareholders exchange common stock for proportionate amounts of common and preferred stock, the preferred stock will be § 306 stock. Reg. § 1.306–3(d), Example (1). Reversing its earlier position, the Service has ruled that § 306 may apply to preferred stock received in a merger involving two widely held corporations. Rev. Rul. 89–63. In light of the Supreme Court's *Clark* decision, however, as discussed in § 9 below, receipt of widely held preferred stock will seldom have the effect of a dividend.

If cumulative preferred stock with dividend arrearages is exchanged for other stock, the transaction will be taxable under § 305(b)(4) (distributions on preferred stock) to the extent of the dividend arrearages. Regs. §§ 1.305–5(d), Example (1) and 1.368–2(e), Example (5). A recapitalization which is part of a plan to produce periodic increases in a shareholder's proportionate interest may also be treated as a taxable stock dividend under § 305. Reg. § 1.305–7(c).

In a typical "estate freeze" recapitalization involving a corporation with a single class of stock, younger-generation family members exchange part or all of their stock for new common stock while older-generation family members exchange their stock for new preferred stock. The usual reason for such a recapitalization is to establish a low value (for estate tax purposes) for the older generation's interest, based on the limited participation of the preferred stock in assets and earnings, while transferring a greater share of potential equity growth to the younger generation. The Regulations provide that such a recapitalization is outside the purview of § 305 if it is a "single and isolated transaction." Reg. § 1.305–3(e), Example 12. Although the new preferred stock is ordinarily § 306 stock, the § 306 taint is removed at the death of the older-generation family member. *See* § 306(c)(1)(C). In 1990, however, Congress curtailed the advantages of such a preferred stock recapitalization through enactment of special gift tax valuation rules. *See* § 2701. If applicable, § 2701 generally assigns an artificially low value to the older-generation's interest at the time of the initial transfer, thereby increasing the amount of the gift to younger-generation family members for gift tax purposes.

(c) *Exchanges of Bonds for New Stock.* If a shareholder exchanges bonds for new stock, the exchange is ordinarily tax free, except to the extent of any interest arrearages discharged in the exchange. § 354(a)(2)(B). If bonds with accrued market discount are exchanged for stock, such discount will carry over to the new stock received and will be taxable as ordinary income upon subsequent disposition of the stock. § 1276(c)(2). If a corporation exchanges stock for its own debt, the corporation is treated as satisfying its indebtedness with an amount of cash equal to the fair market value of the stock transferred. § 108(e)(8). Accordingly, the corporation recognizes cancellation of indebtedness

income to the extent that the fair market value of
the transferred stock is less than the principal
amount of the indebtedness (plus any accrued but
unpaid interest).  The 1993 Act eliminated the
stock-for-debt exception for insolvent or bankrupt
corporations.  Although such corporations may still
exclude all or a portion of cancellation of indebtedness income under § 108(a)(1), the cost of such
exclusion will be reduction of tax attributes under
§ 108(b)(1).

(d) *Exchanges of Bonds for New Bonds*.  An exchange of old bonds for new bonds is generally tax
free, except to the extent that the principal amount
of the new bonds exceeds that of the surrendered
bonds.  *See* § 9 below.  Any "excess" securities
attributable to accrued but unpaid interest may be
taxable as ordinary income.  § 354(a)(2)(B).  The
original issue discount rules of §§ 1272 to 1275 may
also apply to reorganization exchanges, whether or
not the bonds are publicly traded.  Under
§ 108(e)(10), a corporation may recognize cancellation of indebtedness income if the issue price of the
new bonds (determined under §§ 1273 and 1274) is
less than the adjusted issue price of the bonds
surrendered.  Moreover, certain debt modifications
may be treated as deemed exchanges under § 1001,
triggering tax consequences to both the corporation
and its creditors.  *See* Cottage Sav. Ass'n (S.Ct.
1991); Prop. Reg. § 1.1001–3.

(e) *Exchanges of Stock for New Bonds*.  An exchange of stock for new bonds (or other securities)
raises a potential bailout problem.  In *Bazley* (S.Ct.
1947), shareholders exchanged their stock for a
combination of stock and securities in a purported

recapitalization. Under then existing law, the receipt of the securities pursuant to a recapitalization would have been entirely tax free. The Supreme Court, however, recharacterized the distribution of the securities as a taxable dividend under § 301 equal to the fair market value of the securities received in the exchange. This type of bailout is now foreclosed by § 354(a)(2) which treats the receipt of securities as boot, if no securities are surrendered in the reorganization.

In some circumstances, *Bazley* may continue to backstop § 354(a)(2), with potentially harsher tax consequences. *Bazley* treats the entire amount of securities as a dividend (assuming sufficient e & p), regardless of whether the taxpayer has any realized gain. Under § 354(a)(2) and § 356(a)(1), however, recognized gain cannot exceed realized gain. Moreover, any recognized gain attributable to boot securities may generally be deferred under § 453 and taxed as capital gain, provided that the exchange does not have the effect of a dividend under § 356(a)(2). *See* § 9 below. Although the precise scope of *Bazley* remains unclear, the Regulations warn that a pro rata exchange of common stock for common stock and bonds may be treated as a mere distribution of bonds taxable under § 301. Reg. § 1.301–1(*l*).

## § 8. "F" Reorganizations

An "F" reorganization is defined in § 368(a)(1)(F) as a "mere change in identity, form, or place of organization of one corporation, however effected." The words "of one corporation" were added to this definition in 1982 to prevent the use of F reorganizations to amalgamate multiple operating corporations owned by the same shareholders; this limitation, however, does not preclude the use of F reorganizations if multiple corporations are combined but only one of them is an operating company. The 1982 amendment substantially reduced the attractiveness of F reorganizations.

## § 9.  Treatment of Stockholders and Security Holders

(a) *Nonrecognition Property and Boot: §§ 354 and 356.* Under § 354(a)(1), no gain or loss is recognized if stock or securities of one corporate party to a reorganization are exchanged solely for stock or securities of the same corporation or another corporate party to the reorganization, pursuant to the plan of reorganization. Permissible consideration under § 354(a)(1) consists of stock, securities or a combination of both. Reg. § 1.368–2(h). Securities received in a reorganization, however, are nonrecognition property only to the extent that their principal amount does not exceed that of the securities surrendered. § 354(a)(2). Thus, an exchange will be wholly tax free only if (i) stock or securities are exchanged solely for stock, or (ii) securities are exchanged for securities of a lesser or equal principal amount (with or without additional stock). The term securities includes medium to long-term debt obligations; a short-term debt obligation (*e.g.*, a note maturing in less than 5 years) does not qualify as a security.

If a taxpayer receives boot in addition to property permitted to be received tax free under § 354(a)(1), the exchange is partly taxable under § 356. The shareholder receiving boot must recognize any realized gain to the extent of the sum of any cash and the fair market value of any other property constituting boot. § 356(a)(1). No loss is recognized. § 356(c). In the case of securities, the fair market value of any excess principal amount is treated as boot. § 356(d)(2)(B); see Reg. § 1.356–3(b), Example (4). Current proposals would treat as boot an amount equal to the excess of the issue price of the securities received over the adjusted issue price of the securities surrendered. If boot takes the form of an installment obligation (and its receipt is not equivalent to a dividend), any recognized gain may generally be deferred under § 453. See § 453(f)(6); Prop. Reg. § 1.453–1(f)(2). Installment treatment is not available if the stock or securities exchanged are traded on an established securities market. § 453(k)(2).

*Example (1):* Shareholders A, B and C each exchange 100 shares of X stock, pursuant to a reorganization, for Y stock worth $1,500 and $800 cash. The basis of A, B, and C, respectively, in the surrendered stock is $1,000, $2,000 and $3,000. A's realized gain of $1,300 ($2,300 amount realized less $1,000 basis) is recognized to the extent of the boot received ($800) and the remaining gain ($500) is deferred. B's realized gain of $300 ($2,300 amount realized less $2,000 basis) is less than the amount of boot received; accordingly, B's entire gain of $300 is recognized. C's realized loss of $700 ($3,000 basis less $2,300 amount realized) is not recognized.

*Example (2)*: In a reorganization, shareholder A exchanges T stock worth $120 (with a basis of $90) for P stock worth $80 and P's short-term note worth $40. Assume that A's receipt of the boot is not treated as a dividend, and that neither T's stock nor P's note is readily traded. A's realized gain of $30 ($120 amount realized less $90 basis) is less than the amount of boot received ($40); accordingly, A's entire gain is recognized. Under § 453, A's realized and recognized gain of $30 may be deferred, however, until the P note is paid. Since A takes the note with a fair market value of $40 and a basis of $10, one quarter of each payment on the note constitutes basis recovery and three quarters constitutes taxable gain; A's basis in the P stock is $80, as discussed below.

(b) *Dividend Within Gain: § 356(a)(2)*. The character of any recognized gain may be ordinary or capital, depending on the effect of the transaction at the shareholder level. Under § 356(a)(2), if the exchange has the effect of a dividend, the shareholder's recognized gain is treated as a dividend to the extent of his ratable share of accumulated e & p (dividend "within gain" limitation); any remaining gain is treated as capital gain. The restoration of preferential treatment for capital gain has enhanced the significance of dividend versus capital gain treatment of boot. Moreover, § 453 does not apply if receipt of an installment obligation has the effect of a dividend under § 356(a)(2) (regardless of the presence or absence of accumulated e & p). A shareholder with capital losses may prefer capital gain treatment, of course, since capital gains can be used to offset capital losses. A corporate shareholder will almost always prefer dividend treatment under § 356(a)(2), however, because of the § 243 deduction for dividends received. If a corporate shareholder is required to reduce basis under § 1059, the § 243 dividends-received deduction will affect only timing.

*Example:* Shareholders A, B, C and D each own 25% of the stock of X Corp. X is acquired by Y Corp. in a statutory merger, in which A, B, and C each receive Y stock worth $10,000 and cash of $2,000; D receives Y stock worth $1,000 and cash of $11,000. Assume that the cash received by A, B and C has the effect of a dividend but the cash received by D does not, and that each shareholder's ratable share of accumulated e & p is $1,500. Assume further that the shareholders have the following adjusted bases in their respective X stock: $9,000 (A), $11,000 (B), $13,000 (C) and $10,000 (D). A's realized gain of $3,000 ($12,000 less $9,000) is recognized to the extent of boot received ($2,000); $1,500 of the recognized gain is treated as a dividend under § 356(a)(2) and the remainder ($500) as capital gain. B's realized gain of $1,000 ($12,000 less $11,000) is treated entirely as a dividend under § 356(a)(2). C has a realized but unrecognized loss of $1,000; none of the boot is treated as a dividend because of the "within gain" limitation of § 356(a)(2). All of D's realized gain of $2,000 ($12,000 less $10,000) is taxed as capital gain under § 356(a)(1) because it does not have the effect of a dividend.

The test for dividend equivalency is based on § 302 (with application of the § 318 attribution rules). *See* Rev. Rul. 93–61. Prior to the Supreme Court's landmark decision in *Clark* (S.Ct.1989), the courts and Service had adopted divergent views in applying the principles of § 302(a) to boot received in a reorganization. The crucial issue in *Clark* was how the reduction in the shareholder's interest should be measured. Because the taxpayer was the sole shareholder of the acquired corporation, the Service argued that any gain should automatically be treated as a dividend based on a hypothetical redemption by the acquired corporation of a portion of the taxpayer's stock immediately before the reorganization. Rejecting the Service's approach, the Supreme Court analyzed the transaction as (i) a hypothetical exchange by the taxpayer of his stock in the acquired corporation solely for stock of the acquiring corporation and (ii) a hypothetical redemption by the acquiring corporation of part of the taxpayer's stock received in the reorganization for cash. Since the hypothetical redemption reduced the taxpayer's holdings in the acquiring corporation by more than 20% and left the taxpayer with less than 50% of the stock of the acquiring corporation, the Court held that the boot qualified for capital gain treatment under the substantially-disproportionate test of § 302(b)(2).

The Supreme Court's *Clark* analysis is sometimes referred to as a "post-reorganization" approach because the hypothetical redemption is deemed to occur after the reorganization exchange. Under this approach, the greater the amount of boot and the greater the relative size of the acquiring corporation, the more likely that the boot will be taxed as capital gain. If the acquiring corporation is publicly traded, almost any reduction in a shareholder's percentage interest should qualify as "not essentially equivalent to a dividend." *See* § 302(b)(1). Although *Clark* will generally benefit individual shareholders, it may be disadvantageous for corporate shareholders. Even under *Clark*, however, boot may be treated as a dividend if the acquired and acquiring corporations have overlapping ownership. If no qualifying property is received, § 356 does not apply. By analogy to *Clark*, however, a shareholder who receives solely boot should qualify for capital gain treatment under the complete termination provision of § 302(b)(3).

*Example*: A, an individual, owns all of the stock of T Corp. (worth $800) and no stock of P Corp.; P has 800 shares of outstanding stock (worth $10/share). Pursuant to a statutory merger, T is merged into P; in exchange for her T stock, A receives 40 shares of P stock (worth $400) and $400 cash. Under *Clark*, the transaction is analyzed as if A received 80 shares of P stock (worth $800), and P immediately redeemed half of A's stock for $400. Since the hypothetical redemption reduces A's percentage ownership interest from 9% (80/880 shares) to 4.8% (40/840 shares) and leaves A with less than 50% ownership of P, the boot qualifies for capital gain treatment under *Clark*.

Apart from the issue of the appropriate test for dividend equivalency, the further question remains whether the amount of the dividend, if any, should be limited to e & p of the acquiring corporation. Perhaps the e & p of both corporations might be considered in measuring the amount of the dividend, by analogy to § 304. Since *Clark* is likely to result in sale-or-exchange treatment, determination of e & p will generally be less significant.

(c) *Basis: § 358*. The basis of property received in a reorganization is determined under § 358. Under § 358(a)(2), boot (except installment obligations on which recognized gain is deferred) takes a basis equal to its fair market value. Under § 358(a)(1), nonrecognition property takes a substituted basis equal to the shareholder's original basis in the property surrendered, decreased by the amount of cash and the fair market value of any other boot received and increased by the amount of any dividend or other recognized gain. For this purpose, deferred gain attributable to an installment obligation is treated as if recognized immediately. *See* Prop. Reg. § 1.453–1(f). The basis of multiple classes of nonrecognition property received must be allocated in proportion to their respective fair market values. § 358(b)(1); Reg. §§ 1.358–2(a)(2) and 1.358–2(a)(3).

*Example:* In a reorganization, shareholder A exchanges his stock in X Corp. (with an adjusted basis of $10,000) for stock in Y Corp. worth $11,000, Y short-term notes (which are not readily traded) worth $3,000 and cash of $1,000. Assume that receipt of the cash and notes has the effect of a dividend under § 356(a)(2). A's realized gain of $5,000 ($15,000 less $10,000) is recognized to the extent of the boot received of $4,000 ($3,000 of notes plus $1,000 cash). A's basis in the Y stock will be equal to her original basis in the X stock ($10,000), decreased by the cash and fair market value of other boot property ($4,000) and increased by the amount treated as a dividend or capital gain ($4,000). A's basis in the boot notes will be equal to their fair market value ($3,000), under § 358(a)(2). If the exchange qualified for capital gain treatment under *Clark*, A would take a zero basis in the notes and would recognize $3,000 of gain under § 453 as he received payments. A's basis in the Y stock would still be $10,000, since the basis of nonrecognition property is determined as if the boot recipient elected out of installment treatment.

## § 10. Treatment of the Corporate Transferor

(a) *Property Exchanged or Received in Reorganization.* A corporate party to a reorganization recognizes no gain or loss on an exchange of property, pursuant to the reorganization, solely for stock or securities of another corporate party to the reorganization. § 361(a). The transferor (acquired) corporation also recognizes no gain on any other consideration (boot) permitted to be received in addition to stock and securities, as long as the transferor distributes the boot pursuant to the reorganization. § 361(b)(1)(A). Generally, no issue arises in connection with the distribution of boot in a C reorganization, since the transferor is required to liquidate under § 368(a)(2)(G)(i). The transferor never recognizes loss on the exchange. § 361(b)(2).

The acquiring corporation may also assume (or take property subject to) some or all of the acquired corporation's liabilities. Liabilities relieved are part of the amount realized by the acquired corporation, but the acquired corporation normally recognizes no gain because the liabilities relieved are generally not treated as boot for purposes of § 361. *See* § 357(a). If relief of liabilities is for a tax-avoidance or non-business purpose under § 357(b), however, the total liabilities relieved are treated as boot; because there is no way to "distribute" liabilities relieved, the acquired corporation is required to recognize its gain to the extent of the liabilities. Solely in the case of a D reorganization, the transferor may recognize gain under § 357(c) if liabilities relieved exceed the basis of the transferred property. § 357(c)(1)(B).

(b) *Distribution of Property.* Under § 361(c), a corporate transferor generally recognizes no gain or loss on a distribution of "qualified property" to its shareholders pursuant to a plan of reorganization. Qualified property is defined to include stock, stock rights and obligations of the distributing corporation (or another corporation which is a party to the reorganization). § 361(c)(2)(B). The provisions of § 311 and §§ 336–338 (relating to nonliquidating and liquidating distributions, respectively) are expressly made inapplicable to distributions under § 361. § 361(c)(4). If the acquired corporation distributes property other than qualified property, gain (but not loss) is recognized as if such property had been sold to the distributee at its fair market value. §§ 361(c)(2)(A). Moreover, if the acquired corporation distributes property subject to a liability in excess of basis (or if its shareholders assume the liability), § 361(c)(2)(C) treats the fair market value of the property as not less than the amount of the liability.

*Example:* P Corp. acquires all of the assets of T Corp. for consideration consisting of P voting stock worth $1.7 million, P securities worth $200,000 and gold bars with a fair market value of $100,000. Under the boot relaxation provisions of § 368(a)(2)(B), the acquisition is a valid C reorganization. T recognizes no gain or loss on exchange of its assets under § 361(a). The P voting stock and securities are nonrecognition property, and T takes a substituted basis in such property under § 358(a)(1), *i.e.*, T's original basis in the assets transferred, decreased by the amount of cash and the fair market value of any other boot received. The basis of the nonrecognition property in T's hands is generally irrelevant, since T may distribute the nonrecognition property tax free under § 361(c). Moreover, T recognizes no gain on the distribution of the gold bars to its shareholders, even though the gold bars are boot, because they take a basis in T's hands equal to their fair market value under § 358(a)(2). The substituted-basis provisions of § 358(a)(1) do not apply to boot, even if the boot may be received tax free in a reorganization. § 358(f)(limiting substituted-basis treatment to stock or securities of a corporate party to the reorganization).

(c) *Retained Assets.* The "fresh start" basis rule for boot received in a reorganization generally prevents the acquired corporation from recognizing gain on distribution of such boot. Thus, only post-acquisition appreciation in the boot property will trigger gain under § 361(c)(2). Similarly, § 361(c)(2) prevents the acquired corporation from recognizing gain on distribution of stock or securities received in the reorganization, even if such property is appreciated. If the acquired corporation transfers less than all of its assets in the reorganization, § 361(c)(2) will trigger gain (but not loss) on the distribution of the retained assets.

*Example:* T Corp. transfers 80% of its assets to P Corp. in a valid C reorganization; the remaining 20% of T's assets not transferred in the reorganization consists of appreciated real property with a basis of $100 and a fair market value of $200. Under § 368(a)(2)(G)(i), T is required to distribute any retained assets as well as the consideration received in the reorganization in order to qualify the transaction as a C reorganization. Although T recognizes no gain on distributing the property received in the reorganization, T recognizes $100 of gain on distributing the retained asset ($200 fair market value less $100 basis). If T's basis in the retained asset exceeded its fair market value, T would recognize no loss on the distribution. § 361(c)(1).

(d) *Distributions to Creditors.* If an acquired corporation liquidates and distributes stock, securities or other property received in the reorganization to creditors, such distributions are treated as pursuant to the plan of reorganization for purposes of determining whether the transaction qualifies as a C reorganization. § 368(a)(2)(G)(i). The acquired corporation generally recognizes no gain or loss when it distributes property received in the reorganization to creditors. §§ 361(b)(3) and 361(c)(3). These provisions essentially overrule the holding in *Minnesota Tea Co.* (S.Ct.1938), where the court treated the acquired corporation as recognizing gain on a distribution to its shareholders of cash received in the reorganization coupled with the shareholders' assumption of the acquired corporation's liabilities. If the acquired corporation holds back appreciated property for distribution to creditors in satisfaction of liabilities, it will recognize gain to the same extent as if it had sold such property. The acquired corporation may also be able to recognize a loss if it distributes retained assets to its creditors, since such a distribution is technically outside the plan of reorganization under § 361(c)(3).

*Example:* T Corp. has assets with a fair market value of $100, subject to liabilities of $20. In a valid C reorganization, T transfers all of its assets to P Corp. in exchange for P stock worth $100, but P does not assume T's liabilities. T distributes $20 worth of the P stock to its creditor (C) in satisfaction of T's liabilities. T recognizes no gain on the distribution of the P stock to C, even if the P stock is appreciated in T's hands. § 361(c)(3). If T

instead sells the P stock and uses the sale proceeds
to pay C, T may recognize gain, since T's substituted basis in the P stock is likely to be less than its
fair market value.

## § 11.  Treatment of the Corporate Transferee

(a) *Nonrecognition Treatment.*  If the consideration given by a transferee (acquiring) corporation
consists exclusively of its own stock (whether newly-issued or treasury stock), the acquiring corporation recognizes no gain or loss under § 1032.  If the
acquiring corporation issues its own securities in
addition to stock, it essentially purchases property
with its debt obligation and accordingly recognizes
no gain or loss.  If the acquiring corporation transfers some boot (property other than stock or securities), it recognizes any gain or loss realized on such
property under § 1001, but does not receive any
increase in the basis of the acquired property as a
result of the gain recognized.  § 362(b).

(b) *Corporate    Transferee's    Basis.*    Under
§ 362(b), the acquiring corporation generally takes
a basis in property acquired in the reorganization
equal to its basis in the hands of the acquired
corporation, increased by any gain recognized by
the acquired corporation on the exchange.  In a B
reorganization, the acquiring corporation takes a
basis in the transferred stock equal to its basis in
the hands of the acquiring corporation's former
shareholders. §§ 358(e) and 362(b).  Normally, the
acquired corporation recognizes no gain when it
transfers its assets under § 361, unless liabilities
are relieved for a tax-avoidance or non-business
purpose.  If the acquired corporation fails to liqui-

date, however, the transaction may be denied C reorganization status under § 368(a)(2)(G)(i). In this case, the transaction will be a taxable purchase, and the acquiring corporation may be entitled to a cost basis in the acquired property under § 1012.

Even if the shareholders of the acquired corporation recognize gain on the exchange of their stock for stock and securities of the acquiring corporation (together with any boot), the acquiring corporation will not obtain a basis increase in the acquired property. Similarly, the acquiring corporation's basis is not affected by any gain that the acquired corporation may recognize on distributing appreciated property under § 361(c), since such gain is recognized on the distribution rather than in the reorganization exchange. Moreover, the acquiring corporation's basis is generally not affected by relief of the acquired corporation's liabilities, unless such relief of liabilities is treated as cash and triggers gain due to a tax-avoidance or non-business purpose.

Section 362(b)(second sentence) makes the substituted-basis provisions of § 362(b) inapplicable to stock or securities of a corporate party to a reorganization unless such stock or securities are acquired (in whole or in part) in exchange for stock or securities of the corporate transferee (or its parent). Together with § 358(e), this sentence merely ensures that § 362(b) substituted-basis treatment will apply to the corporate transferee in a B reorganization.

(c) *Triangular Reorganizations*.  In a triangular A, B or C reorganization, the acquiring corporation may use stock or securities of its parent as consideration.  Although § 1032 technically applies only to an exchange of a corporation's own stock, the subsidiary will recognize no gain or loss on an exchange of its parent's stock that it received pursuant to the reorganization.  § 1.1032–2.  The subsidiary may nevertheless recognize gain or loss if it transfers parent stock acquired in an unrelated transaction prior to the reorganization.  Reg. § 1.1032–2(d), Example (2).

The Regulations provide rules for adjusting the basis of a parent corporation (P) in its controlled subsidiary (S) following a triangular reorganization (including forward and reverse subsidiary mergers). *See* Reg. § 1.358–6.  For example, assume that P contributes its own stock to newly-formed S;  the P stock has a basis of zero in S's hands and the S stock has a basis of zero in P's hands;  pursuant to a forward subsidiary merger, S acquires the assets of a target corporation (T) in exchange for the P stock.  Although S's basis in the T assets acquired in the exchange is a substituted basis under § 362(b), P's basis in the S stock apparently remains zero.  To eliminate this zero-basis problem, the Regulations treat P as if it had acquired T's assets directly and then transferred them to S.  P's basis in the T assets is determined under § 362(b), and its basis in the S stock is determined under § 358.  *See* Reg. § 1.358–6(c)(4), Example (1).  This treatment seems appropriate since the transaction could have been structured as a direct acquisi-

tion of T's assets by P, followed by a drop down of
T's assets to S.

## § 12.  Reorganizations and § 338

In *Yoc Heating* (Tax Ct.1973), a corporation purchased 85% of the stock of a target corporation for
cash and notes.  As part of the same plan, the
target transferred its assets to a newly-formed subsidiary of the purchasing corporation and dissolved.
The target's minority shareholders received cash in
exchange for their target stock.  Because the stock
purchase and asset acquisition were part of a integrated plan, there was insufficient continuity of
interest to qualify the transaction as a reorganization under § 368.  Accordingly, the purchasing corporation received a stepped-up basis in the target's
assets.  *See also* Kass (Tax Ct.1973)(corporation
purchased target stock and then target merged into
purchaser; target's minority shareholders surrendered their stock in a taxable exchange).

The Regulations reflect the Treasury's view that
the corporate-level result in *Yoc Heating* is inconsistent with the legislative intent of § 338.  Reg.
§ 1.338–2(c)(3).  Accordingly, under the Regulations, the basis of the target corporation's assets
will not be stepped up as a result of a two-step
acquisition when the purchasing corporation makes
a qualified § 338 stock purchase but does not make
a § 338 election.  Technically, this result is accomplished by treating the purchasing corporation's
ownership of target stock as satisfying the continuity-of-interest requirement for purposes of § 368.

With respect to the target's minority shareholders, however, the Regulations follow the result in *Kass*, requiring recognition of gain or loss on the exchange. Apparently, the Treasury does not view the enactment of § 338 as affecting the tax consequences at the shareholder level.

## § 13. Policy Considerations

Reform proposals would replace the existing treatment of corporate acquisitions with an elective carryover-basis or cost-basis regime. *See* American Law Inst., Federal Income Tax Project: Subchapter C—Proposals on Corporate Acquisitions and Dispositions (1982). At the corporate level, nonrecognition treatment would be available as long as the bases of corporate assets were preserved, regardless of the form of consideration. If the parties elected cost-basis treatment, asset basis would be stepped up with a corresponding corporate-level tax. In general, shareholder-level taxation would be determined independent of corporate-level taxation. Thus, a cost-basis acquisition at the corporate level might nevertheless be wholly or partially tax free at the shareholder level. Since the tax consequences would be determined on a shareholder-by-shareholder basis, a shareholder who received qualifying consideration would be entitled to nonrecognition treatment, regardless of the consideration received by other shareholders. The continuity-of-interest and continuity-of-business-enterprise doctrines would no longer be applicable. Although currently in abeyance, these reform proposals may be revived in the future.

# CHAPTER 10

# CORPORATE DIVISIONS

## § 1. Introduction

Section 355 permits a tax-free division of a corporate enterprise into two separate corporations, each owned by shareholders of the original corporation. A § 355 transaction may take the form of a "spin-off", a "split-off" or a "split-up." A spin-off consists of a distribution by a corporation to its shareholders of stock in a controlled subsidiary; by analogy to a dividend, the shareholders of the distributing corporation do not surrender anything in exchange for the distributed stock. A split-off is identical to a spin-off, except that the shareholders of the distributing corporation surrender part of their stock in the distributing corporation for stock in the controlled subsidiary; in this respect, a split-off is analogous to a redemption. In a split-up, the distributing corporation distributes stock in two or more controlled subsidiaries to its shareholders in complete liquidation. Although each of these three patterns may qualify as a tax-free division under § 355, the form of the transaction may have significance with respect to taxation of boot and other matters.

The underlying premise of § 355 is that nonrecognition treatment should be available when the owners of a business merely change the form of the business while continuing to operate it. In a qualifying transaction, § 355 provides that no gain or loss is recognized on the receipt of stock or securities of the controlled corporation. If shareholders receive any other property in addition to such non-recognition property, however, the boot provisions of § 356 are applicable. Finally, the distributing corporation generally recognizes no gain or loss on a distribution of stock or securities of the controlled corporation, although it may recognize gain (but not loss) on a distribution of boot.

## § 2. General Requirements

The three types of qualifying transactions have several elements in common. First, the distributing corporation must be in "control" of at least one subsidiary ("controlled corporation") immediately before the transaction. § 355(a)(1)(A). Control means ownership of stock possessing at least 80% of the total voting power and at least 80% of the total number of shares of all other classes of stock. § 368(c). The controlled corporation may be either a preexisting or a newly-created subsidiary. Second, both the distributing corporation and the controlled corporation (or, if the distributing corporation is a holding company, each of the controlled corporations) must be engaged in the "active conduct of a trade or business" immediately after the distribution. § 355(b)(1). Third, the active business test must also be satisfied for a 5–year period preceding the transaction. § 355(b)(2). Fourth, the distributing corporation must distribute all of the stock or securities of the controlled corporation (or sufficient stock to constitute control under § 368(c), if the remaining stock or securities are not retained as part of a tax-avoidance plan). § 355(a)(1)(D). Fifth, the distribution must not be used principally as a "device" for distributing earnings and profits. § 355(a)(1)(B).

As a result of the qualifying transaction, the shareholders of the distributing corporation will have control of two separate corporations. If the distribution is pro rata, as is the case in most spin-offs, the two corporations will be "brother-sister" corporations owned by the same group of shareholders. A non-pro-rata distribution is often used in split-offs and split-ups, for example, to resolve a dispute among shareholders. Section 355 treatment is available whether or not the distribution is pro-rata. § 355(a)(2)(A).

*Example:* A and B, equal shareholders of X Corp., decide to separate their business interests. Assuming that X has conducted two active businesses for at least 5 years, a tax-free § 355 transaction may be structured as a non-pro-rata split-off or split-up. In a split-off, X would transfer the assets of one business to a new subsidiary (S), in exchange for all of S's stock, and would then distribute the S stock to A in exchange for all of A's stock in X, leaving B as the sole owner of X (with the assets of the second business). In a split-up, X would form two new subsidiaries (S1 and S2), transfer the assets of one business to S1 and those of the other to S2 (leaving

X a mere holding company), and finally distribute the S1 stock to A and the S2 stock to B.

## § 3.  Relationship to Divisive D Reorganizations

A § 355 transaction need not be part of a reorganization.  § 355(a)(2)(C).  If the parent corporation distributes stock of an existing subsidiary in a spin-off, for example, the transaction is governed entirely by § 355.  If the parent transfers part of its assets to a newly-formed subsidiary and then distributes the subsidiary stock in a spin-off, however, the transaction as a whole will constitute a divisive D reorganization under § 368(a)(1)(D).  Under § 361, the parent will recognize no gain or loss on the initial asset transfer, and the new subsidiary will have a substituted basis under § 362(b).  The distribution of the subsidiary's stock must qualify under § 355 in order to meet the distribution requirement of § 368(a)(1)(D).  Although a § 354 exchange satisfies the distribution requirement in non-divisive D reorganizations, § 354 is not applicable to divisive D reorganizations; thus, the requirements of § 355 are, in effect, mandatory for all divisive D reorganizations.  *See* §§ 354(b) and 368(a)(1)(D).

## § 4.  Divisive Bailout Problem

The elaborate anti-avoidance provisions of § 355 were originally enacted in response to a bailout problem illustrated by the facts of *Gregory* (S.Ct. 1935).  In *Gregory,* the taxpayer owned all of the shares of a corporation (United Mortgage), which in turn owned highly appreciated shares of another corporation (Monitor Securities). In order to dispose of the Monitor shares without triggering a corporate-level tax, the taxpayer caused United Mortgage to form a subsidiary (Averill), transfer the Monitor stock to Averill in a § 351 transaction, and then spin off the Averill stock to her. Immediately thereafter, Averill was liquidated and distributed the Monitor stock to the taxpayer. If the transaction had been successful, the taxpayer would have obtained a basis in the Monitor shares equal to their fair market value (thus allowing her to sell the Monitor shares with no additional gain), without any corporate-level tax and at the cost of only a capital gain tax at the shareholder level. The Supreme Court, however, found that the transaction had "no business or corporate purpose" and was a "mere device," masquerading as a corporate reorganization, to avoid tax.

To prevent such tax-avoidance schemes, Congress repealed the tax-free spin-off provisions in 1934, only to reinstate them in substantially their present form in 1954. Present § 355 contains a set of rules designed to prevent bailouts. The restoration of a capital gains preference has revitalized the need for these anti-bailout rules. Even more significantly, § 355 now serves the function of backstopping the repeal of *General Utilities*.

## § 5.  Active Business Requirement

The principal anti-bailout provision of § 355 is the active business test. § 355(b). The requirement that both the distributing corporation and the controlled corporation must actively conduct businesses immediately after the distribution is sufficient to block a transaction like the one in *Gregory*, because the controlled corporation would fail to meet this requirement if it held only cash or investment assets. In addition, § 355(b)(2)(B) requires that both corporations must have conducted active businesses for the 5–year period immediately preceding the distribution. The 5–year requirement is designed to prevent a temporary investment of liquid assets in a new business in preparation for a spin-off. If the 5–year requirement is met, then the controlled corporation was presumably not created for the purpose of tax avoidance with respect to the subsequent corporate division.

Two additional requirements must also be considered. Under § 355(b)(2)(C), the active business requirement is not satisfied if any of the businesses was acquired within the preceding 5–year period in a taxable transaction. Moreover, § 355(b)(2)(D) provides that the active business requirement is not satisfied if the distributing corporation or the distributee corporation acquired control (directly or indirectly) of a corporation conducting an active business within the preceding 5–year period in a taxable transaction. Control means ownership of stock possessing at least 80% of the total voting power and 80% of the total number of shares of all other classes of stock. § 368(c).

*Example:* P Corp. purchases all of the stock of T, and one year later distributes the T stock to P's shareholders in a spin-off. Since P acquired control of T in a taxable transaction within the preceding 5–year period, P's distribution of the T stock fails the requirement of § 355(b)(2)(D) and constitutes a taxable dividend to the P shareholders. Alternatively, if P purchases all of the stock of T, liquidates T tax free under § 332, and then distributes the stock of S Corp. (formerly a subsidiary of T, now a subsidiary of P) to P's shareholders, the transaction will fail the requirement of § 355(b)(2)(D), because P indirectly acquired control of S in a taxable transaction during the preceding 5–year period.

Section 355(b)(2)(D) also denies tax-free treatment of the distribution if the distributee corporation acquires control of the distributing corporation in a taxable transaction during the 5–year period. For example, if P acquires control of T in a taxable transaction, T's distribution of the stock of S (T's subsidiary) to P cannot qualify as a tax-free distribution under § 355 until 5 years after P's acquisition of T, regardless of how long S has conducted an active trade or business. If the distributee corporation acquires less than 80% of the stock of the distributing corporation, however, § 355(b)(2)(D) does not apply because the distributee corporation has not acquired "control." *But see* § 14 below.

## § 6. Definition of Active Business

Section 355 does not define the term "active business," but the Regulations provide some guidelines. A corporation is engaged in an active business if it carries on a specific group of activities for income-producing purposes, including every step in the income-earning process from such activities. Reg. § 1.355–3(b)(2). Two types of assets that are likely to cause problems under this definition are investment assets (*e.g.*, stock, securities, land or other property held for investment) and owner-occupied or leased real property with respect to which the owner does not provide significant services. *Id.* Generally, an active business requires substantial managerial and operational activities conducted directly by the corporation; activities performed by third parties such as independent contractors are not taken into account. *Id.* Mere holding of vacant real estate does not satisfy the active business requirement if the owner has engaged in no "significant development activities." Reg. § 1.355–3(c), Example (2). Similarly, if a parent corporation leases real property used in its trade or business from a newly spun-off subsidiary, the subsidiary's leasing of the property may be treated as a mere investment activity rather than an active trade or business. *See* Rafferty (1st Cir. 1971); Reg. § 1.355–3(c), Example (13). Rental activities may constitute an active trade or business, however, if the owner directly provides sufficient management and maintenance services. Reg. § 1.355–3(c), Example (12); Rev. Rul. 92–17 (corporate general partner actively engaged in real estate business).

The Service formerly insisted that there must be two separate active businesses, each with a separate 5-year history. After taxpayer victories in *Coady*

(6th Cir.1961) and *Marett* (5th Cir.1963) on this issue, the Treasury issued final Regulations in 1989 which explicitly permit a "vertical" division of a single preexisting business into two separate, independent businesses. Reg. § 1.355–3(c), Examples (4)-(5). For example, two equal shareholders of a construction business may divide the business in half by forming a new corporation (with part of the old corporation's construction contracts, equipment and cash) and distributing the stock of the new corporation tax free to one of them. Reg. § 1.355–3(c), Example (4). A tax-free "horizontal" division of an integrated business along functional lines is also permitted, at least if each separate function is economically viable. Reg. § 1.355–3(c), Examples (9)-(11). For example, an integrated steel company may spin off its coal-mining activities to a separate corporation which continues to supply coal to the steel company. Even if the coal-mining business has no customers other than the original steel company, a tax-free horizontal division may be permitted. Reg. § 1.355–3(c), Example (11)(captive coal mine). The Regulations warn, however, that a bailout device may be inferred from post-distribution dealings between the distributing corporation and the controlled corporation. *Reg.* § 1.355–2(d)(2)(iv)(C); *see* § 7 below.

If two separate businesses exist, and the earnings of one have been used to finance expansion of the other within 5 years of the distribution, § 355 treatment may be inapplicable. Rev. Rul. 59–400 (earnings of hotel business used to expand rental business). Similarly, creation of a new business, as opposed to mere expansion of an existing business, may prevent a tax-free spin-off if the new business is not sufficiently "seasoned." The Regulations provide that a new activity in the "same line of business" will be treated as an expansion of the existing business, unless the changes are "of such a character as to constitute the acquisition of a new or different business." Reg. § 1.355–3(b)(3)(ii). Thus, the Regulations adopt the *Lockwood* approach that activities in the same line of business comprise a single business, even if located in different geographical regions. *See* Lockwood (8th Cir. 1965). The acquisition by purchase of a similar business may also qualify as an expansion. *See* Reg. § 1.355–3(c), Example (8) (purchased hardware business).

## § 7. Device

Section 355(a)(1)(B) requires that a corporate division not be used principally as a "device for the distribution of the earnings and profits" of the distributing corporation or the controlled corporation. Historically, the "device" restriction was intended primarily to prevent use of § 355 transactions to convert dividend income into capital gains. Although the restoration of a capital gains preference enhances the significance of the device limit, the Regulations warn that "a device can include a transaction that effects a recovery of basis." Reg. § 1.355–2(d)(1). The Regulations use a facts-and-circumstances test to determine whether a transaction fails the device test. *Id.* Under this balancing approach, the relative strength or weakness of "device" and "nondevice" factors is taken into account.

(a) *Device Factors*. The Regulations identify three factors that are "evidence of device": (i) a pro rata distribution, (ii) a subsequent sale or exchange of stock, and (iii) the nature and use of the assets of the distributing and controlled corporations immediately after the transaction. Reg. § 1.355–2(d)(2). A pro-rata distribution, which normally presents the greatest potential for a bailout of e & p (unless neither corporation has e & p), is subject to particularly close scrutiny. Reg. § 1.355–2(d)(2)(ii). This evidence of device may be overcome, however, by the presence of a strong business purpose. *See* Reg. § 1.355–2(d)(4), Example (2).

Section 355(a)(1)(B) provides that the mere fact that, after the distribution, stock or securities of either corporation are sold or exchanged (other than pursuant to a prearranged plan) will not be construed to mean that the transaction was used principally as a device. The Regulations interpret this language narrowly, indicating that any subsequent sale or exchange (whether or not prearranged) is evidence of device. Reg. § 1.355–2(d)(2)(iii). The greater the percentage of stock sold (and the shorter the interval between the distribution and sale), the stronger the evidence of device. *Id.* Moreover, a prearranged sale is "substantial evidence of device." *Id.* A sale is prearranged if actually negotiated before the distribution or, generally, if discussed by the buyer and seller

before the distribution and "reasonably to be anticipated by both parties." *Id.*

The restriction on prearranged sales is intended
to ensure continuity of interest, *i.e.*, to prevent an
immediate cashing out of the shareholders' investment at capital gain rates. If stock is transferred in
a tax-free exchange following a § 355 distribution,
continuity of interest will also generally be preserved. Accordingly, the Regulations specifically
permit a subsequent reorganization in which "only
an insubstantial amount of gain is recognized."
*Id.; see also* Morris Trust (4th Cir.1966). In such
cases, the shareholders merely maintain their proprietary interest through stock in the acquiring
corporation. If stock acquired in the reorganization
is subsequently sold, however, the sale may be
treated as evidence of device.

For purposes of the device limit, the Regulations
also focus on the "nature, kind, amount, and use of
the assets" of both the distributing and controlled
corporations. Reg. § 1.355–2(d)(2)(iv). The existence of excess liquid assets in either corporation
may be indicative of a device. *Id.* The strength of
this factor depends on the ratio of business to
nonbusiness assets in each corporation. *See* Reg.
§ 1.355–2(d)(4), Examples (2)-(3). Evidence of device also exists if either corporation is a "secondary
business" (one whose primary function is to serve
the business needs of the other corporation) and
could be sold without adversely affecting the business of the other corporation. Reg. § 1.355–
2(d)(2)(iv). Such a "captive" business may repre-

sent essentially an investment rather than an active business. *See* Reg. § 1.355–3(c), Example (11)(related function device).

(b) *Nondevice Factors.* The Regulations list three factors which are evidence of nondevice. First, a corporate business purpose indicates that the transaction was not used principally as a device. Reg. § 1.355–2(d)(3)(ii). The stronger the evidence of device, the stronger the corporate business purpose required to outweigh such evidence. *Id.* Second, evidence of nondevice exists if the distributing corporation is publicly traded and no shareholder owns (directly or indirectly) more than 5% of any class of stock. Reg. § 1.355–2(d)(3)(iii). Third, the fact that a corporate distributee would be entitled to a § 243 dividends-received deduction, in the absence of § 355, is evidence of nondevice. Reg. § 1.355–2(d)(3)(iv).

(c) *Transactions Ordinarily Not a Device.* Notwithstanding the presence of any device factors, three categories of distributions are "ordinarily considered not to have been used principally as a device." Reg. § 1.355–2(d)(5)(i). The first category comprises distributions in which neither the distributing nor the controlled corporation has any current or accumulated e & p, including any e & p that would arise if the distributing corporation distributed any appreciated property immediately before the transaction. Reg. § 1.355–2(d)(5)(ii). The absence of e & p indicates that the shareholders have not used the transaction to avoid dividend income. The usefulness of this exception is limited, however, since most distributing corporations are likely to have appreciated property that would generate e & p if distributed.

The second and third categories consist of distributions that would have qualified for exchange treatment with respect to each distributee under § 302 or § 303, in the absence of § 355. Reg. § 1.355–2(d)(5)(iii), (iv). Since the device test focuses on the distributee's ability to extract e & p at capital gain rates by selling stock, it should not preclude § 355 treatment for a distribution, regardless of how promptly the distributed stock is sold, if the distributee would have been entitled to capital gain treatment on the actual distribution in the absence of § 355. In a typical split-off where a shareholder exchanges all of his parent stock for subsidiary stock, resulting in a complete termination of his interest in the parent, the device restriction of § 355 should thus be inapplicable. The exception for §§ 302/303–type transactions is unavailable, however, if stock of more than one controlled corporation is distributed. Otherwise, the shareholders could avoid dividend income by selling stock of one corporation while retaining stock of the other. Reg. § 1.355–2(d)(5)(i).

## § 8. Business Purpose

The Regulations define a corporate business purpose as a "real and substantial non-Federal tax purpose" of the distributing or controlled corporation. Reg. § 1.355–2(b)(2). The business purpose requirement is intended to restrict tax-free treatment to distributions incident to "readjustments of corporate structures required by business exigencies." Reg. § 1.355–2(b)(1). A shareholder purpose (as distinguished from a corporate business purpose) will suffice only if it is "so nearly coextensive with a corporate business purpose as to preclude any distinction between them." Reg. § 1.355–2(b)(2). If the transaction is motivated solely by a personal purpose of the shareholder (*e.g.*, estate planning), it will not qualify under § 355. *Id.* *See* Rafferty (1st Cir.1971).

Valid business purposes include compliance with federal antitrust laws as well as an amicable separation of a business to permit shareholders to pursue different business interests. Reg. § 1.355–2(b)(5), Examples (1)-(2). A spin-off to facilitate a public offering of the distributing corporation's stock is also permissible. Rev. Rul. 85–122. Similarly, the business purpose requirement is satisfied if stock of a controlled corporation is distributed in order to reduce substantially the amount of administrative time and expense necessary to comply with state regulatory requirements. Rev. Rul. 88–33. *See also* Rev. Rul. 88–34 (business purpose satisfied where distribution enabled subsidiary to hire key employee).

The Regulations indicate that reduction of nonfederal taxes is not a valid business purpose if (i) the transaction will reduce both federal and nonfederal taxes because of similarities in the respective laws, and (ii) the federal tax savings are "greater than or substantially coextensive with" the nonfederal tax savings. Reg. § 1.355–2(b)(2). Thus, a valid business purpose is generally lacking if a § 355 transaction is intended merely to facilitate an S election, since the federal tax savings are almost certain to exceed the nonfederal tax savings. *See* Reg. § 1.355–2(b)(5), Examples (6)-(7). Notwithstanding the expected tax savings from an S election, § 355 may nevertheless apply if the transaction is "substantially motivated" by another legitimate business purpose, such as permitting a key employee to acquire stock. Reg. § 1.355–2(b)(5), Example (8). The Regulations have been criticized for their hostility toward § 355 transactions undertaken to qualify the distributing or controlled corporation for S status. Although an S election generally eliminates the future corporate-level tax, such transactions arguably bear little relationship to the bailout concerns that prompted § 355.

The required business purpose must relate to the distribution rather than merely the incorporation of a separate business. Reg. § 1.355–2(b)(3). The Regulations provide that the business purpose requirement is not satisfied if the corporate objective could be achieved through a nontaxable transaction that does not involve a distribution of stock and is "neither impractical nor unduly expensive." *Id*. In effect, the § 355 transaction must represent the only practical and cost-efficient method of accomplishing the business objective. Thus, the desire to protect one business from the risks of another may justify the incorporation of a subsidiary to operate a risky business but does not constitute an adequate business purpose for distributing the subsidiary's stock. Reg. § 1.355–2(b)(5), Example (3); Wilson (9th Cir.1965). If a distribution of subsidiary stock represents the only means of solving a regulatory rate problem, however, the business purpose requirement is satisfied. Reg. § 1.355–2(b)(5), Example (4).

## § 9. Continuity of Interest

The § 355 Regulations impose the same continuity-of-interest requirement that applies to reorganizations generally. *See* Chapter 9. The requirement that shareholders maintain sufficient continuity is intended to prevent tax-free treatment of transactions that are substantially equivalent to sales. The Regulations require that persons who, directly or indirectly, owned the enterprise prior to the § 355 transaction must own, in the aggregate, sufficient stock to establish "continuity of interest in each of the modified corporate forms in which the enterprise is conducted after the separation." Reg. § 1.355–2(c). Although the Regulations do not specify any minimum continuity, 50% should clearly be sufficient. *See* Reg. § 1.355–2(c)(2), Example (2).

The continuity-of-interest requirement is not violated by a non-pro-rata distribution which leaves some shareholders owning the distributing corporation and other shareholders owning the controlled corporation. *See* § 355(a)(2)(A); Reg. § 1.355–2(c)(2), Example (1). In this situation, each of the modified corporate forms is owned 100% by persons who owned the enterprise prior to the § 355 transaction. If some shareholders sell their stock shortly before a § 355 transaction, the new shareholders may not be counted for continuity purposes, thereby potentially disqualifying the transaction. Although the Regulations apparently focus on pre-distribution sales, post-distribution sales could also violate the continuity-of-interest requirement or the overlapping device restriction.

*Example:* A and B each own 50 of the 100 outstanding shares of X Corp., which owns all of the stock of Y Corp. The businesses of X and Y are of equal value. An unrelated party, P, purchases 40 of A's X shares, and shortly thereafter X distributes all of the Y stock to B in exchange for her X stock. Immediately after the distribution, A owns 20% of X and B owns 100% of Y; P may not be counted for continuity purposes. Since the former shareholders of X (A and B) have failed to maintain minimum continuity with respect to each of the modified corporate forms (X and Y), the transaction fails to qualify under § 355. *See* Reg. § 1.355–2(c)(2), Example (4). It is irrelevant that A and B together have maintained 60% of their interest in the former combined enterprise, since continuity is tested separately with respect to X and Y. If P had instead purchased only 25 of A's X shares, A and B would own, in the aggregate, sufficient stock to establish continuity immediately after the distribution, *i.e.*, A would own 50% of X and B would own 100% of Y. *See* Reg. § 1.355–2(c)(2), Example (2).

## § 10.  Treatment of Boot

Section 355(a) provides that no gain or loss is recognized on receipt of stock or securities of the controlled corporation, if the other requirements of § 355 are satisfied. The boot rules of § 356 will apply if any other property is distributed. For this purpose, boot includes (i) cash or other property, (ii) the fair market value of the excess principal amount of any securities or, if no securities are surrendered, the fair market value of any securities received, and (iii) stock of the controlled corporation if acquired within 5 years of the distribution in a taxable transaction. §§ 355(a)(3), 356(a) and 356(b). The special rule concerning recently-acquired stock of the controlled corporation is intended to prevent the distributing corporation from investing excess funds in stock of the controlled corporation in preparation for a tax-free spin-off. For example, if the distributing corporation has owned 85% of the stock of a controlled subsidiary for more than 5 years and acquires the remaining 15% six months before a spin-off of all the subsidiary stock, the recently-acquired stock will be treated as boot in the distribution. Reg. § 1.355–2(g)(2), Example.

The governing provision for exchanges (split-offs and split-ups) is § 356(a). Under the normal rules of § 356(a)(1), any realized gain is recognized to the extent of the boot received. If the exchange has the effect of a dividend (applying the rules of §§ 302 and 318), however, such recognized gain is treated as a dividend under § 356(a)(2) to the extent of the shareholder's ratable share of accumulated e & p, and the balance is treated as capital gain. In a split-off, dividend equivalence is tested by determining the percentage decrease that would have occurred had the shareholder received only the boot in redemption of part of his parent stock and retained the rest of his parent stock. Rev. Rul. 93–62. If the aggregate fair market value of the distributed property (stock, securities and boot) is less than the adjusted basis of stock and securities surrendered, § 356(c) prevents recognition of loss.

The governing provision for distributions (spin-offs) is § 356(b). Under § 356(b), receipt of boot is treated as a distribution of property under § 301; this result is appropriate since a spin-off is essentially analogous to a dividend distribution. Unlike § 356(a), § 356(b) treats the entire amount of the boot as a dividend to the extent of the corporation's e & p (without regard to the amount of realized gain or the distributee's ratable share of e & p).

## § 11.  Basis to Distributee

The basis of property received by a distributee shareholder in a § 355 transaction is determined under § 358. If the distributee receives no boot, the aggregate basis of his original stock (or securities) will be allocated among the stock (or securities) received or retained in proportion to their respective fair market values. If boot is received, the boot will take a basis equal to its fair market value under § 358(a)(2), and the basis of the non-recognition property must be decreased by the amount of any boot received and increased by the amount of any dividend or gain recognized. § 358(a)(1).

*Example:* X Corp. distributes stock and securities of Y, a controlled subsidiary, to X's sole shareholder A in a § 355 spin-off. Immediately before the transaction, A's X stock had a basis of $4,200 and a fair market value of $22,000; immediately after the transaction, the fair market value of A's retained X stock is $11,000. In the distribution, A receives Y stock worth $10,000 and Y securities worth $1,000. The receipt of the securities is taxed as boot to A, resulting in a $1,000 dividend under § 356(b), and A takes a $1,000 basis in the securities under § 358(a)(2). A's original basis in her X stock ($4,200), decreased by the amount of boot received ($1,000) and increased by the amount taxed as a dividend ($1,000), must be allocated in proportion to fair market value between the retained X stock ($11,000) and the Y stock received ($10,000). Thus, the basis of the retained X stock will be $2,200 ($4,200 × $\frac{11}{21}$), and that of the Y stock will be $2,000 ($4,200 × $\frac{10}{21}$). *See* § 358(c); Reg. § 1.358–2(c), Example (4).

## § 12. Tax Treatment of Distributing Corporation

Historically, § 355 prescribed only the tax consequences to the distributee shareholder; the treatment of the distributing corporation was governed by other provisions. Under current law, the tax treatment of the distributing corporation is generally governed by § 355(c) unless the transaction is preceded by a D reorganization, in which case § 361(c) applies. Whether § 355(c) or § 361(c) applies, the results are generally quite similar. Sections §§ 311 and 336, which govern nonliquidating and liquidating distributions, are both inapplicable to § 355 transactions. *See* §§ 355(c)(3), 361(c)(4). The special gain-recognition rules of § 355(d) are discussed in § 14 below.

Under § 355(c)(1), the distributing corporation generally recognizes no gain or loss on a distribution to which § 355 applies. Gain is recognized, however, on a distribution of appreciated property other than "qualified property," defined as stock or securities in the controlled corporation. § 355(c)(2). Thus, no gain will be recognized at the corporate level even if all or part of any securities distributed are treated as boot under § 356(d). Corporate-level gain will be recognized, however, on a distribution of recently-acquired stock of the controlled corporation, which is treated as nonqualified property. *See* § 355(a)(3)(B).

Section 355(c) applies only to distributions that are not made pursuant to a plan of reorganization. If a § 355 transaction included a D reorganization as a preliminary step (*e.g.*, if the distributing corporation initially transferred assets to a newly-formed subsidiary in preparation for a spin-off of the subsidiary's stock), then § 361(c) would control the treatment of the distributing corporation. Under § 361(c)(2)(A), the distributing corporation would recognize gain on a distribution of appreciated property other than "qualified property." For purposes of § 361(c), qualified property includes (in addition to stock and securities of the controlled corporation) the right to acquire stock and nonsecurity debt obligations. § 361(c)(2)(B).

*Example:* A and B, equal shareholders of T Corp., receive stock of T's existing subsidiary (S) in a pro-rata spin-off. Under § 355(c), the distribution of the S stock would be tax free to T. If T also distributed appreciated property in addition to the S stock, T would recognize gain on the distribution. If S were a newly-formed subsidiary instead of a preexisting one, T's initial transfer of assets to S would constitute part of a D reorganization. Accordingly, the tax treatment of T would be governed by § 361(c) rather than § 355(c), but the results would be identical.

## § 13.  Failed Divisions

(a) *General.* Although § 355 generally prescribes similar treatment for spin-offs, split-offs and split-ups, the consequences of a failed § 355 transaction may depend on the form of the division. A spin-off that fails to qualify under § 355 will be taxed as a § 301 distribution (dividend to the extent of e & p, balance treated as basis recovery or capital gain). A failed split-off will presumably be tested under the rules of § 302, and treated accordingly either as a § 302(a) exchange (*e.g.,* a non-pro-rata split-off resulting in a complete termination) or as a § 301 distribution (*e.g.,* a pro-rata split-off). The tax consequences of a failed split-up are less clear. On one hand, a failed split-up might be treated as a complete liquidation under § 331, allowing the shareholders to recognize capital gain or loss. On the other hand, if the split-up represents a segregation of liquid assets in preparation for a stock sale, § 301 treatment may be more appropriate. The Regulations provide that § 301 may apply to a distribution which takes place at the same time as another transaction if it is in substance a separate transaction. Reg. § 1.301–1(*l*). If the failed split-up is preceded by a § 351 transfer, the Service is likely to seek dividend treatment under a liquidation-reincorporation theory. *See* Telephone Answering Service Co., Inc. (Tax Ct.1974). *See also* Chapter 7.

(b) *Gain or Loss to Distributing Corporation.* If property is distributed in a failed spin-off or split-off, the distributing corporation must recognize gain on any unrealized appreciation; no loss is recognized. §§ 311(a)(2) and 311(b)(1). In a failed split-up, the distributing corporation generally recognizes gain or loss under § 336(a), subject to the loss disallowance rules of § 336(d). If a failed split-up also qualifies as a reorganization, however, the nonrecognition rules of § 361(c) override § 336. *See* § 336(c).

## § 14. Avoidance of General Utilities Repeal: § 355(d)

The repeal of the *General Utilities* doctrine has placed great stress on § 355. A tax-free division of a corporate business in preparation for a sale of the stock of the distributing corporation or controlled corporation may contravene the policy underlying the repeal of *General Utilities*, if that policy is interpreted broadly as calling for imposition of a tax at the corporate level when assets are transferred outside an economic group while remaining in corporate solution. Section 337(d) authorizes Regulations to prevent circumvention of the purpose of the 1986 Act (*e.g.*, the repeal of *General Utilities*) by the use of § 355 or otherwise. In 1990, Congress added § 355(d) to prevent use of § 355 to avoid recognition of corporate-level gain on sale of a business.

Section 355(d)(1) requires the distributing corporation to recognize gain on a "disqualified distribution" of stock or securities of the controlled corporation. Under § 355(d)(2), a disqualified distribution is any § 355 distribution in which, immediately after the distribution, any person holds "disqualified stock" representing a 50% or greater interest (by vote or value) in either the distributing or controlled corporation. Disqualified stock consists generally of stock purchased within the 5–year period prior to the distribution. § 355(d)(3). If applicable, § 355(d) requires the distributing corporation to recognize gain from a deemed sale of the controlled corporation's stock, but does not affect shareholder-level nonrecognition. It is important to note that § 355(d) tests stock ownership immediately after the distribution. In effect, § 355(d) imposes a 5–year holding period in connection with a 50% or greater change of ownership in either the distributing or controlled corporation. Moreover, § 355(d) applies only if the transaction otherwise qualifies under § 355. Thus, failure to satisfy the continuity-of-interest requirement could render the transaction taxable at both the shareholder and corporate level.

*Example*: A has owned 100% of the stock of P Corp. for 10 years. On January 1, 1998, B purchases 50% of A's P stock, and 2 years later P distributes all of the stock of S (P's wholly-owned subsidiary) to B in exchange for her P stock. Immediately after the distribution, A and B each own 100% of P and S, respectively. Since B received the S stock in exchange for her disqualified stock in P, the S stock is also disqualified stock in B's hands. *See* § 355(d)(3)(B)(ii). Thus, P must recognize gain on distribution of the S stock under § 355(d), as if P had sold such stock for its fair market value. The result would be the same if P distributed the S stock to A rather than B, since B would own disqualified stock representing a 50% or more interest in P. If B had owned the P stock for more than 5 years, § 355(c) rather than § 355(d) would govern the tax treatment of the distributing corporation.

The controlled corporation is not permitted to increase the basis of its assets to reflect any gain recognized by the distributing corporation under § 355(d). Thus, a second level of corporate tax will be incurred in the future when the controlled corporation sells its assets. This double taxation could be avoided by treating the stock distribution as a deemed sale of the controlled corporation's assets. *See* § 336(e). The distributing corporation's gain on the stock distribution would be ignored; instead, gain would be determined as if the controlled corporation had sold its assets for fair market value. The controlled corporation would receive a corresponding step-up in its basis for the assets.

# CHAPTER 11

# CARRYOVER OF CORPORATE ATTRIBUTES

## § 1. Introduction

When one corporation acquires another corporation's assets in certain tax-free transactions, § 381(a) provides generally that the acquiring corporation "shall succeed to and take into account" certain tax attributes of the acquired corporation specified in § 381(c). Section 381 applies to asset acquisitions under § 332 (subsidiary liquidations) and to A, C, non-divisive D and F reorganizations under § 368(a)(1). The corporate tax attributes enumerated in § 381(c) include net operating loss carryovers, earnings and profits, capital loss carryovers and accounting methods. Special operating rules are contained in § 381(b).

One of the most significant carryover tax attributes of the acquired corporation tends to be its net operating loss (NOL). Section 382, which restricts the use of NOLs in certain circumstances, originated in the 1954 Code as a response to a perceived problem of "trafficking" in NOLs, *i.e.*, the tax-motivated acquisition of a corporation in order to take advantage of its NOLs. As a policy matter, it may be argued that NOLs should be freely transferable, without restriction on the availability of these attributes to the acquiring corporation. If free trading were permitted, taxpayers who could not use their NOLs could derive the full economic benefit of the NOLs by selling their assets to a purchaser at an increased price reflecting the tax value of the NOLs. On the other hand, free trading in tax attributes may be viewed as a windfall to the purchaser because the increase in the purchase price attributable to the NOLs would presumably be less than the tax savings generated by the NOLs. The 1986 Act completely rewrote § 382 in an attempt to ensure that a change of ownership or combination affecting a loss corporation would neither enhance nor impair the value of its carryovers.

## § 2.  Overview of § 382

The provisions of § 382 come into play only if a loss corporation undergoes a significant change of ownership. After an ownership change, § 382 limits the amount of the old loss corporation's "pre-change losses" that may be used to offset post-change taxable income of the new loss corporation for any subsequent taxable year. The term "pre-change loss" includes NOL carryforwards that arose before the year of the ownership change, an allocable portion of the NOLs incurred during the year of the ownership change, and certain unrealized built-in losses and deductions. §§ 382(d) and 382(h)(1)(B). The statute uses the terms "old loss corporation" and "new loss corporation" to refer to a loss corporation before and after the ownership change, respectively. §§ 382(k)(2) and 382(k)(3).

The same corporation may be both the old loss corporation and the new loss corporation, *e.g.*, if the ownership change that triggers § 382 involves a shift in the stock ownership of a single corporation.

Section 382(b) defines the annual limitation generally as equal to the value of the old loss corporation multiplied by the long-term tax-exempt rate (published monthly by the Service). The annual § 382 limitation is intended to approximate the amount of income that the loss corporation could have earned, absent an ownership change, if it had invested its equity in tax-exempt securities. This "limitation on earnings" approach contrasts markedly with the old § 382 rules which reduced or eliminated the amount of losses that could be carried over.

*Example:* A loss corporation (L) is merged into a profitable corporation (P) in a transaction which triggers § 382. Immediately before the merger, the value of L is $900 and the tax-exempt rate is 10%. The annual limit under § 382(b) will be $90 (10% of $900). To the extent that there is insufficient income to absorb the entire $90 of available losses in any year, the excess amount of the loss will be carried forward to the next year. § 382(b)(2). The higher the loss in relationship to the loss corporation's value, the longer the period over which use of the losses will be spread.

## § 3. Definition of Ownership Change

(a) *General.* The triggering event under § 382 is an "ownership change," as defined in § 382(g). An ownership change requires two components. The first component may consist of either (i) an "owner shift" involving a 5% shareholder or (ii) an "equity structure shift" (referred to as "testing events"). The second component is an increase of more than 50 percentage points in the stock ownership of the loss corporation by one or more 5% shareholders (referred to as a "triggering event") within a 3–year testing period. Regulations § 1.382–2T contain an exhaustive discussion of ownership changes.

(b) *Owner Shift*. An owner shift is defined as any change in the ownership of stock in a loss corporation which affects the holdings of a 5% shareholder (generally, any person owning 5% or more of the loss corporation's stock, directly or by attribution, during the testing period). The percentage of stock owned is based on fair market value. An owner shift may be triggered by a stock purchase, issuance of stock, § 351 exchange or redemption. Certain transfers, however, cannot give rise to an owner shift: transfers between an individual and family members, gifts, bequests, and transfers incident to divorce. § 382(*l*)(3)(A)–(B). Any change in a shareholder's percentage ownership attributable solely to fluctuations in the relative fair market value of different classes of stock is not taken into account. § 382(*l*)(3)(C).

(c) *Equity Structure Shift*. An equity structure shift includes any A, B, C, non-divisive D, or E reorganization. Section 382(g)(3)(B) contemplates Regulations that may treat taxable reorganizations, public offerings and similar transactions as equity structure shifts. Under the current Regulations, a loss corporation is only required to determine whether an ownership change has occurred immediately after an owner shift. Reg. § 1.382–2(a)(4). Thus, an equity structure shift has no operative significance.

(d) *Ownership Change.* After each testing event, the loss corporation must determine whether there has been an increase of more than 50 percentage points in the stock ownership of a 5% shareholder within the 3–year testing period immediately preceding the testing event. Thus, a series of unrelated transfers within the 3–year period may trigger § 382. Each testing event gives rise to a separate 3–year testing period ending on the date of such testing event, but no testing period extends back further than the most recent preceding ownership change.

(e) *Public Groups.* A loss corporation may have a group of shareholders none of whom owns as much as 5% of the corporation's stock. Rather than ignore the less-than-5% shareholders, § 382(g)(4)(A) aggregates such shareholders and treats them as a single hypothetical shareholder (referred to as a "public group"). *See* Reg. § 1.382–2T(f)(13). Tranfers of stock among members of a public group (*i.e.*, less-than-5% shareholders) are not treated as owner shifts and cannot give rise to ownership changes. For certain purposes (*e.g.*, a reorganization or a redemption), a public group may be divided into 2 or more public groups, constituting separate 5% shareholders. § 382(g)(4)(B). Generally, members of one public group are presumed not to be members of any other public group. *See* Reg. § 1.382–2T(j)(1)(iii). In the case of a public offering solely for cash, however, the Regulations create a presumption of 50% cross-ownership, thereby reducing the likelihood of an ownership change. *See* Reg. § 1.382–3(j)(3).

(f) *Examples.* The types of transactions that trigger § 382 are best illustrated by the extreme cases of closely held and publicly held loss corporations.

*Example (1):* Three unrelated individuals, A, B, and C, each own 50 of the 150 shares of outstanding stock of loss corporation L. Any change in stock ownership will be an owner shift because A, B, and C are all 5% shareholders. Assume that A sells her ⅓ stock interest to D (an unrelated individual) on January 1, 1997. D's acquisition of A's stock will be an owner shift involving a 5% shareholder, but will not trigger an ownership change because D's percentage ownership increases only 33⅓ percentage points (from 0 to 33⅓%). If B sells her ⅓ stock interest to E (another unrelated individual) on January 1, 1998, there will be a second testing event. Since D and E together have increased their percentage ownership in L by more than 50 percentage points (from 0 to 66⅔%), there will be an ownership change on January 1, 1998. If C sells her ⅓ stock interest to E on February 1, 1998, there will not be a second ownership change on that date because the testing period for the February 1 transfer extends back only to January 2, 1998 (the day following the most recent preceding ownership change).

*Example (2):* Loss corporation L is a publicly owned corporation. All 1,000 shares of L's stock are owned by 100 unrelated shareholders, none of whom owns as much as 5% of the L stock (Public L). If various members of Public L sell 30% of L's stock to individual A on January 1, 1997, there will be an owner shift (but not an ownership change) because A's stock ownership increases from 0 to 30%. After the transfer to A, L will have two 5% shareholders, A (who owns 30% individually) and Public L (which owns the remaining 70%). Assume that during 1998 each of the remaining individuals in Public L sells her stock to other unrelated individuals, none of whom acquires as much as 5%. Since public trading among non–5% shareholders is disregarded, the sales by members of Public L will not constitute an ownership change. *See* Reg. § 1.382–2T(e)(1)(iii), Example (3).

*Example (3):* The facts are the same as in Example (2), except that L makes a public offering of its stock on January 1, 1997. Pursuant to the public offering, 2,000 additional shares of L stock are sold to new investors, none of whom acquires as much as 5% of L's stock. The Regulations divide L's stockholders into two public ownership groups, the pre-public offering group (Public L) and the new investors acquiring L stock pursuant to the public offering (New Public L). In the absence of any overlapping ownership, the public offering would trigger an ownership change because New Public L's stock ownership would increase by 66⅔ percentage points. Because of the 50% cross-ownership presumption, however, Public L is deemed to have acquired half of the newly-issued stock. Reg. § 1.382–3(j)(13), Example (2). Accordingly, New

Public L's stock ownership increases by only 33⅓ percentage points and there is no ownership change. After the public offering, L will have two hypothetical 5% shareholders, Public L and New Public L.

*Example (4):* Loss corporation L is merged into profitable corporation P in an A reorganization. Before the merger, shareholder A owns all the stock of L and shareholder B owns all the stock of P. As a result of the merger, A receives 25% of P's stock, with B retaining the rest of P's stock. The merger is an equity structure shift which is also an owner shift. There is also a triggering ownership change because B is deemed to have acquired 75% of L in the merger. *See* Reg. § 1.382–2T(j)(2)(iii)(B)(2), Example (1). Since the old loss corporation disappears as a result of the merger, the acquiring corporation is regarded as the new loss corporation and becomes entitled to the old loss corporation's pre-change losses, subject to the § 382 limitation. To avoid an ownership change, A must receive at least 50% of the P stock in the merger, because this would prevent B's deemed increased ownership from exceeding 50 percentage points.

*Example (5):* The facts are the same as in Example (4) except that L and P are both publicly held corporations, and no single shareholder of either corporation (Public L and Public P) owns 5% of L or P stock. On January 1, 1997, L is merged into P in an A reorganization, and the L shareholders receive 50% of P's stock. The merger is an equity structure shift which is also an owner shift. Section

382(g)(4)(B)(i) requires that Public L and Public P be treated as separate hypothetical 5% shareholders. Since Public P has increased its percentage ownership in L by just 50 percentage points, the equity structure shift does not constitute an ownership change. After the merger, Public P and Public L will continue to be treated as two separate 5% shareholders.

*Example (6)*: Loss corporation L has 1,000 shareholders (Public L), each of whom owns one share of L's outstanding stock. Pursuant to a redemption, L acquires 250 shares of its stock for cash. Public L must be divided into 2 separate public groups, consisting of the redeemed shareholders (Public RL) and the continuing shareholders (Public CL). There is no ownership change, however, because Public CL's ownership interest has increased by only 25 percentage points, *i.e.*, from 75% pre-redemption (750/1,000 shares) to 100% post-redemption (750/750 shares). *See* Reg. § 1.382–2T(j)(2)(iii)(C)(2), Example (1).

## § 4. Attribution and Tracing Rules

In determining stock ownership, the attribution rules of § 318 generally apply, with the following modifications (unless otherwise provided by Regulations). First, an individual and all family members (as defined in § 318(a)(1)) are aggregated and treated as one individual. § 382(*l*)(3)(A)(i). Thus, if a father sells stock to his daughter, the sale is disregarded and does not cause an owner shift. Second, stock owned by various entities (corporations, partnerships, trusts or estates) is attributed to the beneficial owners in proportion to their beneficial interests, regardless of the size of such interests, and is not treated as owned by the entity. § 382($l$)(3)(A)(ii). Third, stock is not attributed from a beneficial owner to an entity. § 382($l$)(3)(A)(iii). Fourth, an option to acquire stock is treated as exercised if such exercise would cause an ownership change. § 382($l$)(3)(A)(iv). The Regulations treat an entity that owns less than 5% of the loss corporation's stock as an unrelated individual, *i.e.*, stock owned by such an entity will not be attributed from the entity to its beneficial owners. *See* Reg. § 1.382–2T(h)(2)(iii). The purpose of these rules is to track the ultimate beneficial ownership of stock.

*Example:* A, who owns all of the stock of a loss corporation (L), creates a new corporation (X) to which A contributes her L stock in exchange for all of X's stock. There is no owner shift because all of X's L stock is treated as owned by A, not X. In effect, X is "looked through" for purposes of determining beneficial ownership of the L stock.

A loss corporation may generally rely on required filings under the Securities and Exchange Act of 1934 to determine the identity of 5% or more shareholders. Reg. § 1.382–2T(k)(1)(i). To the extent that the loss corporation has actual knowledge of stock ownership, it must take such actual knowledge into account. Reg. § 1.382–2T(k)(2). The Regulations do not define "actual knowledge" or provide any guidance as to when a loss corporation will be deemed to have actual knowledge concerning stock ownership. Although mere negligence clearly should not trigger this provision, "reckless disregard" of the facts might be sufficient. The loss corporation must also file annual statements with its tax return which identify any testing events and ownership changes during the year. Reg. § 1.382–2T(a)(2)(ii).

## § 5.  Definition of Stock

(a) *General*.  The term "stock" generally includes any type of equity interest, except straight preferred stock (*i.e.*, nonvoting, nonconvertible stock which is limited and preferred as to dividends, does not participate in corporate growth to any significant extent and does not have an unreasonable liquidation or redemption premium). §§ 382(k)(6)(A) and 1504(a)(4). Thus, straight preferred stock is disregarded in testing ownership changes, but is included in determining the value of the loss corporation. Furthermore, certain equity interests that nominally constitute stock (*e.g.*, voting preferred stock) may be disregarded and certain "non-stock" interests (*e.g.*, options and convertible debt) may be treated as "stock." § 382(k)(6)(B). *See also* Reg. § 1.382–2T(f)(18).

(b) *Worthless Stock*.  Section 382(g)(4)(D) treats a 50%-or-more shareholder who claims a worthless-stock deduction as having acquired such stock from an unrelated person, potentially triggering an ownership change. This provision is intended to curtail the double benefit of a worthless-stock deduction and unrestricted use of the loss corporation's NOLs.

## § 6.  Value After Redemptions and Bankruptcy Proceedings

Generally, the value of the old loss corporation is the value of all of its outstanding stock (including preferred stock) immediately before an ownership change.  § 382(e)(1).  In the case of redemptions and similar transactions, however, the value is determined immediately after the ownership change. § 382(e)(2).  Thus, if a loss corporation is acquired in a "bootstrap" acquisition, distributions to redeemed shareholders will reduce the value of the loss corporation (and hence the annual loss limitation).

In the case of insolvency, a loss corporation's value will generally be $0.  If the general rules of § 382 applied, this would effectively eliminate all NOLs after an ownership change.  Section 382($l$)(5), however, provides special rules for loss corporations involved in bankruptcy or similar proceedings.  The effect of these special rules is generally that losses will not be limited after an ownership change, if at least 50% of the loss corporation's stock immediately after the change is owned by former shareholders and certain long-term creditors.  § 382($l$)(5)(A).  The loss corporation's NOLs must be reduced by interest deductions for the prior 3 years attributable to debt converted to equity, on the theory that the creditors were already de facto shareholders.  § 382($l$)(5)(B).  If a second ownership change occurs within 2 years after the initial ownership change, the § 382 loss limitation is re-

duced to zero for any year ending after the second
ownership change.   § 382(*l*)(5)(D).

Because of the interest cutback and limit on
subsequent ownership changes, a loss corporation
may choose to elect out of § 382(*l*)(5).   *See*
§ 382(*l*)(5)(H).   If § 382(*l*)(5) does not apply, the
value of the loss corporation is determined under
§ 382(*l*)(6) immediately after the insolvency transaction.   Thus, the § 382 limit reflects the increase
in value of the loss corporation attributable to surrender or cancellation of creditors' claims.

## § 7.  Anti-Stuffing Rules

Congress was concerned that a loss corporation's
value might be artificially inflated by additional
capital contributions prior to the ownership change.
Under the anti-stuffing rules, any capital contribution made as part of a plan with a principal purpose
of avoiding or increasing the § 382 loss limitation is
disregarded in determining the value of the loss
corporation.   § 382(*l*)(1)(A).   For this purpose, any
capital contribution made within 2 years before the
ownership change is presumed to be part of such a
plan.   § 382(*l*)(1)(B).   The legislative history provides that Regulations may exempt certain contributions made for business purposes.

## § 8.  Reduction of Value for Investment As-
### sets

If ⅓ or more of a corporation's assets are "non-
business" assets (*i.e.*, cash and investment assets),
the value of the loss corporation is reduced by the

value of those assets (net of any allocable debt) for purposes of the § 382 loss limitation.  § 382(*l*)(4). A corporation that owns at least 50% of the stock of a subsidiary, however, is treated as owning its ratable share of the subsidiary's assets rather than the subsidiary's stock.  § 382(*l*)(4)(E).  In some instances, it may be unclear whether certain types of assets (*e.g.*, real estate) are passive investment assets or operating assets.

## § 9.  Increase for Recognized Built-In Gains

If a loss corporation has a substantial "net unrealized built-in gain" at the time of an ownership change, the § 382 loss limitation is increased by the "recognized built-in gain" for any taxable year within a 5–year "recognition period" following the ownership change. § 382(h).  The § 382 loss limitation is also increased by gain triggered under § 338. § 382(h)(1)(C).  Since the old loss corporation could have used its losses to offset such gains in the absence of the ownership change, it is appropriate to allow the new loss corporation to use such losses similarly.

Net unrealized built-in gain is defined as the amount by which the aggregate fair market value of the corporation's assets exceeds their aggregate basis immediately before the ownership change. § 382(h)(3)(A).  The net unrealized built-in gain is deemed to be zero, however, unless it exceeds the lesser of (i) 15% of the fair market value of the corporation's assets (other than cash and certain marketable     securities)    or    (ii)   $10,000,000.

§ 382(h)(3)(B).  For example, the 15% threshold requirement is met if the corporation has assets with an aggregate fair market value of $4,000,000 and an aggregate basis of $3,200,000, because the appreciation ($800,000) exceeds 15% of $4,000,000 ($600,000).  Recognized built-in gain is any gain attributable to disposition of an asset held by the old loss corporation, to the extent that such gain does not exceed the unrealized built-in gain attributable to the asset on the date of the ownership change.  § 382(h)(2).  The total increase in the § 382 loss limitation for recognized built-in gain during the 5–year recognition period may not exceed the net unrealized built-in gain immediately before the ownership change.  § 382(h)(1)(A)(ii).  In the case of installment sales, the 5–year recognition period may be extended.  *See* Notice 90–27.

## § 10.  Limit on Net Built-In Losses

Section 382 limits the recognition of net built-in losses as well as NOLs.  If a corporation has net unrealized built-in losses, § 382(h) subjects those losses to the § 382 limitation if they are realized within a 5–year recognition period following the ownership change.  § 382(h)(1)(B).  As in the case of built-in gains, built-in losses are determined immediately before the ownership change and must meet the 15% (or $10,000,000) threshold requirement.  § 382(h)(3).  If a corporation has a built-in gain of $50 for one asset and a built-in loss of $100 for another asset, the net unrealized built-in loss is $50.  If a built-in loss is disallowed under § 382 for a taxable year, that loss may be carried over and

used in a later year, subject to the § 382 limit.
§ 382(h)(4). Built-in depreciation deductions are
generally treated as built-in losses. § 382(h)(2)(B).

## § 11.  Continuity of Business Enterprise

Under § 382(c), loss carryovers are retroactively
reduced to zero if the new loss corporation fails to
continue the business enterprise of the old loss
corporation for the 2–year period beginning on the
ownership change. The business continuity test is
the same as for tax-free reorganizations under Regulations § 1.368–1(d), *i.e.*, the new loss corporation
must either continue the old loss corporation's business or must use a significant portion of the old loss
corporation's assets in a business. If the business
continuity test is not met, § 382(c)(2) nevertheless
allows loss carryforwards to the extent of recognized built-in gains and § 338 gains.

## § 12.  Section 383 Limit on Other Items

Upon an ownership change with respect to a loss
corporation, § 383 limits certain other items (unused general business credits, unused minimum tax
credits, capital loss carryforwards and foreign tax
credits) under rules similar to those of § 382. The
Regulations provide rules for coordinating the limitations under §§ 382 and 383. *See* Reg. § 1.383–
1T.

## § 13.  Section 384 Limit on Sheltering Built–In Gains

Section 384 limits a corporation's ability to offset
built-in gains against "preacquisition losses" (*i.e.*,

NOLs and built-in losses) of another corporation during a 5–year recognition period following certain stock or asset acquisitions. § 384. The stock acquisition rule applies if one corporation acquires "control" of another corporation and either corporation is a gain corporation (*i.e.*, a corporation with a net unrealized built-in gain at the time of acquisition). Control is defined as stock representing 80% of the voting power and value of a corporation within the meaning of § 1504(a)(2). The asset acquisition rules apply to any tax-free A, C or D reorganization if either the acquired or acquiring corporation is a gain corporation. A special rule for successor corporations ensures that the § 384 limitation remains applicable if one corporation is liquidated tax-free into another corporation under § 332. Section 384 does not apply if both corporations were under common control (using a more-than-50% ownership test) during the previous 5–year period (or the entire period of the gain or loss corporation's existence, if shorter).

If § 384 applies, preacquisition losses may not be used to offset built-in gains which are recognized during the 5–year recognition period; this restriction does not apply, however, to preacquisition losses of a gain corporation. *See* § 384(a)(parenthetical phrase). Thus, a gain corporation may use its preacquisition losses to offset its own built-in gain. Prior to the enactment of § 384, loss corporations were generally permitted to use their losses against income of an acquired profitable business, subject to the § 382 restriction that the loss corporation did not undergo a significant change of ownership. Section 384 adopts a different approach: it prevents melding of pre-acquisition losses and built-gains through corporate combinations, regardless of whether the acquiring corporation has net built-in gain or loss. If both provisions apply, the § 382 limit is applied before determining the § 384 limit.

Section 384 derives much of its terminology from § 382. *See* § 384(c)(8). As under § 382(h)(3), the threshold for determining whether a corporation has net unrealized built-in gain (or loss) is the lesser of 15% of the fair market value of the corporation's non-cash assets or $10,000,000. Under § 384, gain from disposition of an asset is presumed to be recognized built-in gain, unless the corporation demonstrates otherwise. § 384(c)(1)(A). By contrast, the corporation bears the burden of showing that gain from disposition of an asset is recognized built-in gain under § 382. While recognized built-in gain increases the § 382 limit, it is disadvantageous for purposes of the § 384 limit.

*Example (1):* Gain corporation G is acquired by loss corporation L in a transaction which is subject to § 384 (but not § 382). The two corporations subsequently file a consolidated return. G has a net unrealized built-in gain of $200,000 and L has an NOL of $500,000. In the first post-acquisition year, G recognizes a $50,000 built-in gain. L's loss carryforward cannot be used to offset any portion of G's gain. In the second post-acquisition year, G realizes a gain of $200,000. Only $150,000 ($200,-000 net unrealized built-in gain less $50,000 previously recognized built-in gain) of the $200,000 gain is treated as a recognized built-in gain subject to § 384. Since G has recognized its entire net unrealized built-in gain, L's $500,000 NOL may be used to offset G's remaining $50,000 of gain (and any subsequent gains) until the NOL is used up or expires.

*Example (2)*: The facts are the same as in Example (1), above, except that G also has an NOL of $50,000. Since G is a gain corporation, its preacquisition loss of $50,000 may be used to offset its built-in gain of $50,000 during the first post-acquisition year.

## § 14. Relationship of § 269 and §§ 382–384

Section 269 authorizes the Service to deny certain tax benefits following an acquisition of control of a corporation or a tax-free acquisition of a corporation's assets, if the principal purpose of the acquisition was tax evasion or avoidance. Although § 269 remains in full force, its role is greatly reduced because §§ 382–384 automatically limit the desired tax benefits in nearly all transactions within the scope of § 269. The Regulations provide that § 269 may nevertheless disallow a deduction or credit that is limited or reduced under § 382 or § 383; the §§ 382 and 383 limitations are relevant, however, in determining whether the principal purpose of the acquisition is tax avoidance. Prop. Reg. § 1.269–7.

Section 269(b) focuses narrowly on tax-motivated liquidations pursuant to a plan adopted within 2 years of a "qualified stock purchase" for which no

§ 338 election is made. Congress was concerned
that former § 269 might literally not apply to such
transactions, since the liquidation rather than the
acquisition was tax motivated. The potential abuse
addressed by § 269(b), however, is relatively remote. In the absence of a § 338 election, an acquiring corporation inherits the § 382 limit applicable
to the acquired corporation following a § 332 liquidation. *See* § 382(*l*)(8). Alternatively, an acquiring corporation may elect § 338 and use the acquired corporation's NOLs to eliminate gain on the
deemed asset sale. Since the failure to elect § 338
is unlikely to be abusive under these circumstances,
the role of § 269(b) is quite limited. *See* Prop. Reg.
§ 1.269–7.

Other statutory provisions and judicial doctrines
may limit the use of NOLs. For example, § 172(h)
limits NOL carrybacks created by interest deductions attributable to a "corporate equity reduction
transaction" (CERT), as discussed in Chapter 8.
The legislative history of the 1986 Act notes specifically that the judicially-developed doctrine of *Libson
Shops* (S.Ct.1957)(limiting use of loss carryovers to
income of the same business that generated the
losses) does not apply to transactions covered by
§ 382.

# CHAPTER 12

# SUBCHAPTER S

## § 1. Introduction

Subchapter S (now §§ 1361–1379), originally added to the Code in 1958 and amended in 1982, is intended to minimize federal income tax considerations in deciding whether to conduct a business in the form of a corporation, partnership or other entity. A corporation that elects Subchapter S treatment (an "S corporation") is roughly comparable to a partnership for federal income tax purposes: in each case, the entity's income (whether or not actually distributed) and losses generally pass through directly to shareholders, without being separately taxed at the entity level.

The analogy between the "pass-through" treatment of S corporations under Subchapter S and partnerships under Subchapter K, however, is imperfect. An S corporation represents a hybrid of corporate and partnership-type characteristics, and remains subject to the rules of Subchapter C except to the extent preempted by those of Subchapter S or otherwise made inapplicable. § 1371(a). Section 1371(a)(2) provides that an S corporation in its capacity as a shareholder of another corporation is treated as an individual. This provision is intended to deny S corporations the benefit of certain provisions applicable to C corporations, such as the § 243 dividends-received deduction, if the result would be inconsistent with pass-through treatment. Although the precise scope of § 1371(a)(2) is unclear, it does not prevent S corporations from participating in corporate transactions such as § 368 reorganizations, § 332 liquidations and § 338 acquisitions. See GCM 39768; TAM 9245004.

S corporations combine the advantages of corporate business form with those of a single-level income tax. Income from an S corporation's business operations will generally be subject to a single shareholder-level tax at a maximum rate of 39.6%, which is less burdensome than the double-level tax (as high as approximately 61%) imposed on C corporations. Even if a corporation retains its earnings for its own growth, an S corporation will generally bear a lower tax burden in the long run because its retained earnings can be distributed tax free in a liquidation or on a sale of the shareholder's stock.

## § 2. Eligibility

(a) *General.* An S corporation is defined as a "small business corporation" for which a Subchapter S election is in effect. § 1361(a)(1). A small business corporation is a domestic corporation with only one class of stock and no more than 35 shareholders; each shareholder must be an individual (other than a nonresident alien), an estate or an eligible trust. § 1361(b)(1). Moreover, an S corporation must not be an "ineligible corporation," defined in § 1361(b)(2) to include members of an affiliated group, financial institutions and certain other entities. For purposes of the 35–shareholder limit, a husband and wife (and their respective estates) are treated as a single shareholder, regardless of whether they hold stock jointly or separately. § 1361(c)(1). All other co-owners are treated as separate shareholders. Reg. § 1.1361–1(e).

The Service has ruled that use of a partnership of S corporations does not violate the purpose of the 35–shareholder limit. Rev. Rul. 94–43. According to the Service, the 35–shareholder limit is intended to preserve administrative simplicity. Under this "purpose" analysis, the S status of corporate partners should be respected, since a partnership arrangement does not undermine administrative simplicity at the S corporation level. Whether partnerships may be used to circumvent other S limitations may thus depend on the purpose of the particular provision.

(b) *Trusts as Shareholders.* Eligible trusts include grantor-type trusts treated under §§ 671–678 as owned by an individual who is a United States citizen or resident. § 1361(c)(2)(A). In addition, eligible trusts include "qualified Subchapter S trusts," essentially trusts having a single current income beneficiary who makes a timely election to have the provisions of § 1361(d) apply. A typical trust of this sort is a "qualified terminable interest property" trust established for the benefit of a decedent's surviving spouse and qualifying for the estate-tax marital deduction. *See* Reg. § 1.1361–1(j)(4).

(c) *One-Class-of-Stock Requirement.* The one-class-of-stock requirement is designed to ensure that each share of stock represents an equal share in the profits and assets of the corporation, and obviates the need to allocate income among different classes of stock. After much controversy, the Treasury issued final Regulations in 1992 on the one-class-of-stock requirement. Reg. § 1.1361–1($l$). Generally, a corporation has only one class of stock if "all outstanding shares ... confer identical rights to distribution and liquidation proceeds." Reg. § 1.1361–1($l$)(1). A corporation will not be treated as having more than one class of stock merely because of differences in voting rights among the shares of common stock. § 1361(c)(4). Also, stock of a second class that is authorized but unissued does not violate the one-class-of-stock requirement. *See* Reg. § 1.1361–1($l$)(3). *See also* Reg. § 1.1361–1(b)(3)(restricted stock).

The determination of whether all outstanding shares of stock confer identical rights to distribution and liquidation proceeds is based on the "governing provisions" (*i.e.*, the corporate charter, articles and bylaws, binding agreements relating to distribution and liquidation proceeds, and applicable state law). Reg. § 1.1361–1($l$)(2)(i). Normal commercial arrangements (*e.g.*, leases, employment contracts, and loans) are generally not treated as governing provisions unless a principal purpose of the arrangement is to circumvent the one-class-of-stock requirement. *Id.* Provided that the governing provisions confer identical rights, distributions that differ in timing or amount do not give rise to a second class of stock but may be recharacterized for other tax purposes (*e.g.*, as a below-market loan under § 7872). *See* Reg. § 1.1361–1(*l*)(2)(v), Example (5). *See also id.*, Example (3)(excessive compensation).

The Regulations generally disregard buy-sell agreements, agreements restricting transferability and redemption agreements unless (i) a principal purpose of the agreement is to circumvent the one-class-of-stock requirement and (ii) the agreement establishes a purchase price that, when the agreement is entered into, is significantly above or below fair market value. Reg. § 1.1361–1(*l*)(2)(iii)(A). An agreement to purchase or redeem stock does give rise to a second class of stock if the price is set at book value or anywhere between fair market value and book value. *Id*. Moreover, the Regulations provide a safe harbor for "bona fide" agreements to purchase stock upon death, divorce, disability or termination of employment. Reg. § 1.1361–1(*l*)(2)(iii)(B).

When a change in stock ownership occurs, distributions that reflect the shareholders' varying interests during the year do not violate the one-class-of-stock requirement. Reg. § 1.1361–1(*l*)(2)(iv). Such distributions should generally occur within a reasonable time to avoid recharacterization for other tax purposes. *Id*. A state-law requirement that the corporation withhold state income taxes on behalf of some shareholders does not give rise to a second class of stock if it affects only the timing (not the amount) of distributions. Reg. § 1.1361–

1(*l*)(2)(ii). In effect, the corporation's payment of state income tax on behalf of some shareholders is treated as a constructive distribution, which must be taken into account in determining whether all shareholders are entitled to equal distributions. Reg. § 1.1361–1(*l*)(2)(v), Example (7). The one-class-of-stock requirement is violated, however, if a corporation attempts to equalize the shareholders' after-tax burdens by distributing greater amounts to those shareholders with heavier state tax burdens. *Id.*, Example (6). Even though the shareholders receive identical after-tax distributions, the arrangement alters their right to equal pre-tax distributions.

Under prior law, the Service often litigated unsuccessfully the issue of whether corporate debt owed to shareholders, if reclassified as equity, counted as a second class of stock. A safe harbor now exists for so-called "straight debt," which will not be treated as a second class of stock for purposes of the one-class-of-stock requirement. § 1361(c)(5). The safe-harbor rules require an unconditional written promise to pay a sum certain in money on demand or on a specified date; the interest rate must not be contingent on profits or on the borrower's discretion; the debt cannot be convertible into stock; and the creditor must be an individual or entity eligible to own stock in an S corporation. *See* Reg. § 1.1361–1(*l*)(5)(i). The safe harbor is available even if straight debt is subordinated to other debt. Reg. § 1.1361–1(*l*)(5)(ii).

The Regulations provide that a debt instrument
will be treated as a second class of stock only if (i)
the debt instrument constitutes equity under general
principles of federal tax law, and (ii) a principal
purpose of issuing the debt instrument (or entering
into the arrangement) is to circumvent the requirement for identical rights to distribution and liquidation proceeds or to circumvent the limitation on
eligible shareholders. Reg. § 1.1361–1(*l*)(4)(ii)(A).
A safe harbor exists for debt instruments held by
shareholders in the same proportion as nominal
stock. Reg. § 1.1361–1(*l*)(4)(ii)(B)(2). An obligation that qualifies under the straight-debt safe
harbor is not treated as a second class of stock,
regardless of whether it constitutes equity under
general principles of federal tax law. Reg.
§ 1.1361–1(*l*)(5)(iv). If straight debt bears an unreasonably high interest rate, however, the purported interest payments may be recharacterized for
other tax purposes. *Id*.

Under the Regulations, hybrid debt-equity instruments are unlikely to be treated as a second class of
stock which would disqualify an S corporation.
This liberal approach seems justified because the
one-class-of-stock requirement is intended primarily
to ensure that an S corporation's capital structure
remains relatively simple.

## § 3.  Election, Revocation and Termination

(a) *Election*.  An S election for any taxable year
may be made during such taxable year on or before
the 15th day of the third month thereof or at any

time during the preceding taxable year. § 1362(b)(1). The timing requirement must be strictly observed: an S election that is filed late is treated as being made for the following taxable year. All persons who are shareholders on the day of the election (and former shareholders, in some cases) must consent. § 1362(a)(2); Reg. § 1.1362–6(b)(3). Once made, an S election remains effective until revoked or terminated.

The Service has generally been lenient in permitting technical defects to be cured, despite the absence of statutory discretion. Taxpayers have occasionally taken advantage of the strict procedural rules to disavow an S election. *See Smith* (Tax Ct.1988)(no "substantial compliance" when original form lacked proper signature). Proposed legislation would authorize the Service to provide relief when an S election is invalid because of untimeliness or inadvertence.

(b) *Revocation.* An S election may be revoked only with the consent of shareholders owning more than half of the corporation's stock on the day of the revocation. § 1362(d)(1)(B); Reg. § 1.1362–2(a)(1). Generally, a revocation takes effect as of the first day of the corporation's current taxable year if made on or before the 15th day of the third month thereof, or as of the first day of the following taxable year if made after the 15th day of the third month. The revocation may, however, specify any prospective effective date. §§ 1362(d)(1)(C) and 1362(d)(1)(D). For example, a revocation filed on April 1 for a calendar-year S corporation will generally be effective on the following January 1; if the revocation specifies April 15 as the effective date, however, it will be effective as of that date.

(c) *Involuntary Termination.* An S election may also be terminated involuntarily if the corporation ceases to be a "small business corporation," *e.g.*, because stock is transferred to a nonresident alien or a partnership. § 1362(d)(2); Reg. § 1.1362–2(b)(1). An inadvertent termination may be disregarded if action is promptly taken to requalify the corporation as a small business corporation and the shareholders agree to make any required adjustments. § 1362(f); Reg. § 1.1362–4(a). *See* Rev. Proc. 94–23 (automatic inadvertent termination relief). An involuntary termination may also occur if an S corporation (with accumulated e & p from operations as a C corporation) for 3 consecutive taxable years has passive investment income exceeding 25% of gross receipts. § 1362(d)(3). In addition to automatic termination, the corporation is subject to a penalty tax on "excess net passive income" under § 1375, discussed in § 8 below.

(d) *Effect of Termination.* If a revocation or involuntary termination takes effect in mid-year, the corporation's taxable year is divided into 2 short years, representing the portion of the year preceding the effective date (the "S short year") and the portion of the year beginning on the effective date (the "C short year"), respectively. § 1362(e). *See* Reg. § 1.1362–3. Generally, items of income, loss, deduction and credit are allocated between the S short year and C short year in proportion to the number of days in the respective short years (the daily allocation rule). § 1362(e)(2). Alternatively, if all persons who were shareholders at any time during the S short year and on the first day of the C short year so elect, items may be allocated to the respective short years based on normal tax accounting rules (the specific allocation rule). § 1362(e)(3). If more than 50% of the corporation's stock is sold or exchanged during the termination year, then the specific allocation rule is mandatory. § 1362(e)(6)(D). The corporation's tax liability for the C short year must be computed on an annualized basis, thereby preventing the corporation from exploiting the low corporate tax brackets. § 1362(e)(5)(A).

(e) *Election After Termination*. After revocation or involuntary termination of an S election, the corporation is ineligible to make a new election for a 5–year period without the consent of the Service. § 1362(g). *See* Reg. § 1.1362–5.

## § 4. Taxable Year and Accounting Methods

An S corporation's income or loss flows through to a shareholder in his taxable year in which (or with which) the corporation's taxable year ends. § 1366(a). For example, if the S corporation's first taxable year begins on February 1, 1997 and ends on January 31, 1998, an individual shareholder will report income for that period in his individual return for calendar year 1998. In effect, the corporation's fiscal year permits a deferral of tax at the shareholder level on the first 11 months of the corporation's income.

To eliminate such deferral, § 1378 requires that an S corporation use a calendar year unless it establishes a business purpose (other than deferral of income to shareholders) for a different fiscal year. *See* Rev. Proc. 87–32 (guidelines for requests to adopt, retain or change taxable years). The 1987 Act left § 1378 unchanged, but added two new provisions, §§ 444 and 7519. Under § 444, an S corporation may elect a fiscal year that results in no more than 3 months of deferral at the shareholder level (generally, a taxable year ending in September, October or November). The price of the election is that the entity must pay a tax under § 7519 intended to compensate for the shareholder-level deferral attributable to the § 444 election.

An S corporation is generally not subject to the mandatory accrual accounting method under § 448. Moreover, under § 267(e)(1), an S corporation and any person who owns (directly or indirectly) any of its stock are treated as related parties within the meaning of § 267(b). As a result, an S corporation is not permitted to deduct salary payments to a shareholder until such payments are includible in the shareholder's income. *See* § 267(a)(2).

## § 5. Pass–Through of Income or Loss

(a) *General.* Generally, an S corporation is treated as a conduit, and is not subject to corporate-level tax except for special taxes imposed under §§ 1374 and 1375. Taxable income of an S corporation, which flows through to the shareholders, is computed in the same manner as that of an individual with certain modifications. § 1363(b). Under § 1366(a)(1), each shareholder must report his pro-rata share of the corporation's separately and non-separately stated items of income, loss, deduction or credit. Separately-stated items are those which could affect the tax liability of different shareholders differently depending on their particular tax situations, *e.g.*, capital gain, § 1231 gain, charitable contributions, and tax-exempt income. All other items (*e.g.*, operating income) are combined at the corporate level, and passed through to shareholders as an item of non-separately stated net income or loss. Each item included in a shareholder's pro-rata share has the same character as in the hands of the corporation. § 1366(b).

(b) *Basis Adjustments to Stock and Debt.* A shareholder's basis in stock and debt of an S corporation is important in determining the amount of losses and deductions that can be passed through, as well as the tax treatment of corporate distributions, sales or exchanges of stock, and repayment or retirement of debt. Initially, a shareholder's basis in stock acquired in a § 351 transaction is the amount of cash or the adjusted basis of any property contributed to the S corporation, adjusted for any liabilities assumed or taken subject to. § 358. Under § 1367(a)(1), a shareholder's stock basis is increased by separately and non-separately stated items of income. *See* Reg. § 1.1367–1(b). Under § 1367(a)(2), stock basis is decreased by separately and non-separately stated items of loss and deduction, tax-free § 1368 corporate distributions, and items of expense which are neither deductible to the corporation in computing its income nor properly capitalized (*e.g.*, a bribe or illegal payment). *See* Reg. § 1.1367–1(c).

*Example:* A, an individual, contributes $10,000 to X, a newly-formed calendar-year S corporation, in exchange for all of its stock. In Year 1, X earns $5,000 of taxable income and distributes $1,000 to A on December 31. Under § 1363(a), X is not taxed; under § 1366(a), the $5,000 of income passes through and is taxed directly to A. A's original basis in her X stock ($10,000) is first increased by $5,000 under § 1367(a)(1), and then reduced by $1,000 under § 1367(a)(2)(A) to reflect the tax-free distribution to A. *See* § 1368(b). If X instead distributed the $1,000 to A in Year 2 (and had no taxable income that year), the result would be the same. If X had an operating loss rather than operating income of $5,000 in Year 1, the loss would flow through to A, who could use it to offset $5,000 of otherwise taxable income, subject to the at-risk and passive loss limitations of §§ 465 and 469. The loss would also reduce A's basis in her stock from $10,000 to $5,000 under § 1367(a)(2)(B).

Adjustments to stock basis are determined on a per-share, per-day basis. § 1377(a)(1); Reg. § 1.1367–1(b)(2). A shareholder's basis in stock may not be reduced below zero. § 1367(a)(2). If stock is acquired at different times, some shares may have positive bases when the bases of other shares have been fully recovered. Whenever downward adjustments applicable to a particular share exceed its basis, the excess is applied to the shareholder's other shares in proportion to their bases. Reg. § 1.1367–1(c)(3).

*Example*: A, an individual, owns 2 of the 5 outstanding shares of X, a calendar-year S corporation. One of A's shares has a basis of $5 and the other has a basis of $10, so that the aggregate basis of A's stock is $15. During the year, X has no income and incurs a loss of $20; A's allocable share of the loss is $8 ($4 per share). After the basis of each share is reduced by $4, the adjusted bases of A's shares are $1 and $6, respectively. If X had instead incurred a loss of $30, A's allocable share of the loss would be $12 ($6 per share). Accordingly, the basis of one of A's shares would be reduced from $5 to zero; the remaining $7 of loss would reduce the basis of A's other share from $10 to $3. *See* Reg. § 1.1367–1(g), Example (2).

Once the basis of a shareholder's stock has been reduced to zero, downward adjustments (other than for distributions) are applied against the basis of any indebtedness. § 1367(b)(2)(A); Reg. § 1.1367–2(b)(1). Any net increase in basis is applied first to restore any previous reduction in the basis of debt for taxable years beginning after December 31, 1982, and then to increase the shareholder's stock basis. § 1367(b)(2)(B); Reg. § 1.1367–2(c)(1). For this purpose, the net increase is equal to the excess of all upward adjustments over all downward adjustments (determined after taking distributions into account). If the net increase (before distributions) does not exceed the amount of distributions, there is no net increase. Accordingly, debt basis is restored only after stock basis has been increased to the extent necessary to maximize tax-free distributions. *See* Reg. § 1.1367–2(e), Examples (4)-(5). In the case of multiple indebtedness, any net increase is applied first to restore the basis of debt repaid during the year and then to restore the basis of remaining debt in proportion to outstanding prior reductions. Reg. § 1.1367–2(c)(2).

*Example:* A, an individual, contributes $2,000 to X, a calendar-year S corporation, in exchange for all of its stock, and simultaneously lends $5,000 to X. In Year 1 (after 1982), X has an operating loss of $6,000. Under § 1367(b)(2)(A), A's basis in her stock is first reduced from $2,000 to zero, and the remaining $4,000 of loss is applied to reduce A's basis in the debt from $5,000 to $1,000. In Year 2, X has operating income of $3,000. Under § 1367(b)(2)(B), A's basis in the debt is increased from $1,000 to $4,000, and A's stock basis remains zero. In Year 3, X has operating income of $10,000 and distributes $9,000 to A. After the distribution is taken into account, the net increase in basis is $1,000 ($10,000 income less $9,000 distribution), which is applied to increase A's basis in the debt from $4,000 to $5,000. At year end, A's basis in her stock is zero (zero plus $9,000 income remaining after debt restoration less $9,000 tax-free distribution).

(c) *Shareholder Guarantee.* Corporate debt generally creates basis in the hands of a shareholder only if it runs directly from the corporation to the shareholder. Moreover, the shareholder must make an actual economic outlay; for example, a shareholder who merely delivers his promissory note to the corporation receives no basis. Rev. Rul. 81–187. *But see* Lessinger (2d Cir.1989). An S shareholder, unlike a partner, does not receive basis for debts incurred by the corporation to third-party lenders. A shareholder guarantee of third-party debt ordinarily does not provide basis until the shareholder actually makes payments under the guarantee, or shareholder notes are substituted for corporate notes to the lender. *See, e.g.,* Rev. Rul. 75–144; Estate of Leavitt (4th Cir.1989); Harris (5th Cir.1990); Uri (10th Cir.1991). Some courts, however, have permitted a basis increase in the guarantee context if the particular facts demonstrate that the lender looks primarily to the shareholder for repayment and the S corporation is thinly capitalized. *See* Selfe (11th Cir.1985).

(d) *Timing of Adjustments*. The adjustments to stock basis are normally determined at the end of the S corporation's taxable year. Reg. § 1.1367–1(d). If stock is sold during the taxable year, however, any adjustments are effective immediately prior to the sale. *Id*. Stock basis is increased by pass-through items of income, and decreased by pass-through items of loss or deduction, before the reduction for distributions. § 1368(d); Reg. § 1.1367–1(e). Proposed legislation would revise these ordering rules so that distributions would reduce stock basis before losses, thereby conforming S treatment to the partnership model.

*Example*: A, an individual, is the sole owner of X (a calendar-year S corporation). At the beginning of the year, A owns 10 shares of X stock with a per-share basis of $5. Half-way through the year, A sells 2 of her 10 shares to B for $20 per share. During the taxable year, X has income of $100. Effective immediately prior to the sale, the basis of each share of stock sold is increased by $5 ($100 income divided by 10 shares, multiplied by ½); accordingly, A reports gain of $10 per share on the stock sale ($20 less $10 basis). In addition, A includes pass-through income of $90 for the taxable year, consisting of $5 of income allocable to each share held for half the year and $10 of income allocable to each share held for the entire year. At year end, the basis of each of A's 8 remaining shares is increased from $5 to $15.

(e) *Termination of Interest.* If any shareholder disposes of his entire interest in an S corporation during the taxable year, the S corporation may elect under § 1377(a)(2) with the consent of all persons who are shareholders during the taxable year to treat its taxable year as if it consisted of two separate taxable years, the first of which ends on the day on which the shareholder's entire interest is terminated. If a terminating election is made, separate-year treatment applies for purposes of allocating items of loss, deduction and credit, making adjustments to various corporate-level accounts, and determining the tax consequences of distributions to shareholders. *See* Prop. Reg. § 1.1377–1(b).

## § 6. Limitation on Losses

(a) *Section 1366(d) Limit.* Section 1366(d)(1) limits the amount of losses or deductions passing through to a shareholder for any taxable year to the sum of (i) the shareholder's aggregate basis in stock of the corporation and (ii) debt owed by the corporation to the shareholder. The purpose of § 1366(d)(1) is to limit the allowable pass-through losses and deductions to the amount of the shareholder's actual investment in the corporation. Any disallowed loss or deduction is carried over indefinitely to subsequent years and may be used when the shareholder's basis is increased through additional capital contributions, loans or net operating income. § 1366(d)(2).

(b) *At-Risk and Passive Loss Limitations.* Individual S shareholders are subject to the at-risk rules of § 465 which limit the amount of loss from certain activities (expanded by the 1986 Act to include real estate activities) allowable as deductions to the aggregate amount the taxpayer has "at risk" in the activity at the close of the taxable year. An S shareholder's amount at risk is initially equal to the amount of personal funds and the adjusted basis of unencumbered property which he contributes to the activity. § 465(b)(1). *See* Prop. Reg. §§ 1.465–22(a) and 1.465–23(a). Amounts borrowed for use in the activity (*e.g.*, funds borrowed by an S shareholder and lent to the corporation) increase the shareholder's amount at risk only to the extent that he is personally liable for repayment of the borrowed amount or has pledged property not used in the activity as security. § 465(b)(2). An S shareholder is generally not considered at risk for debt owed by the corporation to third parties, even if the shareholder guarantees the debt. Prop. Reg. §§ 1.465–24(a) and 1.465–6(d). An S shareholder's amount at risk is increased by any pass-through income (including tax-exempt income), and correspondingly decreased by any pass-through losses, distributions and repayment of debt. Prop. Reg. §§ 1.465–22(b), 1.465–22(c), and 1.465–23(c). If losses exceed the S shareholder's amount at risk at the end of the taxable year, such excess losses are suspended and carried over indefinitely until the shareholder's amount at risk is increased. § 465(a)(2); Prop. Reg. § 1.465–2.

Individual S shareholders are also subject to the passive activity loss limitations of § 469. A passive activity generally includes any rental activity and any other trade or business in which the taxpayer (S corporation shareholder) does not "materially participate"; rental activities are treated as passive activities without regard to material participation. § 469(c); *but see* § 469(c)(7)(exception for real property developers). A taxpayer is treated as "materially participating" if he satisfies any one of 7 alternative tests (including participation in the activity for more than 500 hours in the year). Temp. Reg. § 1.469–5T(a). Passive activity losses may generally be used only to offset income from passive activities, not income from active sources or portfolio income (*e.g.*, dividends, interest and royalties). A special rule, however, permits an individual to offset non-passive income by up to $25,000 of losses from rental real estate activities in which the individual "actively participates." § 469(i). Passive losses and credits that cannot be used for the current taxable year are "suspended" and carried over indefinitely to subsequent years. Suspended passive losses are recognized and may be used to offset any other income on a fully taxable disposition of the taxpayer's entire interest in the activity. § 469(g)(1)(A).

The at-risk and passive loss rules serve as additional limitations on an S shareholder's ability to deduct losses passed through from the S corporation. The shareholder's basis is reduced under § 1367 regardless of whether the loss is subject to further limitation under § 465 or § 469. Similarly, the shareholder's amount at risk under § 465 is reduced regardless of whether the loss is suspended under § 469. The shareholder's basis and amount at risk are not further reduced, however, when the loss is ultimately allowed under § 469.

*Example:* A contributed $20,000 to X (a calendar-year S corporation) in exchange for X stock. X is engaged in an at-risk activity in which A does not materially participate. In Year 1, A's share of X's operating loss is $50,000. Since the loss ($50,000) exceeds A's amount at risk ($20,000), A may deduct only $20,000 of loss currently. Even if the $20,000 loss is subject to further limitation under § 469, A's stock basis and amount at risk are reduced to zero at the end of Year 1.

## § 7.  Cash Distributions

(a) *General.* Distributions made by an S corporation with respect to its stock that would otherwise (if made by a C corporation) be taxed under § 301(c) are instead taxed under § 1368. Such distributions may be attributable to original shareholder capital contributions, borrowed funds, S earnings, or e & p accumulated while the corporation was a C corporation.

(b) *No Accumulated E & P.* If an S corporation has no accumulated e & p from any source, a distribution of cash will be tax free to a shareholder to the extent that it does not exceed the shareholder's stock basis. § 1368(b)(1). Any excess will be treated as gain from a sale or exchange of property. § 1368(b)(2). This simplified treatment applies to all distributions from S corporations formed after 1982 for which an S election has been in effect since inception; such corporations will never have accumulated e & p (unless a former C corporation is acquired in a tax-free reorganization).

*Example:* A, an individual, owns all 10 shares of X (a calendar-year S corporation) with a basis of $1 per share. On March 1, X distributes $60 to A; for the entire taxable year, X has net income of $40. Under § 1367(a)(1), A's per-share basis in the X stock is first increased to $5 ($1 + $40/10) before taking the distribution into account. The amount of the distribution attributable to each share of A's stock is $6 ($60/10). *See* Reg. § 1.1367–1(c)(3). The tax-free portion of the distribution ($5 per share) reduces the basis of each share to zero. §§ 1368(b)(1) and 1367(a)(2)(A). Under § 1368(b)(2), the remaining portion of the distribution ($1 per share) is treated as gain from a sale or exchange. The total gain ($10) is equal to the excess of the distribution ($60) over the sum of A's prior aggregate stock basis ($10) and the pass-through income for the taxable year ($40). *See* Reg. § 1.1368–3, Example (1).

(c) *Accumulated E & P.* The distribution rules are considerably more complex if an S corporation has accumulated e & p from its previous existence as a C corporation. Under § 1368(c)(1), a distribution from an S corporation with accumulated e & p is treated the same as a § 1368(b) distribution (basis recovery or gain from a sale or exchange) to the extent of the S corporation's "accumulated adjustments account" (AAA). The AAA represents essentially the post–1982 undistributed net income of the S corporation; it is a corporate-level account which begins at zero and is adjusted for the S corporation's income or loss in a manner similar to the basis adjustments of § 1367. § 1368(e)(1)(A). *See* Reg. § 1.1368–2. Unlike basis adjustments, however, the AAA is not increased by tax-exempt income and may be reduced below zero. If the AAA is reduced below zero, it must first be restored to a positive balance before tax-free distributions may be made to shareholders. Any distribution in excess of the AAA is taxed as a dividend to the extent of the S corporation's accumulated e & p. § 1368(c)(2). Once distributions have exhausted accumulated e & p, any further distributions will be nontaxable to the extent of the shareholder's remaining stock basis and any excess will be taxed as proceeds from a sale or exchange. § 1368(c)(3).

*Example:* A, an individual, is the sole shareholder of X, a calendar-year S corporation. At the end of Year 1, A has a basis of $70,000 in her X stock; and X has accumulated e & p of $10,000 and an AAA of $50,000. On December 31, X distributes $100,000 to A. The $100,000 distribution is nontaxable to the extent of X's AAA ($50,000), and reduces A's basis in her stock from $70,000 to $20,000. §§ 1368(c)(1) and 1368(b)(1). Of the remaining distribution, $10,000 is attributed to X's accumulated e & p, and is taxed as a dividend to A under § 1368(c)(2). The portion taxed as a dividend has no effect on A's stock basis, because basis is reduced under § 1367(a)(2)(A) only by tax-free § 1368 distributions. Once X's accumulated e & p is exhausted, the remaining $40,000 is treated as tax-free basis recovery to the extent of A's remaining basis ($20,000) and the balance ($20,000) is taxed as gain from a sale or exchange under § 1368(c)(3).

The AAA must be adjusted downward by the amount of any distribution to which § 1368(b) or § 1368(c)(1) applies. *See* Reg. § 1.1368–2(a)(3). If distributions during the taxable year exceed the AAA at year end, the AAA generally must be allocated among distributions in proportion to their respective amounts. § 1368(c). In the case of a "qualifying disposition," the Regulations provide an exception to the pro rata rule: an S corporation may elect to treat its taxable year as consisting of two separate taxable years, the first of which ends on the date of the qualifying disposition. Reg. § 1.1368–1(g)(2). A qualifying disposition occurs if, within a 30–day period, a shareholder disposes of more than 20% of his stock, the corporation redeems 20% or more of its stock from a shareholder, or the corporation issues stock equal to 25% of its previously outstanding stock to one or more new shareholders. *Id*. *See* § 1377(a)(2)(terminating election).

In the case of a redemption of stock which is treated as an exchange, a special rule provides that the AAA (whether positive or negative) is reduced by a percentage equal to the percentage of stock redeemed. § 1368(e)(1)(B). The AAA is adjusted first for distributions governed by § 1368(a) and then for redemptions treated as exchanges if both occur during the same taxable year. Reg. § 1.1368–2(d)(1). Adjustments to accumulated e & p are made independently of any adjustments to the AAA. The corporation's accumulated e & p is adjusted downward by the amount of a distribution treated as a taxable dividend under § 1368(c)(2). § 1371(c)(3). A special rule also permits an S corporation, with the consent of all affected shareholders, to elect to treat distributions as attributable first to accumulated e & p. § 1368(e)(3). *See* Reg. § 1.1368–1(f). This election may be useful if a corporation wishes to purge itself of accumulated e & p.

## § 8. Corporate–Level Taxes

(a) *General.* An S corporation without accumulated e & p is generally not subject to corporate-level tax. Under §§ 1374 and 1375, however, special penalty taxes are levied on S corporations that have prior operating histories as C corporations.

(b) *Excess Net Passive Income.* Under § 1375(a), an S corporation may be subject to a corporate-level tax if it has accumulated e & p at the end of the year and its passive investment income exceeds 25% of its gross receipts. For this purpose, gross receipts are defined as the "total amount received or accrued" under the corporation's accounting method. Reg. §§ 1.1375–1(b)(4); 1.1362–2(c)(4)(i). To prevent easy manipulation of the gross receipts test, only the excess of gains over losses from disposition of capital assets (other than stock and securities) is included in gross receipts; gross receipts from sales or exchanges of stock or securities are taken into account only to the extent of gains, without netting for losses. §§ 1375(b)(3) and 1362(d)(3)(C); Reg. § 1.1362–2(c)(4)(ii). The term passive investment income includes gross receipts from royalties, rents, dividends, interest, annuities and gains from the sale or exchange of stock or securities. § 1362(d)(3)(D). Rental income does not constitute passive investment income, however, if the lessor provides "significant services" or incurs "substantial costs." *See* Reg. § 1.1362–2(c)(5)(ii)(B)(2).

Total passive investment income must exceed 25% of gross receipts to trigger the § 1375 tax. The § 1375 tax is imposed, however, only on "excess net passive income" (ENPI). To determine ENPI, the total passive investment income must first be reduced by directly attributable expenses to arrive at net passive income (NPI). NPI is then multiplied by the amount of passive investment income which exceeds 25% of gross receipts, and divided by passive investment income for the year. The result is ENPI, which is taxed at the highest corporate rate of 35%. *See* Reg. § 1.1375–1(a). The amount subject to tax is limited, however, to the corporation's total taxable income for the taxable year. For example, if a corporation has net passive income of $20,000, passive investment income of $25,000 and gross receipts of $40,000, the excess net passive income is $12,000 ($20,000 × $15,000/$25,000).

(c) *Built-In Gain Tax.* Section 1374 is intended to prevent C corporations from avoiding the repeal of *General Utilities* by converting to S status prior to a liquidation. The § 1374 tax applies to built-in gain (or built-in income) recognized during a 10–year recognition period after S status takes effect. The built-in gain tax generally does not apply to a corporation that has been an S corporation since inception. § 1374(c)(1).

Under § 1374(b), the built-in gain tax is imposed at the highest corporate rate on the corporation's "net recognized built-in gain," reduced by certain net operating loss carryforwards and capital loss carryforwards. An overall limitation restricts the amount of the net recognized built-in gain to the "net unrealized built-in gain," *i.e.*, the excess of the aggregate fair market value of all of the corporation's assets over the aggregate adjusted basis of the corporation's assets at the time of conversion from C to S status. §§ 1374(c)(2) and 1374(d)(1). For example, if a corporation has unrealized built-in gains of $100 and unrealized built-in losses of $60 on the conversion date, only the net unrealized built-in gain of $40 is subject to tax under § 1374. Thus, the appreciation in assets purchased after the conversion date and subsequent appreciation in existing assets is generally not subject to the § 1374 tax. The fair market value of inventory is determined as if, on the date of conversion, the S corporation sold its inventory to a willing buyer in a nonliquidating sale. Reg. § 1.1374–7(a).

Net recognized built-in gain for any taxable year may not exceed the corporation's taxable income (as determined under § 1375(b)(1)(B)). § 1374(d)(2). If the "taxable income limitation" applies, any excess built-in gain is carried forward to a subsequent year. *Id.* For example, if an S corporation has a recognized built-in gain of $100 and a current operating loss of $100 in the same year, the recognized built-in gain is not taxed under § 1374 for the current year because the corporation's recognized built-in gain ($100) exceeds its taxable income ($0). The untaxed portion of the recognized built-in gain ($100) is carried forward and taxed under § 1374 in the succeeding year (during the recognition period), subject to the taxable income limitation for such succeeding year.

The Regulations provide a useful summary of the manner is which an S corporation's net recognized built-in gain is determined. Net recognized built-in gain for any taxable year is the least of three amounts: (i) the amount of the S corporation's taxable income (applying C corporation rules), determined as if only recognized built-in gains, losses and carryovers were taken into account; (ii) the taxable income limitation; or (iii) the corporation's net unrealized built-in gain reduced by net recognized built-in gain for all prior taxable years during the recognition period (the "net unrealized built-in gain limitation"). Reg. § 1.1374–2(a).

Recognized built-in gain includes any income which accrued before the corporation's first taxable year as an S corporation but which is recognized for tax purposes during the recognition period. § 1374(d)(5)(A). *See* Reg. § 1.1374–4(b)(accrual test). For example, if a cash-method C corporation elects to become an S corporation, § 1374 potentially applies upon collection of any accounts receivable owed to the former C corporation. *See* Reg. § 1.1374–4(b)(3), Example (1). Recognized built-in losses include amounts which are allowable as a deduction during the recognition period but which accrued before the corporation's first taxable year as an S corporation. § 1374(d)(5)(B). *See* Reg. § 1.1374–4(b)(3), Example (2)(contingent liabilities not properly accruable).

The built-in gain tax applies to assets acquired from C corporations (or from another S corporation subject to § 1374) in certain nonrecognition transactions. § 1374(d)(8). Built-in loss property contributed to a corporation before or during the recognition period is subject to "anti-stuffing" rules similar to the rules of § 336(d)(2). Reg. § 1.1374–9. Generally, these rules disregard losses or deductions attributable to built-in loss property contributed with "a principal purpose" of avoiding the built-in gain tax. *Id.* Under the installment sale method, realized built-in gain may be deferred until after the recognition period. *See* Notice 90–27. To forestall this potential abuse, the Regulations impose the built-in gain tax on installment sale proceeds reported during or after the recognition period, subject to the taxable income and other limitations. Reg. § 1.1374–4(h).

The Regulations also provide a "look-through" rule to prevent an S corporation that owns a partnership interest from using the partnership entity to avoid built-in gain. Reg. § 1.1374–4(i)(1). Generally, an S corporation must treat its distributive share of partnership items, for purposes of § 1374, in the same manner as if such items had been earned directly by the S corporation. These rules apply, for example, when an S corporation contributes appreciated property to a partnership in exchange for a partnership interest, and the partnership subsequently sells the asset during the recognition period. A de minimis exception applies to certain "small" partnership interests, unless the S corporation forms or uses the partnership with "a principal purpose" of avoiding the § 1374 tax. Reg. § 1.1374–4(i)(5).

Section 1374 is both underinclusive and overinclusive. On the one hand, if the corporation is sufficiently patient, it can avoid the § 1374 tax by waiting out the 10–year period before liquidating or otherwise disposing of its assets. On the other hand, the burden is on the taxpayer to establish the amount of the net unrealized built-in gain. If the taxpayer is unable to meet this burden, not only pre-election but also post-election gain may be swept in under § 1374, even though appreciation in assets while held by an S corporation is normally subject to only a single level of tax.

(d) *Coordination With § 1375.* The special taxes on passive investment income and built-in gain are coordinated to prevent double taxation if income would otherwise be subject to both provisions. The amount of passive investment income is determined by excluding any recognized built-in gain or loss for any taxable year during the 10–year recognition period. § 1375(b)(4). Thus, net recognized built-in gain is subject only to the § 1374 tax.

(e) *Reduction in Pass-Through for Taxes Imposed.* The special taxes on passive investment income and built-in gains are also coordinated with the pass-through rules of § 1366. If the built-in gain tax is imposed for any taxable year, § 1366(f)(2) treats the amount of tax as a loss for that year. As a result, the loss passes through to the shareholders, effectively offsetting a portion of the recognized built-in gain taxed at the shareholder level. The character of the loss is determined by reference to the built-gain that gave rise to the § 1374 tax. § 1366(f)(2). Similarly, under § 1366(f)(3), the amount of passive investment income passing through to shareholders is reduced by a proportionate share of the tax imposed under § 1375. The combined corporate and shareholder-level tax rate under these special taxes is as high as in the case of a C corporation; moreover, both levels of tax are imposed at once, regardless of when the income is distributed.

(f) *LIFO Recapture.* Under § 1363(d), a C corporation electing S status must include in income its LIFO "recapture amount." The LIFO recapture amount is the excess of the FIFO value of the corporation's inventory over its LIFO value at the close of the corporation's last taxable year as a C corporation. § 1363(d)(3). The basis of the inventory is increased to reflect the amount subject to the recapture tax, which is payable in four equal installments. §§ 1363(d)(1) and 1363(d)(2).

(g) *Installment Treatment.* If an S corporation distributes certain installment obligations in complete liquidation, § 453B(h) permits nonrecognition of gain at the corporate level to the extent that receipt of the obligations by the S shareholders does not constitute payment for their stock under the rules of § 453(h)(1). *See* Chapter 7. The shareholders report gain or loss upon receipt of payments under the obligation, and the character of such gain or loss is determined under the pass-through rules of § 1366(b). In addition, the corporation recognizes gain on distribution of an installment obligation to the extent that gain from sale of the underlying property is subject to the built-in gain tax.

## § 9.  Property Distributions

Liquidating and nonliquidating distributions of appreciated property (other than the corporation's own obligations) are treated as recognition events at the corporate level. §§ 311, 336, and 1371(a). This rule prevents S shareholders from receiving a stepped-up basis in appreciated property without corporate-level recognition of the unrealized appreciation in the property. Accordingly, the corporation is treated as if it had sold the appreciated property to the distributee at its fair market value. The deemed sale may trigger the built-in gain tax and may also affect the character of the gain (*e.g.*, ordinary income treatment under § 1239 if the property is depreciable in the hands of a related shareholder). If the basis of property exceeds its fair market value, § 311(a) disallows recognition of loss on a nonliquidating distribution. Under § 336(a), however, loss may be recognized on a

liquidating distribution, subject to the limitations of
§ 336(d).

*Example:* The sole shareholder of an S corporation has a basis of $10 in her stock at the beginning
of the year, and the corporation distributes appreciated property with a basis of $10 and a fair market
value of $100 on December 31. Assuming that the
built-in gain tax does not apply, the corporation's
entire recognized gain of $90 will pass through to
the shareholder, increasing the shareholder's basis
in her stock to $100 ($10 plus $90 of pass-through
income). § 1367(a)(1). The shareholder's basis
will be reduced by $100, the fair market value of
the distributed property, and the shareholder will
take a $100 basis in the distributed property.
§§ 1368(b)(1) and § 301(d). The shareholder will
recognize no gain on the distribution, but her stock
basis will now be zero.

## § 10. Family Income–Splitting

An S corporation may be a useful device for
channelling profits from a business into the hands
of lower-bracket family members. Under
§ 1366(e), however, the Service may reallocate income among members of the family group if a
family member furnishes services or capital to the
corporation without "reasonable compensation."
In addition, a transfer of shares in an S corporation
to children must not be a mere "paper" transaction,
*i.e.*, the children must enjoy beneficial ownership of
the stock as well as possess legal title. Section 1(g)
curtails the benefits of family income-splitting by

taxing certain minor children's unearned income at their parents' marginal rate.

## § 11. Worthless Stock or Debt

If the stock or debt of an S corporation becomes worthless, the shareholder may be entitled to a deduction under § 165(g) or § 166(d). Under § 1367(b)(3), the adjustments to stock and debt basis for the S corporation's separately and non-separately stated items of income or loss are made before the deduction for worthlessness of stock or debt is determined. The effect of this rule may be to prevent all or a part of the corporation's operating losses from being treated as capital losses under § 165(g) or § 166(d). Shareholders of an S corporation that meets the requirements of § 1244 may also be entitled to an ordinary loss on sale or worthlessness of their stock within the limits of § 1244, just as in the case of a C corporation. *See* Chapter 2.

## § 12. Post–Termination Transition Period

Under § 1371(e), S shareholders are entitled to tax-free treatment of cash distributions from an S corporation which has previously taxed but undistributed income at the time its S election terminates, to the extent that the distribution does not exceed the AAA as defined in § 1368(e). The distributions must occur within the so-called "post-termination transition period," generally the one-year period after termination. § 1377(b). Distributions of cash (but not other property) are treated as tax-free during the post-termination transition period, and reduce stock basis.

*Example:* A calendar-year S corporation's election terminates on July 1, 1997, when its AAA is $25,000, and it has $15,000 of taxable income during its C short year. On December 31, 1997, the corporation distributes $30,000 to its shareholders. The shareholders will treat $25,000 of the distribution as tax-free recovery of their stock basis and the remaining $5,000 as an ordinary dividend from the corporation's current e & p.

If an S shareholder has accumulated disallowed losses which exceed his stock basis at the end of the last taxable year for which the corporation is an S corporation, such suspended losses are treated as if they were incurred on the last day of the post-termination transition period. § 1366(d)(3)(A). Thus, to the extent that the shareholder's stock basis increases during the post-termination transition period (*e.g.*, through additional capital contributions), the loss will be allowed currently and reduce stock basis. §§ 1366(d)(3)(B) and 1366(d)(3)(C). Only stock basis (not debt basis) is considered in determining whether suspended losses may be used during the post-termination period.

## § 13.　Future of Subchapter S

The principal advantages of an S election are that income from business operations or liquidation will generally be subject to only a single shareholder-level tax. Although an S corporation is less flexible than a partnership with respect to allocations of income or loss, the limited liability offered by the corporate form may be an important consideration. Limited liability companies (LLCs), however, combine corporate and partnership characteristics in a hybrid form which offers most of the advantages of an S election without such disadvantages as the one-class-of-stock requirement and eligibility restrictions. If LLCs become the preferred form of business organization for small business, they may undermine the viability of Subchapter S.

# CHAPTER 13
# INTEGRATION

## § 1. Introduction

In the early 1990's, the debate over corporate-shareholder integration intensified. Many countries other than the United States have already achieved integration in some form, and commentators have developed a variety of theoretical and practical integration models. Integration raises issues both of equity (whether corporate income should be taxed at the individual shareholder or corporate rate) and of efficiency (eliminating tax-induced distortions by taxing corporate income only once). The current interest in integration reflects the destabilizing effect of tax law changes during the 1980's, which encouraged leveraged buyouts, share repurchases and other nondividend distributions. While these particular concerns have become somewhat less urgent, the goal of integration is likely to remain economically and politically important.

To place the integration debate in perspective, this Chapter first examines proposals to reduce or eliminate existing biases and then considers several recent integration proposals. It concludes by suggesting that the current system may be moving toward a public versus private distinction: large publicly traded entities would be eligible for integrated treatment, while other entities would qualify for pass-through treatment.

## § 2. Eliminating Existing Biases

Based on the assumption that the double tax is fundamentally flawed, the integration proposals seek to reduce or eliminate one level of tax. An alternative approach would be to retain the basic double tax structure while adopting narrowly targeted reforms to address specific biases. These biases include disincentives for distributions in dividend form as well as preferential treatment of debt as compared to equity. Although these biases reflect longstanding problems under the double tax system, they have been exacerbated by recent tax law changes and financial innovations. During the 1980's, publicly held corporations turned increasingly to share repurchases and similar techniques to substitute debt for equity. Capital markets proved willing to accept riskier financial structures as both new and old investors benefited from reductions in the burden of the corporate double tax.

Before examining some specific reform proposals, it is useful to consider how a typical debt-equity conversion generates tax savings. Although the following discussion focuses on the mechanics of share repurchases, leveraged buyouts often serve a similar function. Closely held corporations have long recognized the significant tax advantages of share repurchases and other nondividend distributions. It is therefore somewhat puzzling why publicly held corporations have only recently engaged in share repurchases on a large scale. Possibly, compensating biases in favor of retention of corporate earnings tended to offset the tax advantages of nondividend distributions.

The use of retained corporate earnings to repurchase shares eliminates the corporate tax on future earnings from the distributed amounts, with no adequate offsetting burden at the shareholder level. Once stock basis is recovered tax free, any excess distribution is taxed to shareholders at favorable capital gain rates. During the 1980's, financial arbitrageurs helped corporate managers use leverage to exploit these benefits by borrowing to finance share repurchases. The combined effect of leveraged share repurchases—the corporate-level interest deduction and the reduction in the number of shares outstanding—permitted companies to report higher after-tax earnings per share, even though a larger portion of their pre-tax earnings was diverted to creditors. Higher earnings per share may in turn support higher share prices after a share repurchase than would be the case if the available funds were distributed in dividend form.

*Example*: Assume that X Corp. has 100,000 shares of outstanding stock and no debt. X has pre-tax earnings of $1,500,000 and pays tax of $500,000 (approximately 33%); thus, X has after-tax earnings of $1,000,000 ($10 per share). X's stock sells at approximately $70 per share (7 times earnings). On the advice of an investment banker,

X issues $6,000,000 of debt bearing 12% interest and uses the funds to repurchase 65.9% of its stock at $91 per share (65,900 shares × $91 per share = $6,000,000). The effect of the transaction on X's cash flow can be summarized as follows:

| Cash Flows | Before | After |
|---|---|---|
| Shareholders | $1,000,000 | $ 520,000 |
| Bondholders | 0 | 720,000 |
| Corporate income tax | 500,000 | 260,000 |
| Total operating income | $1,500,000 | $1,500,000 |

After the borrowing and share repurchase, X must pay $720,000 of interest to the new bondholders. Because the interest deduction shelters a portion of X's pre-tax earnings, X pays tax on only $780,000 rather than $1,500,000. Thus, X's tax burden is reduced from $500,000 to $260,000. After payment of interest and taxes, X has available $520,000 for distribution to continuing shareholders. Given the smaller number of shares outstanding (34,100), X's after-tax earnings per share increase from $10 before the transaction to just over $15 after the transaction. *See* American Law Inst., Federal Income Tax Project: Reporter's Study Draft, Subchapter C (Supplemental Study) 18–21, example (1)(1989).

At first glance, the transaction appears to increase X's overall profitability. In fact, however, X's pre-tax return remains constant. The only significant difference is that a portion of this amount (the $240,000 tax savings) has been redirected from the government to X's creditors and continuing shareholders. In the example, X is willing to pay $91 per share to repurchase its stock, a substantial premium over the trading price of $70 per share prior to the transaction. One reason why X's shares might sell at a discount is that the market price implicitly reflects the burden of the corporate tax. Even without any increased efficiency on the part of management, the elimination of a portion of the corporate tax burden is sufficient to account for the increased share values.

The impact of the increased use of debt in corporate capital structures during the 1980's has given rise to considerable debate. While some view higher debt-equity ratios as imposing beneficial "discipline" on corporate managers, others have expressed concern that over-leveraged companies pose a greater risk of bankruptcy. The changes in the tax law cannot fully explain the dramatic increase in share repurchases and other types of debt-equity conversions during the 1980's. Nevertheless, it seems likely that tax-induced distortions played a significant role in these financial restructurings. Even if one believes that market forces may be relied upon to determine the proper level of such corporate activity, this does not make a "level-playing field" any less desirable. Thus, the case for reducing or eliminating existing biases in the corporate tax system remains strong regardless of one's views on the merits of highly leveraged capital structures.

The 1989 ALI Reporter's Study seeks to accomplish this goal by an ingenious set of proposals that would neutralize existing biases. These proposals would impose a minimum corporate-level tax on nondividend distributions (set at 28%) as a "toll-charge" for removing future earnings from the burden of the corporate tax. Shareholders would be allowed a credit for the corporate-level excise tax on nondividend distributions. The excise tax would effectively ensure that all distributions bear a minimum level of tax, approximating the burden imposed on ordinary dividend distributions. To alleviate the bias in favor of debt, the proposals would disallow an interest deduction for corporate debt incurred to replace existing equity. In addition, an interest-type deduction would be allowed with respect to "new equity." The rationale for restricting this relief to new equity is to reduce windfalls for shareholders who purchased stock at a price that reflected the burden of the double tax system.

These proposals may be viewed as an alternative to integration or perhaps as a transitional step from an unintegrated to an integrated system. Such incremental reform may be preferable to integration because it avoids full-scale shifting of tax burdens and potential windfalls to existing shareholders. The continued reliance on the corporate double tax, however, may lead integrationists to view these proposals as defective. The proponents of integration bear the burden of demonstrating that some form of integration is not only preferable in theory but also workable in practice.

## § 3. Integration Proposals

(a) *General.* Several methods of implementing "full" or "partial" integration have been proposed as alternatives to the existing double-tax system. The principal integration approaches are: (i) repeal of the corporate income tax and attribution of corporate income directly to shareholders (the partnership-type model), (ii) retention of the corporate tax as a withholding tax to be credited against the ultimate shareholder-level tax (the imputation credit method), (iii) dividend relief in the form of a corporate deduction for dividends paid (the dividend-deduction method) or exclusion of dividends from shareholder income (the dividend-exclusion method), or (iv) taxation of distributed and undistributed earnings at different rates (the split-rate method).

Both dividend relief and the imputation credit method provide relief for distributed corporate income. Similarly, the split-rate method used in some European countries generally taxes distributed corporate earnings at a lower rate than retained corporate earnings. In comparison to dividend relief or the split-rate method, the imputation credit method provides a greater degree of "transparency" and thus more closely approximates full integration. These different methods of partial integration would not necessarily alleviate overtaxation of retained corporate earnings or gains from sale of corporate stock. In a partially integrated system, corporations would continue to be taxed as entities separate from their shareholders.

Full integration typically implies treatment of the corporation as a "conduit" by analogy to the partnership model. Although partnership-type treatment has long been considered the ideal method of implementing integration, it is generally considered administratively unworkable. In the case of large, publicly held corporations with complex capital structures, taxing corporate income directly to shareholders would require extremely complex allocations. The problem of allocating income to specific shareholders would be magnified when corporate stock is traded frequently. Full attribution of corporate income might also require taxation of individual shareholders who had not yet received a corresponding distribution of income. Although the Treasury has devised methods for auditing large partnerships, tracking numerous shareholders may pose difficult procedural problems. Even if full or partnership-type integration remains the ideal, partial integration may be pursued on pragmatic grounds.

(b) *Treasury Proposals.* After careful consideration of various integration alternatives, a recent Treasury study recommends the dividend-exclusion method. *See* U.S. Dep't of the Treasury, Report on Integration of the Individual and Corporate Tax Systems—Taxing Business Income Once (1992); U.S. Dep't of the Treasury, A Recommendation for Integration of the Individual and Corporate Tax Systems (1992). Under the Treasury proposals, shareholders would exclude from their individual income distributions of previously-taxed corporate earnings. Thus, the corporate tax would represent the ultimate tax levied on dividend distributions. Retained earnings would also be afforded partial relief. A corporation could elect to treat retained earnings as if distributed to shareholders and then reinvested in the corporation. The deemed distribution would trigger an appropriate basis adjustment in the shareholders' stock, thereby mitigating the problem of overtaxation upon a subsequent sale of the stock.

The Treasury's dividend-exclusion method is intended not so much to integrate the corporate and shareholder taxes as to ensure that corporate income is taxed only once. According to the Treasury, elimination of distortions in the double tax system will lead to significant efficiencies. The dividend-exclusion method seeks to attain these efficiencies with a schedular system in which all corporate income is taxed at a uniform rate, independent of the individual shareholders' tax rates. One significant drawback is that the dividend-exclusion method is extremely vulnerable to changes in the relationship between individual and corporate tax rates. When the maximum individual rate exceeds the maximum corporate rate, dividend exclusion represents a windfall to high-bracket shareholders. Critics claim that the Treasury's dividend-exclusion method represents a defective form of integration because it sacrifices equity to efficiency concerns.

(c) *ALI Reporter's Proposals*. In terms of fairness, the "imputation credit" method recommended by the 1993 ALI Reporter's Study seems superior to the Treasury's dividend-exclusion method. *See* American Law Inst., Federal Income Tax Project:

Integration of the Corporate and Individual Taxes, Reporter's Study of Corporate Tax Integration (1993). While introducing some additional complexity, the imputation credit method achieves the integrationist objective of taxing corporate-source income at the individual shareholders' rates. The imputation credit method operates by "grossing up" each actual distribution to a shareholder by a ratable share of the corporate tax previously imposed on the distributed earnings, and then allowing the recipient shareholder a credit for the corporate tax. In effect, the corporate tax serves as a downpayment at the corporate level for the tax which is ultimately imposed at the shareholder level.

*Example*: Assume that X Corp. and A (an individual shareholder) are taxed at rates of 35% and 20%, respectively. If X earns pre-tax income of $154, X is left with only $100 to distribute to A after paying a corporate-level tax of approximately $54 (35% × $154). Under the imputation credit method, A is treated as having received a total distribution of $154 ($100 distribution plus $54 "gross up"), which is accompanied by a refundable tax credit of $54. Accordingly, A receives a tax refund of $23, *i.e.*, $54 credit less $31 shareholder-level tax (20% × $154). If A instead were taxed at a rate of 40%, she would owe an additional tax of $8 on the distribution, *i.e.*, $62 shareholder-level tax (40% × $154) less $54 credit.

The amount of the grossed-up dividend is equal to the amount of the actual cash distribution divided by $(1 - c)$, where $c$ is the corporate tax rate. Thus, if the corporate rate is 35%, an actual distribution of $100 is equal to a grossed-up distribution of $154 ($100 ÷ (1 − .35)). The refundable credit ($54) is equal to the excess of the grossed-up distribution ($154) over the actual distribution ($100). The additional shareholder-level tax (or refund) is thus equal to the difference between the tax imposed at the individual shareholder's rate and the tax previously paid at the corporation's rate. The imputation credit method would also permit constructive dividend treatment of retained corporate earnings, with an accompanying credit and appropriate basis adjustments. If the corporation's rate equals or exceeds the rate applicable to individual shareholders, a constructive distribution would generate no additional tax (or generate a refundable credit) at the shareholder level.

(d) *Alternatives*. The Treasury also considered a more ambitious proposal in the form of a "comprehensive business income tax" ("CBIT"). If fully implemented, a CBIT would radically alter business taxation by imposing a uniform entity-level tax on virtually all enterprises, including partnerships and sole proprietorships. Under a CBIT, all distributions from business entities would be taxable to the recipient, and no deduction would be allowed for interest or dividends. Thus, a CBIT would equate the treatment of debt and equity. To avoid disruption of existing business arrangements, a CBIT would be implemented over a lengthy transition period (10 years). While other integration models would lose revenue, a CBIT would be revenue neutral or might, under certain assumptions, even increase revenues.

(e) *Special Problems*. Each of the various integration models poses its own peculiar technical and political difficulties. Given the tortuous process of implementing any new proposal, any integration model is unlikely to prove much simpler in operation than the existing system. Moreover, political pressures to raise revenue or accommodate various groups may add significantly to the complexity of integration.

One troublesome issue concerns the treatment of tax-exempt investors, who hold nearly half of all corporate equity and debt. The dividend-exclusion method would treat taxable and tax-exempt investors exactly alike, since neither would owe any tax on excludable dividends. All shareholders would bear an implicit tax, however, equal to the corporate-level tax. If the corporate tax is viewed as a surrogate for the individual tax, tax-exempt shareholders should arguably be entitled to relief, perhaps in the form of a refund of the implicit corporate-level tax. Under the imputation credit method, the availability of a refundable credit to tax-exempt shareholders might mean that corporate earnings bear no tax at all. To deal with this problem, the ALI Reporter's proposals would impose an explicit tax (at an unspecified rate) on corporate dividends and interest paid to tax-exempt shareholders. As a political and economic matter, however, it might prove quite difficult to determine the appropriate rate of the surcharge.

The treatment of corporate tax preferences represents another serious problem under an integrated system. To the extent that existing corporate tax preferences, such as accelerated depreciation, have served to mitigate the burden of the double tax, their continued existence may be called in question in an integrated system. If a repeal of such preferences is politically unfeasible, some mechanism may be necessary to prevent "superintegration" as a result of the flowthrough of these preferences. Superintegration occurs whenever a full shareholder-level credit is allowed for dividends distributed out of earnings that have been taxed at less than the maximum corporate rate. For example, assume that a corporation earns income from tax-exempt bonds and taxable bonds. Since a portion of the corporate income has escaped corporate tax entirely, the distributee shareholder should not be allowed a full credit for the corporate taxes deemed paid. A full credit would result in negative tax rates on the preferential income, *i.e.*, a credit in excess of actual taxes paid.

In the international context, there are two principal issues: (i) whether integration benefits should be extended to foreign shareholders of domestic corporations and (ii) how foreign taxes paid by domestic corporations on foreign-source income should be treated for purposes of subsequent distributions. The dividend exclusion and imputation credit methods would not automatically extend the benefits of integration to all shareholders; foreign shareholders might be eligible to receive such benefits only through negotiated treaties, not by statute, or might be subject to a special "foreign investor's tax." Similarly, foreign taxes paid by a domestic subsidiary would not necessarily "flow through" for purposes of allowing the parent corporation's shareholders to exclude (or receive an imputation credit for) an equivalent amount of distributed income. The extension of integration benefits as far as possible is sometimes advocated as advancing the goal of "capital export" neutrality and maximizing efficient allocation of international capital. In light of potential revenue losses, however, it is not surprising that the Treasury and ALI proposals adopt a cautious approach to unilateral extension.

## § 4. Future Directions

(a) *General.* The rise of alternative business forms, such as limited liability companies, highlights continuing problems in the taxation of business entities. Under the current system, whether business income is taxed twice or only once is in effect elective, since entity classification turns essentially upon contractual or state law provisions. In a fully integrated system, classification issues would largely disappear. If, however, only partial integration proves feasible, it is essential to develop a coherent set of classification rules to determine which entities should be subject to double tax.

(b) *Rationale for Double Taxation.* There is little consensus concerning the rationale for taxing corporate income twice. The corporate tax has often been justified as a charge for the special privileges or benefits of conducting business in corporate form. The benefits theory is flawed, however, because it is impossible to measure accurately any benefits attributable to the corporate form. Moreover, such benefits are unlikely to bear any discernible relationship to the burden of the corporate-level tax. One of the most significant corporate characteristics—limited liability—is now freely available to businesses organized in noncorporate form. Another significant corporate characteristic—access to capital markets through public trading—is no longer unique to corporate stock since some partnership interests are also publicly traded.

Some commentators have suggested a "liquidity" standard for determining whether business entities should be subject to a double-level tax. Under a liquidity standard, a separate corporate tax may be justified as an excise on economic rents or excess profits attributable to corporate capital. As a practical matter, however, it is virtually impossible to devise a tax that differentiates between normal and excess returns to capital. Other commentators have argued that tests based on gross revenues or active participation should be used to distinguish between double tax and pass-through entities. While an integrated system focused on small, actively-managed businesses may have substantial political appeal, such criteria make relatively little sense from a tax policy perspective.

The imposition of a separate corporate tax is increasingly difficult to justify when no similar tax is imposed on unincorporated businesses that are functionally indistinguishable from corporations. Nevertheless, as a practical matter, the existing system may be moving toward a "public versus private" distinction based on the liquidity of the underlying ownership interests. Nearly all firms which are not publicly traded can already obtain the benefits of pass-through treatment. If the distinction between widely held and closely held businesses is considered sufficient to justify different approaches, partial integration along the lines of the Treasury or ALI proposals might be reserved for the former, with pass-through treatment available for the latter.

(c) *Preservation of Pass-Through Treatment.* In a partially integrated system, it would be necessary to consider what forms of pass-through treatment should be preserved. On the one hand, S corporations might be viewed as superfluous in an integrated system. On the other hand, S corporations arguably provide an ideal model for pass-through integration because of their relative simplicity and ease of operation. It would seem unfair to deprive existing businesses of the benefits of Subchapter S until some form of pass-through treatment is available generally to businesses. In view of the complexity of Subchapter K, few would urge partnership taxation as a model for simplification. Accordingly, it would seem sensible, under a partial integration model, to make Subchapter S available for as many nonpublicly traded businesses as possible.

(d) *Consumption Tax Alternatives.* The debate over integration must be viewed in the broader context of ongoing efforts to reform the federal income tax system. The separate corporate tax could be viewed as compensating for the realization doctrine, which shields shareholders from being taxed annually on their ratable share of corporate income. In an integrated system, many of the existing problems of the individual income tax would persist. Current criticisms of the individual income tax as unfair and overly complex have served to focus attention on possible alternatives, including a value-added tax (VAT) or consumption-type tax. Because these alternatives are generally perceived as regressive, they are unlikely to win broad political support as a complete replacement for the current income tax. As a revenue-raising supplement to the income tax, however, a modified VAT or progressive consumption tax might provide a needed source of financing for corporate-shareholder integration.

Alternatively, the existing corporate tax might be replaced with a business cash-flow tax for both corporate and noncorporate businesses. Similar to an individual consumption tax, a business cash-flow tax would permit immediate deduction or expensing of new investments. Under certain assumptions, the present value of deducting an investment immediately from taxable income is equivalent to exempting the investment's return. A business cash-flow tax would equate the treatment of interest and dividends. Financial receipts such as loans would generally be excluded from the tax base, and financial outflows such as loan repayments and payments of interest and dividends would not be subtracted from the tax base. Thus, only cash flows from non-financial activities would affect the tax base. Implementation of a business cash-flow tax seems likely, however, only in connection with a more fundamental decision to substitute a consumption tax base for the existing income tax base.

As a practical matter, corporate-shareholder integration remains the most likely path for comprehensive reform of business taxation. Because integration is almost certain to prove costly in terms of lost revenue, however, it will require difficult economic and political choices. The modest efficiency gains of integration must be weighed against the offsetting tax changes that would be necessary to maintain revenue neutrality while preserving the progressivity of the existing tax system. In the absence of thoroughgoing reform, it is important to consider the practical impact of incremental changes on the existing tax system. On the one hand, the evolution of hybrid forms of business organization may be viewed as a transitional step toward an integrated system. On the other hand, piecemeal de facto integration may only hinder serious efforts to fashion a coherent federal system of taxing business entities. The longer Congress delays, the more difficult it may become to implement rational and comprehensive reform of the corporate tax system.

# INDEX

†